TIL
DEATH
DO
US
PART

TIL
DEATH
DO
US
PART

MIKE & PATTI PASCHALL

COPYRIGHT

Til Death Do Us Part Copyright © 2015 by Michael D. Paschall and Karen C. Paschall.

FIRST EDITION
Library of Congress Cataloging-in-Publication Data has been applied for.

Cover & Title Page design: Jonathan C. Egan

Cover photographs: Sean Champ Smith

Subjects photographed: Sean Champ Smith

ISBN 978-0-9827944-7-0
ISBN (ebook) 978-0-9827944-8-7

We dedicate this project to our parents:

Jerry Ray and Martha Ruth Cox
&
Joseph D. and Marcelaine Paschall

Thank you for showing us what it looks like to stay
in a marriage until the very end.

We love you!

Acknowledgements

First, we need to thank our children, their spouses, and our beautiful grandchildren: Nicole and Steve, Paige and Jon, Isabel, Jones, Lewis, Grace, and Esther. We're a tight-knit bunch and these wonderful people present a constant reminder that they're taking notes and we need to notice our own vapor trail. They've lived this project with us. Their words of encouragement and suggestions have been extremely valuable. We know how this book will hit the heart of any young couple because they've told us. We believe in them so deeply. Apparently they feel the same way about us also.

There are a fairly large number of spiritual sons and daughters, longtime friends, and supporters who continually sow into us. Their tangible support and love bolsters our every effort to do what we are called to do. Some of the cost we've paid in ministry has brought forth some of the most beautiful fruit we've ever known. There are too many of you to name. You know who you are. Oh, how we love you!

We've also been blessed with garden friends who have been there for us as we've taken this sacred journey with the people we've interviewed in this project. Michael and Kathy, Jay and Maryann, Dave and Bonnie, Jack and Rose have always provided us with a soft place to process what we've gleaned. What a gift you are to us!

A special thank you to Ryan and Tina Essmaker for showing us the charming powers of rhythmic interviews inside their beautiful: The Great Discontent. Your suggestions and insights for capturing the interviews were so helpful. Thanks for sharing your time and expertise!

We needed a professional photographer to introduce the faces that go along with the voices in these interviews. Sean Champ Smith was the one we wanted from the beginning to capture those images. He's a busy man who lives all over the world. But when we asked him, he said, "I'm in." We love you, Sean. You are a good son. Thank you.

Once we had a commitment for the photography, we needed to raise extra funds for the project. There were flights and logistics to manage in order to make it all happen. As the interviews were starting to pile up, some of our friends asked, "What can we do to help?" We promised that we'd let them know what we needed once we had an idea ourselves. Jay and Maryann Lathern, Jack and Rose Egan, Glenn and Sandy Landry, and Earl and Barbara Patrick all gave generously to make the photography project happen. A "thank you" seems so small in comparison to what you gave, but we are grateful beyond words.

Our youngest daughter's husband, Jon C. Egan, took some of Sean Smith's photography and then crafted the overall concept for the book cover. Jon's creative talent is obviously ridiculous. He always serves us with his best. Thanks son!

David Reyes gave himself to us by editing these interviews. He's a busy guy with a growing family, but he always seems to make time. Thanks David. You honor us well.

Friend and author, Chad Conine, also helped us on a multitude of levels. He edited the introductions and gave a final look at the entire project. Chad's feedback has been extremely valuable and encouraging throughout the editing process. We've known Chad and his family since he was a small child. It has been a true joy to witness his growth into such an honorable man. Thanks Chad. It's been awesome to have you along on the ride.

We canvassed the publishing community long and hard in an effort to find a book agent for this project. Once it became clear that we needed to self-publish and began to get our hearts resolved to that path, it seems that a divine intervention occurred. From out of nowhere, Vern Hyndman showed up. Vern is a brilliant man who has pushed us with a plan to get this book out there. It was an instant connection. Many thanks, friend! Your confidence in this project is pure encouragement!

Lastly, we must give our heartfelt thanks for Marsha Blessing and the design team at Orison Publishers, Inc. You delivered everything that you promised: professional direction, insight, creativity, integrity, the loving hand of peace, and a quality product. Yeah, that has been a gift.

Contents

From Mike

"Do you promise to love, honor, trust, and serve in sickness and in health, in adversity and prosperity, and to be true and loyal until death do you part?"

For over 30 years, I've been reading those words to young couples at the altar on their wedding day. As they face each other, clasping hands and peering deeply into the window of their partner's soul, they say their weighty vows of pledge and promise. Aside from all the legalities of the action, it is probably one the most spiritual moments they will ever have. In that mystical moment, they "tie the knot" and bind their soul to the one who supposedly completes their life and person. Once those vows are made and the rings are given, I make a simple pronouncement: These two are husband and wife! And so it is. Game on.

Although I've seen it repeated hundreds of times, I'm not convinced that any of us truly understand the significance of what is being promised with those words. Do we marry because we're in love or because we're in lust or both? Lust probably had much more to do with my own marriage to my girl, but somehow our love grew and overshadowed all the other incidentals. It's been that way for almost 40 years. So far, life has been kind to us as a couple. We've been tested, but not to finality. We're both old enough and astute to know there is a fence on the backside of this lovely pasture.

As many hours as Patti and I have spent doing premarital counseling with couples, we have felt that we've probably benefitted much more than any prospective bride or groom. We've tried to be brutally honest about the challenges of marriage. Even though we've given them the "goods" as we understand it, we've felt that there is so much more that they need to see and experience before it makes real sense to them. We've wondered how one goes about showing someone what real love looks like. About the only way love is really proven is over time and under pressure. Is a promise to love really worth anything if it hasn't been tried? Doesn't love cost us something? Romantic love is valid, but only about an inch deep. But, when you're 24-years old, can you really be convinced of anything other than the romantic expectation of marital bliss? Life can dish out such bitter bites and that is when those deep-rooted vows come into play. Something has to anchor us to the deep and each other. Beauty and sexuality will eventually fade. Then what?

Our original intent was to put something on paper that we could hand to engaged couples and say, "This is what it means to make a vow and then live it to the end." Now this book project has morphed into something that is more multi-faceted. Yes, it is very insightful for pre-marital prospects, but it also serves up healthy doses of wisdom for any married couple that might be paying attention to the dialogue in the interviews. If you decide, along with your mate, to begin to dig in to each other again and stoke the fires that forge depth and intimacy, the book will have done its work. Ultimately, the hope is that any person might sensibly read Til Death Do Us Part and then face their significant other with a renewed aspiration that says: We can do better in this relationship! Right?

Every widow or widower is asked the same questions and there is no one true pat answer for anything. That is what is so awesome about an interview format. There is no speculation or theory. The information is directly from a widow or widower who has already proven their staying power. In fact, they stayed until the very end of their best friend's life. They loved, served, and wavered not as death crouched at the door. There is so much to learn from each of these brave souls, and the reader is free to grab and apply what is so unselfishly given.

The need for love to manifest uniquely in every relationship is vitally important. The overall value of this book should stimulate honest questions between life partners. Hopefully, those questions make room for each couple to find their own answers. Like spilled water that seeps into the cracks of the sidewalk, their answers settle into what they resolve in their own heart. Their agreement is where the magic is found.

The goal is not to traumatize anyone with these beautifully brutal stories. They are only kisses of truth, yet sometimes those kisses hold the inescapable fact of our fragile mortality. But that's the overall value of the truth. What is it that we're willing to receive and give with our most intimate life partner and mate? Can we really face anything together?

To spice it up a bit, we canvassed about 15 couples that I had previously married over the past couple of years. We asked them, "What three questions would you ask a widow or widower about marriage?" Some of them graciously responded and we took the best questions and built them into the interviews with our candidates. Thus the sections "From the Newlyweds." Again, there were no pat answers, but by the time you get to that section you sense that you feel and know the person being interviewed. Their answers seem to make perfect sense.

Patti and I are convinced that these precious stories gained from these raw interviews are powerful enough to drastically affect how any couple might relate or communicate. We think it will stimulate questions within a person that only they can answer with their mate. If the feedback we've gotten from our trial readers is any indicator of this book's true potential, then we have something here. What this compilation of interviews has done for our own marriage is tangibly positive. There is more patience and willingness to invest in real dialogue about what's important in the time that we do have together. It really does challenge the thought, we've got time... maybe tomorrow.

One of the things that we need to point out here is that the goal was not to write a religious book. Our hope was that the book would be read and valued by everyone regardless of his or her faith. We interviewed some people we have known over the course of our lifetime, and some of those people played vital roles in our own professional ministry. There was more than enough room for spirituality to surface in the interviews, but again, it wasn't the point. There were no direct questions about faith in any interview. The focus was on the staying power of a couple even when it got unbearably hard. At times, there is heavy God talk in these interviews, but there is also unbridled pain and emotion that manifest in the normal vernacular of our overall culture. We welcomed whatever they said and have filtered nothing. We asked them for the truth and to not hold back how they felt. Every person interviewed had the right to change his or her words and expressions in the editing process. One or two of them did that, but most did not. These interviews are very raw and very real. We do not apologize for that. These precious people gave us what we asked for.

There are twelve chapters in this book. Each chapter is signified only by the person's first name that we are interviewing. I wrote each introduction to the interview. We have gathered pictures from each person interviewed that highlight the timeline of the marriage. Photographer Sean Smith captured the portraits of each interviewee. Sean's involvement was a labor of love on his part, but once he met the people you're about to meet in these interviews he was sold on the overall vision. One of the persons lives abroad in the UK, and the rest are scattered over the United States. There was a serious cost to complete that task, but this book and these people deserve that kind of investment.

Why would I say that? It's simple—these stories given by twelve brave souls need to be heard. From the bowels of the earth there is a shadowy resonance that eerily touches us all. Something will take each of us out eventually. No one escapes the date with death. Even with that being said, it implores us to value life today. Love today. Be thankful today. That's the advice from those who have lost their best friends. The testimony of the bereaved teaches us to pay attention to today. Nothing stays the way it is forever. Nothing.

Patti and I are forever grateful to those who shared their story with us. But, we would be remiss if we did not also thank you also for picking up a copy. If you love this book, buy copies for your friends and loved ones. We all need to be reminded of what we promised on our wedding day. I said it. Patti said it, and you probably promised it too: Til death do us part. But, until that day, we can do better.

—Mike Paschall

From Patti

NO! This book can't be over. The story isn't finished. I still have an hour left in my flight and I'm a wreck. Surely the woman sitting next to me is wondering what is going on. As I sat there thinking about the book I'll Be Seeing You, by Deane Johnson, I am in total tears thinking about this woman's journey! Only a few weeks ago, Deane's grandson Jackson recommended her book. He thought it might help me. It did that and more. We had just moved back to Texas to help take care of my Mother who is struggling with Alzheimer's. Little did Jackson know, the book was a huge help and encouragement and, not only that, it planted a seed in my heart that helped birth this book.

I believe my husband is an incredible writer. So when I landed that day at the airport, I had a request for Mike. At lunch I shared my thoughts with him.

"I want you to write my Mother's story," I said.

People need to know more about this disease and the struggles of it. He sat quietly and then said, "Honey, I'm not sure I can do that. I would have to know what is going on in her head to do it justice and I don't think I can do it. Let me think about it." That afternoon, Mike got a revelation about this book. I was not immediately on board, but the more I thought about it, I knew his idea was brilliant.

People have stories that need to be told. People matter. Their lives matter. We are always hearing or reading about the rich and famous, which is great. But un-rich and un-famous people are just as important and it's stories like these that remind us what life is really about. Through the good, hard, sick, and even death—people matter!

I have to thank the wonderful dozen for this gift they have given Mike and I! You have become family to us and you are eternally in our hearts! Mike, Lawanna, Bruce, Bebe, John, Ruthie, Tommy, Jackie, Marcy, George, Jordan and Deane, you are all rock stars in my book! Your faithfulness, courage, strength and love will be encouragement to all mankind! We love you dearly!

—Patti Paschall

Bebe

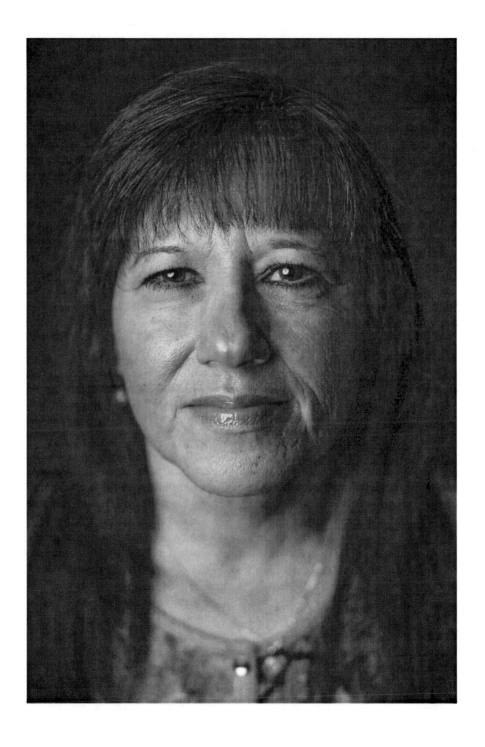

Introduction

Picture one of the majestic rivers of Texas: The Brazos, the Rio Grande, or the Guadalupe. At times, they meander through the territory like spilled honey. But that is when you can best see that beautiful tiny tree that is anchored in the caliche river bottom. That little tree stands straight and firm, providing so much shade and cover for the schools of fish that hang out in the shadows of its outspread limbs. It's peaceful, still, and serene, like a painting that always remains true. The tree stands, enjoying the cool waters, and the gently lapping breeze.

Yet, there are times when the river pushes forward in rage. It swells with rains and angry boiling. It eats its way through the land, dismantling those things that are not anchored down or secure. Despite all of that, our tiny tree stands firm. It bends, but it does not break. It twists, but it does not turn. Whatever the river brings with it downstream, no matter how high the waters rise, the tree holds it's ground. Water and debris swirl around the tree — never through it. It has a job. In it's core, there are rings of solid promise.

In this elemental vision, Beatrice "Bebe" Felan Garcia is that 5' 1" tree and, of course, the river is life. The strength that you are about to discover in this interview is staggering. I suspect it's most uncommon and remarkably rare. I must confess that I was completely undone by my few short hours with this woman. I feel we have been given something precious — a piece of Bebe's heart. I love her, and I pray you will love her too.

How can someone be so afraid, yet ferociously fearless in the battle she faced? How did she hold firm, while so many things were taken away? It could only be love. It had to be love. I knew Martin. I bought stamps from him at the post office, but it goes back further than that. We went to the same grade schools in McGregor. He was a sophomore when I was a senior in high school. Martin was quiet, serious, and one of the few Hispanics in my school. I was totally unaware of the burden that guy carried as a kid, and I'm not proud that I didn't know. I worked a couple summers for a road construction company where Martin's dad (Martin, Sr.) was a long time employee. Other than those few little details, that was the extent of my knowledge of the Garcia family. That is my loss.

People can inspire, but selfless people melt us. This story melted me, and it's powerful enough to change us all if we let it. I have wept many times preparing this for your consumption. Martin and Bebe's story is rich, and it's grounded deep, just like that tree. Yes, just like that tiny, yet beautifully magnificent tree.

It is a real privilege to present to you: Bebe. What a woman! –MDP-

Tell us about how you two met and fell in love?

I moved to McGregor in 1981, after I graduated from High School. I had known Martin and his sisters most of my life. His sisters were some of my best friends. I met them through my sister Ramona and her husband Frank Leos who lived here in town. I knew who Martin was, but I didn't really get to know him closely until after I moved to McGregor that summer. He asked me out. I was 18, and he was 22 years old. We started dating and pretty much fell in love right away.

We dated two years, and I got pregnant. That is when we made the decision that we would live together. Martin was a very responsible person. It wasn't in his plans, but things happen. So we took a different approach to the issue. We knew we loved each other, but we were both unsure about marriage. We knew how serious it was to make vows to each other, but we also knew that we had a responsibility to each other. So we moved in together to see if we could live together. That was in 1984. Our daughter Amanda was born, and we were living in Waco, both working to provide for our child. We were living as married people, but we wanted to make sure we were both going to commit. We lived that way for 6 years. In 1990, I got pregnant again, with my son, and we decided it was time to get married. We both knew it was time to make the vow. We loved each other and knew we could make it as a couple.

Was it love at first sight?

Pretty much. Martin was so funny, but also very serious and mature for his age. I was working two jobs myself, paying my way, so the connection was full of mutual admiration and love. But we did want to make sure before we took the final step.

When and where were you married?

October 13, 1990. We had the Justice of the Peace in McGregor marry us. It was a quiet little service with our respective families.

How long were you and Martin married?

Twenty-three years married. By common law it was twenty-nine years.

So let's go with common law... what was the first year of your marriage like?

It was very hard. You think you know someone when you date them. But once you move in with someone, it's a game changer. Finding out their likes and dislikes—how you actually live compared to each other is very different and can be very difficult. We only thought we knew each other.

It was tough. We argued a lot, which is a part of getting to know each other. You have to test the boundaries of what is going to be acceptable or not acceptable. When do you give in, and when do you stand firm? That's the only way to find out. We argued over stupid things **[laughing]**. "Where did you put the foil?" Just dumb stuff like that. We could go a couple days without talking because of our differences over stupid things. We finally realized that we needed to sit down and talk about the things that were upsetting to us. But it took almost two years to get to that point. It was argue... make up. Argue... make up.

I run a daycare for children, and I hear the stories from young parents. They can be done with a relationship because of the smallest issues! There doesn't seem to be a whole lot of commitment to stick it out. We did argue, but no one was going anywhere. It's a part of figuring out the deal. I can see that clearly from here, but there were days back then that I wondered **[laughing]**. You've got to stick in there. It's part of it. It takes time to really get to know one another.

How differently were you both raised?

I had a little more privileged life than Martin. Both of us came from big families. His mother didn't work outside of the home. Both of my parents worked. My dad was a veteran. We had a big farm and also a gas station. He didn't grow up with the stuff that I did. Since he was the oldest of 6 other siblings, he was like another father. I was the youngest of eight kids. I came into the relationship not really knowing much about homemaking, but I did know how to work hard. Martin didn't resent my lack of homemaking skill, but he was hard on me about waste. He was very alert to how we spent our money. I was used to spending what I made on what I wanted. He came from a totally different perspective. He was extremely responsible and could see the needs before they happened. We clashed quite a bit on that topic. He carried that responsibility at a very young age. I didn't have to. He worked at a very young age, but the money went to his mother and his family. My money went to what I wanted and on myself.

Martin taught me a lot about priorities. He grew up in pretty tough circumstances. It was a pretty hard life for a young person. My experience was nothing like that. Being with him has made me a totally different person—for the better.

Early on, what were some of your toughest challenges as a couple?

The governance of finances was hardest on me. We fought a lot about money. But probably how we raised our kids was a major obstacle we had to work through. Martin was a very strict parent—again, probably because of how he grew up. I was spoiled rotten as a kid, so I was much more prone to be lenient with the kids. We learned how to balance that, but it wasn't always easy on the front end of parenting.

We figured out how to compromise and hear the other side of a situation. We had been together long enough to see that an argument didn't have to end a discussion. We didn't have to go silent the next day. That stuff was hurting our relationship, so we'd keep talking until we could find the common ground.

What were your shared goals and ambitions?

Our families. That was it. Taking care of our kids, his family, and my family, was our life. We had a goal for Martin to retire from the post office. He only had a little bit further to go. All we wanted was to be able to retire and enjoy our grandkids and our family [crying].

He had made me a promise that once he retired, we could move back to my hometown. He loved Meridian as much as I did. We'd take the kids to the State Park and spent a lot of our summers at that lake. We were going to find a little house and retire near the Park. We had plans to watch the grandbabies grow up around the lake.

There were no plans to be rich and have a lot of things. That wasn't what we wanted. We wanted to retire, be happy, enjoy ourselves, and pour into our family. That was it. That was the goal.

So as the marriage began to develop and mature, what did "normal" look like for Martin and Bebe's relationship?

Normal meant being together. Another challenge we faced early on was due to the fact that we had different ideas about free time together. I wanted a lot of people around, my friends, and a lot of activity. Martin taught me that you should want to spend quality time with your best friend—everyone else can wait. Your best friend is the one who you have the most fun with. The one you trust with everything.

I'd think it was so boring to just be us two and the baby. But not Martin! He wanted quality time with me and the baby. It took me a while to see it, but eventually I began to know what he was talking about. Martin became my best friend. I eventually realized that nobody compared to him. I wanted to spend as much time with him as possible [crying]. I think we truly became one when we both were totally satisfied with just being together. He was my best friend... 24/7.

Normal was a lot of laughter. We laughed so much at each other and ourselves. Even after Martin got sick, while he was still aware of his condition, he'd walk into the room and say, "Bebe," and then he'd just stand there trying to remember what he was going to tell me. I'd say, "You forgot, didn't you?" And we'd both bust out laughing. We loved laughter so much! I remember the Christmas after he got the diagnosis that he noticed that the star was crooked on the Christmas tree. He wanted to fix it. I said, "Martin, just leave it alone. We'll get Alex to fix it when he gets home." Well, he wasn't having it, and he moved a big chair over by the tree. I said, "Martin, don't do this, you're going to fall." He was adamant, "No, I'm not!" So he climbs up on the chair and actually fixes the star, and he turns around to me and says, "See?" About that time he falls off the chair. We laughed and rolled in tears for two months after that incident. I could just mention the star and he'd bust out laughing. He couldn't remember much, but he could remember trying to fix that star.

What part of your life with Martin was the most rewarding for you?

Watching him care for his family. My family also became his family. That man loved his family. Martin's concern for his family was an amazing thing to see. If I had something come up with my family, he'd be the first to say, "Go Bebe. Go do what you have to do." He was very in tune with what everyone needed. It was incredible to experience life with someone like that.

What have you learned the most in your life that Martin taught you?

He showed me how two people can become one. I know we say that we can't imagine our life without our partner **[crying]**. But I had definitely grown to that point. I could not imagine my life without him. That is what he taught me. I didn't know any of that early on. I didn't know that is what marriage and love is all about.

What do you think you taught him the most?

[chuckle] Wow! What would Martin say? Probably he'd say that I convinced him to let go some times. He was always so serious and meticulous about details. He had a lot of plates spinning, especially with the family. Sometimes I'd just say, "Martin! Let it go. Get your mind off of it. Let's go have some fun."

Martin stressed a lot. He'd have sleepless nights because he was thinking about a problem with one of his brothers or sisters. He was constantly concerned. I'd be the one trying to get him to chill out. Sometimes it is what it is. Worrying doesn't change anything. That was my approach with him often. Again, it's easy to see—he was the oldest, and I was the baby. Martin had been wearing stress for most of his life.

When did Martin's medical complications begin to surface?

In June 2009. We had started noticing a few little changes with Martin. Nothing was too alarming. He was about to turn 50. So it was little things beginning to pile up. He had a uniform that he wore to work every day. Martin was immaculate about his dress. Everything had to be ironed. Every hair was always in place. He came home one day from work and said, "Bebe, you'll never believe what I did today." Of course I said, "What?" "I forgot to put on my belt before I went to work." I was astonished. "You forgot to put your belt on today?" "Yeah, I can't believe I did that!" Well we blew that off and laughed about it. I kidded him, "You're about to hit the big 50!"

A couple weeks later, he came home at lunchtime, and he was totally disgusted with himself. I said, "Martin, what is wrong with you?" He said, "I did not put any deodorant on today!" I said, "Shut up!" He was adamant, "No! I did not put any deodorant on today." Again, we laughed about it and basically shrugged it off.

I hadn't put it all together, but I knew something was going on because he was having problems at work. He was having problems with balancing his cash at work. At first it was like $30 or $40, but later, he was having to put in $130 or $140 toward the balance because he was giving out the wrong change. I would ask, "Martin, what is going on?" He was so frustrated— almost to the point of tears. This was a man that didn't make those kinds of mistakes. Again, I didn't really think it was a big deal. "Come on Martin. You got to pay attention," and then I blew it off. He was beating himself up about it. There was no reason to pile on. But every week he had to put in over $100 to balance the drawer.

The postmaster at Martin's work called me one day, "Bebe, can I ask you a question?" I said, "Sure." He replied, "Is Martin okay?" I said, "Well... yeah. What's wrong?" "Bebe, he's been messing up at work a lot. The reason I'm concerned is because Martin is my best employee. He's trained everyone in this office. He's so consistent. But he's having transaction problems on the computer. And you know about the problems with the cash, right?" I said, "Yeah, I know all about it." "Well, we can't figure out if he's handing out the wrong change, or if he's keying in the wrong information on the computer. But he's having some problems. Maybe you should get him checked out." I was going to talk to Martin later that afternoon about it, but he was so frustrated about it all that I decided not to talk to him about it that day.

The very next morning, about 8:15 a.m., the postmaster called me back and said, "Bebe, I think you need to come up here." It startled me, "What? What's wrong?" "I don't know, but I just think you need to come up here." Of course, I dropped everything and drove up there. When I get there, Martin is standing at the computer, but he's totally frustrated and very stressed. Another employee was trying to help him, but Martin was so agitated. He said to Martin, "I'll get you through this, just calm down. Put in your password." Martin couldn't remember his password. He'd had that same password for twenty years. I said, "Hey, let's go home. It's time to go home." He said, "What are you talking about, I've got work to do." I said, "No. We need to go see the doctor. Something is wrong, and I think you're stressing too much.

That's all I think it is, so let's calm down and go get you checked out." When he walked out that day, he never went back to work. That was it.

So I took him home and made an appointment with the doctor. The doctor said, "It looks like symptoms of Alzheimer's, but it could just be stress." Of course, he referred us to a neurologist in Waco, who ran all kind of tests on Martin. A couple days later, we go back to the neurologist and he point blank said, "It's Alzheimer's, early onset." We were floored. He asked, "Does he have retirement?" We confirmed he did. "Go ahead and apply for it." I said, "What?" I was flabbergasted. The doctor was very blunt and straightforward, "He'll never be able to go back to work. I want to start him on this medication. It might help or at least slow down the progression." Then he said, "Do you know anything about Alzheimer's?" I told him I didn't. "Educate yourself. You need to know what you're facing. You got 5 to 7 years."

As we were walking out of the room, the doctor called me back in. "Bebe, he's young, and so are you. I gave you the lifespan with Alzheimer's early onset of 5 to 7 years. This is going to be very hard on you. I suggest you put him in a nursing home when it's time because he's going to be too much to handle. I'm sure you need to work, so just get on with your life." It was so blunt that it hit my heart hard. I wasn't sure I liked this doctor, but his honesty was a serious wakeup call for me.

So we walked out of there that day, I'm worried about Martin, and he never says a word about any of it to the doctor. We get into the car, and I asked him if he was okay. He said, "Yeah." I continued, "Are you worried?" He said, "A little bit." So I pushed, "Do you want to talk about it?" He said, "Nope." So we drove back home, and I asked him if he wanted me to tell the kids. He thought we probably should tell them. After that, it was a very quiet ride.

About the time we pulled into McGregor on that trip home, I told him [crying], "Martin, you don't have to worry about anything. I'm going to take care of you. You don't have to worry. I'm not putting you into a facility. I'm not going to do anything like that. I'm going to take care of you." He got very emotional. After he calmed down, he said that he knew that I would. He told me that he loved me, that I was a good wife, and he trusted me 100%. I said, "I will take care of you. Don't worry." [crying]

The next day I talked to the kids. Of course they had questions about the diagnosis and all the things that the neurologist had said. I promised them too that I was going to take care of their dad. They were in total agreement and voiced their willingness to do whatever was necessary to take care of their father. I was running a daycare at the time, so I told Amanda that she'd have to take over for me, and I'd stay home and take care of Martin. Amanda stepped right in and took over. She's been awesome. Next we told the families, and of course, everyone took it really hard.

His memory was slipping, but not totally gone. He could have moments of clarity, so I started trying to gather as much information as I could about what he wanted down the road—even after he was gone. I told him, "It would be helpful for me to know what you want. We don't have to talk about it, and I know you very well, but I want to carry out what you want. I know that your kids are your number one priority." He said, "Yes." Most of the time, all you got from him was a "yes" or "exactly." That was a big response [chuckle]. "I know you want me to take care of the kids." He said, "Yes, exactly." I knew he was boiling with worry, so I wanted to assure him that I'd take care of the things he was concerned about.

Martin started the medication, but it wasn't helping, and it was making him sick. After about 3 months, my primary doctor recommended that we get a second opinion. So he sent us to see another neurologist in Round Rock. By this time, I felt that I was losing him really fast. He couldn't control his bladder anymore [crying]. That was the first time I had to put the pull-ups on him. He was so worried about having to make that trip to the doctor without soiling himself. It was one of the hardest things I ever had to do for him. He just couldn't control it anymore. Martin was so hard on himself when he'd have an accident. I'd try to console him, but it really got under his skin.

So he consented to the pull-ups, and we went to get a second opinion. I really felt that this doctor in Round Rock was awesome. He looked at all the tests and agreed that it was early onset Alzheimer's, but he disagreed with Martin being on the medicine. He said, "First, the medicine is making him sick, and second, it slows down the brain." That confirmed why I was having such a hard time motivating Martin to get up. Before the medicine, he was quite mobile. Once we started that medicine, I could barely get him up. I wanted him up to walk and move around. "Then let's take him off the medicine and let him enjoy the time he has with some mobility." Martin perked back up. He became more alert and was able to get around a lot better.

In that interview, I asked the doctor what stage of Alzheimer's did he think Martin was in. He said he believed that Martin was stage-one. By then, I had been to every seminar I could attend. I was reading a lot also, so I knew the symptoms of the stages. I had done my homework. I replied, "Stage one?" I knew that stage-one was like forgetting where you put your keys. I said, "We're way beyond stage one. He can't control his bladder and has some serious memory loss." He said, "Well, he seems like he's only in stage-one." Every question the doctor asked Martin required a "yes" or "no" answer. All Martin had said to the doctor was "yes" or "no." I said, "I think we're in stage four or five already." The doctor replied, "Oh no, he can't be that far along." I shot back, "How can you make that determination? I'm the one who lives with him. I know what he can and cannot do. He's fully dependent on me. I brush his teeth, I comb his hair, I bathe him, I'm taking care of his bladder and bowel functions, I have to feed him, and you say he's stage-one?" Of course, he said he didn't realize that I was doing all of those things for Martin. I said, "You never asked me what I was having to do for him. You asked him "yes" or "no" questions. He's pretty good at saying 'yes' and 'no,' but that's about it." He was shocked when he got that information and said, "Well, you're right. I should have asked you about those things." I had to help Martin walk into the room! The doctor saw a man sitting in a chair who answered "yes" or "no" to his questions. So I filled him in on all the things that were going on with Martin. We basically got the same diagnosis—Azheimer's early onset, with a life expectancy of 5 to 7 years.

Wait. There were too many physical complications too fast for Alzheimer's right? Weren't the doctors suspecting something else?

You would think. I could talk to you about my disappointment with the doctors, but we don't have time for that discussion. Had I not educated myself, I would have been screwed. And there is no education available for early onset Alzheimer's. Most, if not all, of the data is geared towards senior adults. Every seminar I went to was for how to care for the senior adult patient. I had a 49-year-old husband who didn't fit any of the criteria. I'd talk to the presenter of the seminar, explain my situation, and they couldn't grasp how rapidly Martin was declining both physically and with memory health.

Now we know that Martin had Pick's disease, which is a genetically rare form of dementia, similar to Alzheimer's, but it's not Alzheimer's. It's a neurodegenerative disease that progressively causes the destruction of nerve cells in the brain. A lot of the symptoms are the same as with Alzheimer's. I have to give credit to Dr. Boles because he knew that something else besides Alzheimer's was wrong with Martin. Near the end of Martin's life, he was making a house call because we couldn't get Martin out. Dr. Boles said, "Bebe, promise me that you'll have an autopsy on Martin when he passes. If you don't have the money to do it, let me know. It just doesn't add up. Something else is going on here. To see such a healthy man in my office at age 49, and now four years later to see him in this condition... it has to be more than Alzheimer's."

So when Martin died, you thought he died of Alzheimer's?

Yes. We didn't get the diagnosis of Pick's disease until after we had the autopsy done. All we had ever been told by the neurologists was that it was Alzheimer's. The examiner gave the report to Dr. Boles and confirmed that it was indeed Pick's disease. It was a genetic disorder, and Martin had the gene. Pick's disease runs its course in four to five years—much like early onset Alzheimer's. Currently, there is no cure for Pick's disease. Martin died four and a half years after we got the first diagnosis. It is hereditary in the family, so one of his parents had to have the gene. It's a 50/50 chance that his brothers and sisters also have the gene. You can have the gene and never have it activate, but obviously Martin's did. I asked what causes it to activate, and I was told that too much stress could be enough. Martin was overweight for a man of his physicality. That, coupled with the inability to deal with stress, can trigger the gene.

I had learned what I could about Alzheimer's and had prepared as well as I could for dealing with an Alzheimer's patient. I had all these door alarms and locks for the doors. I was ready for the worst. But he was never that patient. He didn't roam; he didn't fight me—nothing like that ever happened. From the day he was diagnosed, he flowed with everything. The Pick's was definitely eating him, but we didn't know what we were really dealing with. He never argued, he did have memory loss, but he never acted like a normal Alzheimer's patient.

Did his personality change at any level?

Only that he stopped talking. He was diagnosed in January of 2010, and by December 2010, he'd nearly stopped talking to us. He could still recognize the kids, but by Christmas 2011, he wasn't responding to any of us, and it really upset Amanda. It was upsetting to all of us, and "yes" and "no" were less and less frequent. We could be in the room with him telling stories, and if something funny was said, he'd just burst out laughing. But there wouldn't be any communication from him. He was listening at times. Every night I'd say, "Goodnight Hon. I love you." [crying] And I'd get back, "Good night. I love you too." By January 2011, I might not get a response. I might get, "night," or "love you," but that was about it. He was done talking. There were no more conversations.

By that point, he was completely dependent upon me. I had to read his mind to meet his needs. I guessed a lot. I was doing everything for him by then. I made sure he drank his water. I had weaned him off of all of the other medications he was on. I was cooking healthy for him. His cholesterol had lowered. His blood pressure was better. Dr. Boles was amazed at how he was able to come off of those meds. Martin was diabetic, so I worked hard to make sure he was getting the right nutrition. He had a monster sweet tooth, so I cut that out. Martin kept his appetite until two weeks before he died. When he backed off on eating, I knew we were making a turn.

By then, Hospice had come in. They were here about six months before Martin died. I was stubborn and just wanted to do it all myself, but once getting him into the shower became a two person job, I called for some help. We (the nurse and I) would walk him up and down the hall [crying]. I refused to let him give up. She'd grab his hips, and I'd hold his arms, and I knew as long as I could get him up, I'd have another day with him. So we'd walk him, then sit him in his chair, and I would feed him his breakfast. He'd listen to his favorite TV show, *The Price is Right*, but he'd never open his eyes. He kept them closed unless I poked at him or made fun of him or I actually physically opened them. I'd say, "You in there? Look at me." I might get a grin out of him at that point.

How did Martin handle his complications emotionally?

Honestly, I never really got any emotional reaction from him. He got emotional on me that one trip back from the neurologist, and the rest of the time there was very little response. Martin did not feel sorry for himself. At times early on, I could see he wanted to talk about something. I'd ask him what he was thinking about, and he'd forgotten before he could verbalize it. I'd say, "Do you want to talk about the kids?" He'd say, "Yes!" But I'd have to guess. I'd say, "The kids are fine Martin. Don't worry about them." But, he'd get a little emotional around that topic. Other than that, he was very even tempered. I'd ask, "Do you want to see the grandbaby?" "Yes!"

My kids felt that he was so even keeled about it all because he knew and trusted that I could handle everything. He was emotionally very stable.

How did you handle his complications emotionally?

Well, I am a Capricorn. We tend to be helpers. We help a lot of people, but we hold a lot inside. I've always held things in for my kids, because I didn't want them upset. My kids are crazy about their dad. So it was one of my biggest concerns. I explained everything to them and kept them in the loop. They were young adults, so I could talk honestly. But my feelings didn't really show. The truth was traumatic enough. I didn't want to put more on them. Because I stuffed the feelings, I worried a lot. If it had only been Martin that I was concerned for, it might not have been that bad. But there was so much more going on than Martin.

I still had the Daycare, but there was no financial help from the Post Office until your retirement kicks in. It took 18-months for Martin's retirement to engage. Honestly, it was 18-months of pure hell. We had just moved into a home that Martin had always wanted when he got sick. We lost most everything we had because I stayed home with Martin. All of the worrying that I did about losing the house and trying to pay bills and deal with bill collectors forced me into an "I don't give a shit about material things. I don't give a shit about not paying that bill. Collect on me. Fine. I don't care. I'm staying right here where I am. You can collect. You can repo. Do what you have to do, but I don't give a shit. I'm taking care of my husband."

You could explain all day to the collectors what the challenges were, but they were ruthless. I explained it over and over, but it made no difference. We lost everything. We didn't have credit cards, but the problems were with utilities and medical supplies. We were evicted and had to move. At that point, my kids were mad at me because they were in the dark about how bad the financial situation had become. I told them, "It's my life. I'm trying to do what your father would want." Martin didn't believe in borrowing money from anyone, for any reason, so I wasn't going to do it unless I had to!

We had to move twice after Martin got sick. With all that hell going on around me, I still had Martin. If I could get a smile or any kind of response, it made my day—a big victory!

Was there a moment of communication when you both acknowledge the seriousness of the complications to each other?

Yes. It was following the very first meeting with Dr. Boles on the day he left the Post Office. Dr. Boles had suggested that it might be early onset Alzheimer's. He and I were sitting outside, and I told him we needed to talk about it. He didn't want to, but I pressed him. He mentioned that he wasn't upset, but he was scared. I asked, "About what?" He thought a moment and said, "My family." He didn't really want me to tell them. I told him that it was unfair of him to ask me not to tell them. But he wanted me to wait until it was certain. That was the extent of the concern and the conversation. He moved to compliance quickly.

What kind of daily care did Martin need from you?

100 percent of everything he got was from me: food, meds, bathing, and hygiene—all of it. Martin was totally dependent on me to meet his needs. He could grip your hand, but most of the dexterity was lost.

When he walked, he would tilt his head back like he was looking at the ceiling. I've never read about that symptom in any description about Alzheimer's. I'd ask Dr. Boles, and he hadn't ever seen it either.

I'd have to massage his jaw to get him to chew his food. He'd forget to chew, so that was a good reminder for him to chew his food. I'd always insist that we try to walk him. The nurses were quick to want to use the wheelchair, and it would have been easier, but I wanted him moving on his own until he absolutely couldn't do it anymore.

How much of that overall burden did you shoulder by yourself?

Absolutely all of it. Call me "hardheaded" and "stubborn." I've been called that by my family—it's okay. But it was hard on us, and I didn't want to ask anyone for anything. I've touched on this, but Martin and I built our relationship on him and me. It was my place to take care of my best friend. I didn't want the help from anyone because I knew how private Martin was.

He loved his family, but he was also all about us two together. Everyone was willing and wanted to help, but Martin would not have wanted his brothers and sisters having to do the things that were necessary for his bodily care. It was probably hard enough on him, even with me being his wife, handling all the duties to keep him clean and hygienically cared for.

I would never allow my daughter Amanda to help. We had discussed it often that her dad wouldn't have wanted her to be in the middle of all of that. I'd need to clean up Martin myself. Finally one day she stormed into the room after he'd had a really bad bowel movement. I told her she needed to wait outside. She was adamant, "Look, mom. My dad doesn't know who is taking care of him anymore, so I can come in here and help you mom. Just let me help you." **[crying]** So I allowed it. That was the first time I actually let her help me. She had a breakdown moment afterwards, because she didn't realize how bad her dad really was. Now she understood what I had been through. I had been handling all that by myself.

You can't imagine how many times I was told to put Martin in a care facility and get on with my life. Most of the medical and nursing community gave me that kind of advice. There is nothing wrong with the advice, but it wasn't for Martin, me, his family, or my family. I appreciated the conventional wisdom, but I had a totally different conviction about what kind of care Martin needed. He was about us. I never had a second thought about it.

How well do you think you did under that stress?

I became a chain smoker. I've never been a drinker, so I didn't go there. I lost 50 lbs. I worried too much and stressed a lot, but I've been told I handled the stress very well. Maybe I did? I think it's made me a stronger person. I cried when I was alone. I've always been driven to work hard and achieve. I did the best that I could. I feel good about it. I can rest with that.

Where did you find your strength and courage?

My family. That was all that I was focused on. Take care of Martin, and take care of my kids. I tried to make everything as easy as possible for them. My granddaughter has had the hardest time with Martin's death. She's still getting some therapy over it all. She held in the pain and is just now dealing with the grief. Trying to protect them all was a distraction from all the heartache. They gave me a reason to be strong.

When they came in every day and could see for themselves that Martin was clean and fed, it validated that I was doing my job. They knew he was being cared for **[crying]**. That is why I pushed him so hard to walk some. I knew we were moving closer and closer to the end when walking became such a chore for him. I loved being able to tell them, "Oh no, he walked for me today!" That was a good day. When he had a good day, we all had a good day. My kids were my inspiration.

Was there a point when you knew that your caretaking days were numbered?

Two weeks before he died. That morning I had gotten him up, and he walked to his chair. There were several things that happened that day that were different. He was always good to open and move his mouth around as I was brushing his teeth. He'd also adjust his bottom lip so I could shave that part right under the center of his bottom lip. It was like it was some kind of automatic response with those two things. It was really funny to me. But on that day, he wouldn't open his mouth. I had spent about 15 minutes trying to get him to eat some scrambled eggs. I opened his eye and spoke to him. He usually at least cut his eyes to look at me. On that day, he didn't look my way, but kept staring straight ahead. I checked his blood pressure, and it was a little bit low. I kept trying to get him to eat something. He wouldn't eat that morning. He didn't eat anything for lunch. And I finally got some soup in him later that afternoon. I had a private crying session because I knew we had made a shift. Something had changed, and it stayed that way until he died.

Did you two ever talk about "your" future without Martin in the picture?

Yes, just very briefly [crying]. One time he told me, "Take care of the kids. Make sure you get them set up. You're smart, and I know you can do it. Set them up, and take our grandbaby to Disneyland." [crying] "And I want you to be happy." I told him that I didn't want to talk about it. I changed the roles on him and didn't want to hear any of it. He said, "No, Bebe. You're young and beautiful. Be happy. If you find someone..." And I cut him off, "No, Martin. I don't want to talk about this. Stop talking about it. There is never going to be anyone else." And he grabbed my hand and said, "Stop waving your hands at me. You know what I mean. I don't even have to say it." I knew what he meant. That was it.

I know he was releasing me to find someone else, but I couldn't even process the thought for one second. I'm still there [crying].

What was going on in your head and heart during the few final days with Martin?

I knew it was getting close and that this was going to hurt, so I was concerned for my kids and Martin's family. We were all worried about Maddy (grandbaby). Amanda had been trying to prepare her, but she was 6 years old. She was adamant that she wasn't going to lose her Papo (her name for Martin). I was dreading the grief that we were all going to face. I knew how hard his brothers and sisters were going to take this. They were are all so close—really crazy about each other.

The last two weeks I was focused on making Martin comfortable and making the families comfortable with everything that was going on. During the last week, the house was full of family, night and day. But deep down, my heart was broken.

Looking back, how prepared were you to let him go?

Totally prepared. There was no way to know if he was having any kind of discomfort. He might scrunch his eyes—maybe he had a headache, who knows, but I'd give him liquid Tylenol. Other than minor things like that, there just wasn't any way to know. Whenever I'd see Dr. Boles, I'd ask him, "Dr. Boles, is he in discomfort?"

Knowing Martin the way that I did, knowing how far he had gone from his normal and healthy self, I'd pray at night for the Lord to just take him from me and not let him suffer with this dreadful disease. Why? Why did he have to go through this? You question God. Why did you put our family through this? Just don't let him suffer. But when I looked at him, he wasn't really in any pain, or didn't appear to be suffering. As the time drew near, I was genuinely ready to let him go. I didn't want him to be in his condition any longer. Our family had watched him deteriorate. They cried their hearts out for him. The last couple days of watching his breathing and giving him the morphine to help him rest—that whole watch was so hard for all of us.

I know that God does miracles. But my miracle was when God took him. He wouldn't have wanted everyone by his bedside crying. That was my decision, not his. But I didn't feel I had a choice. The family needed time for closure and healing. I was ready for that day to come. It was time for the hurt to stop.

Was there an opportunity to say "goodbye" before his final sleep?

Yes. I had actually said my "goodbye" a long time ago. Martin's sister, Dalia, and I had a discussion. Dalia was the sibling that came around the most when Martin was sick. She and I had always had our ins and outs, mainly over stupid stuff. But when Martin was first diagnosed, she was the first one to come around. She and I had a lot of deep soul talks about life and the problems we were facing. Dalia asked me one day, "Bebe, have you said your goodbye to Martin?" I said, "Yes, I have Dalia." It's hard to explain, but when he was first diagnosed, I began to educate myself on what we were going to face with the disease. I knew what was going to happen. When Martin stopped responding to me, it was obvious that this was no longer the man I fell in love with [crying]. It was his body, and I know it was his soul in there, but his spirit was gone. It wasn't my husband any longer. Right or wrong, that is what I felt. He didn't know me anymore. He wasn't responding. When I had that realization, I let him go. I was determined to take care of him, but he was free to God in God's timing. That is how I said my "goodbye." It allowed me to flow with the process in the final days. It was ok that it happened.

I was with him until his last breath. I kept telling him, "Just go, Martin. It's ok. Just go. I'll see you soon. There's nothing to worry about here. Just go."

So it's been 12 months since he passed. How are you doing?

I'm doing ok. I told you that I believe that it's made me a stronger person. I'm motivated to make Martin proud. I know how he felt about everything, so I'm on task with my kids. Martin had friends whose parents had left them an inheritance. Martin didn't have that, so he wanted something more for his children. I have the Daycare business that I'm leaving with Amanda. I'm opening up a little bar and grill in Meridian that I'm hoping to be able to leave to Alex. I'm busy, but it's important because that is what Martin wanted.

I am inching closer to being happier. I'm excited about the move to Meridian. I have my breakdown moments. I think of him every single day. I see something every day in McGregor that reminds me of him. It's a part of why I'm moving. It's not to forget, but this was his hometown, not mine. Everywhere I go here—I see him. There are too many stories from a man who was a mail carrier for so many years. Seeing a mailbox usually has a story attached to it. Or I can go into the grocery store and someone will see me who knew him. People mean well, but I don't want to re-live all the stories every day. That's part of the reason why it was so easy for me to make the decision to move from here.

I'm certain I'm still hurting inside. I can't seem to let all of that go right now. I totally shut down for about four months after Martin died. I wouldn't go anywhere. I didn't want to be approached by people with their condolences. People are kind and want to help, but I just didn't want to re-live it all. I sent the kids on a lot of errands. I'm still hurting, but I'm getting on with my life.

Do you ever sense that Martin is with you?

Oh my God, absolutely! I feel he is with me in everything I do. Especially when I'm with my kids and grandbabies. Even when I'm by myself, I don't feel alone. I know he's gone, but his presence and influence is everywhere. I learned that not just with Martin, but by losing my father, my sister, and my brother. It's different with Martin, because he was my soul mate, but yes, I feel him with me every minute of the day.

Most marriage vows contain the words: "For better or for worse... in sickness and in health... until death do us part." Describe what those words might have meant to Martin & Bebe.

They meant everything. We tested the waters. We didn't take those words lightly. It's probably frowned upon for us to live together, but that commitment was in place from the very beginning. We were very serious about the vows we made. We really loved each other, but you have to go through all kinds of challenges before you can actually affirm whether or not the love is real. If you won't stick it out, you'll never get to the real meaning of what those vows mean. No matter what happens, you have to stick together and work it out.

It's a legitimate give and take. Having someone to work through the process with is the good stuff. That's how you grow together. That's why I wouldn't allow anyone to care for him when he got sick. He was my love, my best friend—the one to whom I pledged my life. That's what you're supposed to do.

Were there times during the illness that you didn't think you could do it anymore?

Never. I made a promise. I was keeping that promise no matter what. It never crossed my mind to stop doing what I was doing. And I never regretted making that promise for a second.

I realize that not everyone can do that. It was the hardest thing I've ever done, but I got through it. Everyone will have to determine what is best for his or her situation. If you make a commitment, then stay true to the commitment. It probably will be hard. Things like that cost us.

From the Newlyweds:

If my spouse were just diagnosed with a terminal illness, what advice would you give me?

Educate yourself. Whatever that takes, educate yourself.

How did your mate's condition affect your normal intimacy patterns as a couple?

Everything was altered immediately. The meds he was taking shut all the sexuality down immediately. By the time he got off the meds 3 months later, he was drastically feeling the effects from the disease. So we were done with that part of our life together.

How did you handle those changes?

It was very hard. I had to face the fact that I had no control over this. It was what it was. I had my own challenges with getting older, but we had bigger issues to deal with than worry about the loss of our sexual intimacy. We were young, and it was much too early to be shut down like that, but Martin's care was the focus. I was fine with it.

It was mind over matter. There was so much to do with Martin's care, there wasn't a lot of time to feel sorry or lament the loss. We were busy trying to take care of him and enjoy every day with him. The kids and I cried quite a bit when he was first diagnosed, but I reinforced constantly that I wanted nothing but positive thoughts around Martin. I wanted us to talk to him, tell stories, laugh, and love as we always had. Even Maddy was so quick to love on her Papo. She'd tell him stories about her day, and of course, he'd never respond or even open his eyes, but we were all engaging with him as normal as possible. I didn't know what he could hear or not hear, nor did I know if he was listening or not. As I said earlier, sometimes he'd crack up laughing. It would surprise us all that he was actually listening and paying attention to what was going on in the room.

How did you find joy together when so much time and emotion was filled with the illness, disability, and disease? How did you avoid not focusing on the bad all the time?

That's why we stayed positive and reassuring to him. That was still the man we loved sitting in that chair.

What's the one piece of advice you'd give someone just starting out in marriage?

Take it seriously. There are going to be lots of ups and downs. But you have to want it to work. The love that brought you together is not enough to sustain you to the end. Your love has to grow. You have to stick with it. Young couples quit too easily. Don't give up. Love is a full-time job. Work at it, and you'll eventually find all the rewards you want. There aren't guarantees about life. So stop wasting time. Commit to make it work, and then work at it. Every marriage is a risk. No one is excluded. So decide to make it work.

What are your most important memories of your marriage?

[crying] All the times we got to spend together. We loved the fun times at the lake. We loved watching our kids grow up. Every little family gathering I hold dear to my heart. Martin hated movie theaters. As far as he was concerned, that was a waste of family time. We'd rent a movie and hang out, but he wanted to be where he could engage with the family.

Do you still think that marriage is a great idea?

Absolutely! I believe fully in marriage. I think it is a wonderful way to live life.

Any final words of advice for married couples of all ages?

Enjoy every day. Don't give up so easily. Work at it. You made a vow. Be serious. Never give up on each other.

In memory of

Martin Garcia, Jr.
June 30, 1959 – May 25, 2013

Bruce

Introduction

"And they'll walk out to the bleachers; sit in shirtsleeves on a perfect afternoon. They'll find they have reserved seats somewhere along one of the baselines, where they sat when they were children and cheered their heroes. And they'll watch the game and it'll be as if they dipped themselves in magic waters. The memories will be so thick they'll have to brush them away from their faces. The one constant through all the years has been baseball. America has rolled by like an army of steamrollers. It has been erased like a blackboard, rebuilt and erased again. But baseball has marked the time. This field, this game: it's a part of our past. It reminds us of all that once was good and it could be again."

—Terence Mann, movie *Field of Dreams*

If you ask baseball people to define "gamer," you'll usually get something like, "That's a guy that shows up to play everyday. He'll sacrifice himself for the team in whatever way he's needed. You want him in the big moment — when it's crucial. His nose is always in the mix. Give him the pressure, and you've made his day."

One of the things you have to realize about a gamer is that what you might see off the field doesn't necessarily mirror what you see on the field. What you see on the field is usually magical, special — a dance involving natural fluidity and athletic grace. In the eyes of the right beholder, it's all quite beautiful. Baseball is truly more than just a game; it's part religion, part science. It often requires a gamble of faith. You bet the odds, but nothing is ever guaranteed. Sometimes luck or bad fortune happens. But that's why the gamer shows up everyday to play. He has to play in order to find the truth of the moment. Today he could win. Tomorrow he might lose. That's just the way it is with baseball. But, there is only one way to find out. He has to play and play hard every single day.

I just recently met Bruce Cotharn, but I've known about him for a really long time. He married a girl I grew up with. Lisa Smith Cotharn was the daughter of one of my mother's best friends. My parents and her parents were closely bonded for many years, so there were a lot of Saturday nights where she and I collected fireflies and caused minimal trouble in the front yard as the parents were busy with the grill and iced cans of Schlitz in the back yard. Some childhood memories live a long time. Lisa's family lived in Waco, Texas, and mine lived 14 miles away. We went to different schools. Life happened, the paths led in different directions, and we grew up, and apart.

As I interviewed Bruce, my heart ached for him. The man lost a lot of love, identity and purpose when he lost his girl. But I've also ached for myself.

I wished I had made the time to pursue a closer friendship with Lisa as we stomped through life to do what we each chose to do. I've struggled emotionally with this story because I've felt my own remorse in not keeping up with her.

Lisa genuinely married well. She married a gamer. Bruce is an honorable man of both internal toughness and compassion. The ways in which he served his wife and his kids' mother is incomprehensible to most of us. From what I've been able to gather, the man blasted one right out of the park!

It has been a huge privilege to capture a piece of their story. Although this interview sheds some light, there is always more to know. Of all you'll read and feel in this interview, don't miss the rhythm of the gamer. The man came to play. Every. Single. Day.

Meet a uniquely committed man: Bruce. I'm proud to call him my friend. -MDP-

Tell us about how you two met and fell in love?

Sure. We were college sweethearts. In the fall of 1979, we were both attending McLennan Community College in Waco, TX. I was there on a baseball scholarship, and she was the local Waco girl living at home to save money on her college education for two years. I had a Tuesday through Thursday tennis class at 7:00 AM. Lisa and her best friend were in the tennis class that immediately followed my class. I always stayed to play against another guy after class, just hoping she might notice me. It didn't work.

Basketball season rolled around, and I'd see her at the games because she was a friend with everyone on my baseball team. She never paid any attention to me then either.   One night she came over to our apartments where the athletes were living. I was in the kitchen and the window was up. Lisa walked by (she had a very distinctive sound, look, and confidence to her walk) and I yelled "hey" out the window as she went by. I popped outside to talk to her for a moment. I said, "You walk past me on the tennis court, and you walk past me at basketball games. What does a guy have to do to get you to pay attention?" She laughed, and then answered, "I guess the proper thing to do would be to take me to dinner tomorrow night." I said, "I can do that."

I remember our first date was on a Friday in March, after baseball practice. I showered, and my roommate asked, "Where are you going?" I told him that I was taking Lisa Smith out to dinner. We went to Leslie's Chicken Shack to eat fried chicken. Afterwards, we ended up at the Melody Ranch for some dancing. I kissed her that night, and I knew I was going to marry her. After kissing me, Lisa went home and told her best friend and her sister that she had met the man she was going to marry.

Was it love at first sight?

Pretty much. If you were to ask the guys I played baseball with at MCC, they'd tell you different.   They would tell you that Lisa picked me, and I didn't have a chance! But I was in love with her mind just as much as I was physically attracted to her.

We didn't marry right away. After finishing our course study at MCC, Lisa left for Texas A & M. I left for Texas Christian University, stayed one year, and returned to finish my last two years of education and play baseball at Baylor. Honestly, I waited way too long to marry her. I was caught up in wondering how far I would be able to go with baseball and what a work career was going to look like. It took time for me to sort all of that out. In my mind, I didn't want to drag her through my mud. We loved each other, but I had serious questions about providing some sort of financial stability and consistency. I missed out on some great years with her because of my indecision about baseball and a work career—which prolonged the courtship for way too long.

I have a friend who is a coach in Louisiana. He won multiple high school football state championships and then accepted the head Division 1 football job at his alma mater. Simultaneously, his wife got a big promotion with Coca-Cola. They were talking about a bigger house and private school for the kids, and he said he told his wife, "I want to just go back to the days of eating bologna sandwiches for dinner, winning football games, and always bumping into each other when you walk around every corner in the house." Knowing now what I didn't know then, "going through the mud together," like my coaching friend talked about, IS the fun part.

Eventually, Lisa confronted me with, "Look, it's ME or baseball—make a decision." So I picked Lisa.

When and where were you married?

We were married on June 7, 1986 in Miller Chapel on the Baylor University campus in Waco, TX.

How long were you and Lisa married?

Twenty-three years. I met her when I was 18 years old, so I tell people we had a 30-year relationship.

What was the first year of your marriage like?

Lisa was pregnant with Courtney within 3 months of us getting married. That wasn't exactly in our plans, but that was God's plan, and we were very excited about becoming parents. That year was also very trying. There wasn't a lot of excitement extended towards us from my side of the family. My older brother had personal circumstances which dominated and controlled my parent's time. My parents were not emotionally invested in Lisa's pregnancy. Lisa needed their support—bringing a new kid into the world. Lisa had lost her mom while in High School, so it was a tough go. That being said, and thinking about it now, this was a bit of foreshadowing because we did get the support from our Sunday school class who brought the party to the hospital when they heard about Lisa checking in.

We were facing the normal challenges of most new marriages: work stress, financial pressure, plus making preparations for a new baby. We were both 25, and it was fast paced. We needed to put on the big boy jeans and the big girl panties in order to face adult responsibility.

How differently were you both raised?

My dad worked in the waterworks business. We were not affluent, but we lived comfortably. There were perks to my dad's job, so there was a membership at Colonial Country Club in Ft. Worth, tickets to TCU, Rangers, and Cowboys games. My brothers and I never wanted for much. I also loved to quail hunt, and we had a lease north of Breckinridge, Texas. I had bird dogs. I have said many times, "Back when I was a spoiled rich kid and my Dad paid for everything, I loved training bird dogs."

Lisa's dad was a football coach before he bought his own business. Things were much tighter financially for their family. Lisa's mom made all the girl's clothes while growing up. They didn't shop retail for clothes.

I grew up with two brothers and cousins who lived just down the street, so my support system was more "family" related. Lisa grew up in a neighborhood where all the kids interacted as family. She thrived in that kind of atmosphere!

We both came from fairly rigid homes in a disciplinary aspect. We had fathers who were not afraid to use the belt if needed. My mom made all of the decisions in my home. I have said many times that I didn't know whom I feared the most: God or my mother, and not necessarily in that order! I never knew Lisa's mom, but I heard many stories about her being very loving and attentive to her daughters. Lisa was also very close to her Me-maw (her grandmother Nona).

Early on, what were some of your toughest challenges as a couple?

We really struggled with financial management. There never seemed to be enough money to meet all the needs. We had different rhythms for time management. I have a tendency to get tunnel vision, and it takes me longer than most to accomplish a task. I lose track of time in those scenarios. Lisa was very regimented and systematized in her approach to prepare for her job. She liked to be early to whatever she was going to be involved in.

I learned early in our relationship that she was tough-minded. That meant that I could express an idea to her, but she might not be convinced immediately. She needed the space and time to process. Once she was on board, she was on board, but there was no rushing that process. She might have to chew on it for a while. You didn't say, "Lisa, you need to do so and so!" It was better to say, "Lisa, have you thought about...?"

Lisa was strong-willed and had ideas about how order was to flow. My tendency was to serve and help carry out those orders. I'm not a controller. So we flowed pretty well together.

What were your shared goals and ambitions?

Lisa had gotten a Master's in Education and was working towards her Doctorate. I was in total agreement with that. She got a lot of satisfaction from her work. In fact, during the post-injury season of Lisa's life, it was her work that saved her. She was a teacher, it was her motivation that helped to endure the intense full body nerve pain she lived with every day post injury.

I was working as a sales representative and hoping to always improve my opportunities to provide for the family. Of course, we wanted to see the kids grow and experience some success in all their endeavors. We wanted them to get a college degree and expand their dreams. We were synchronized in those desires.

So as the marriage began to develop and mature, what did "normal" look like for Bruce & Lisa's relationship before the accident?

I actually believe those 5 years before the accident were some of our toughest years. Lisa had some health issues and she didn't feel well, and consequently, she wasn't happy. Her weight had ballooned, and that added extra stress to her condition. I caught some of the negative effects of her not being happy. My confidence levels took some pretty hard hits during that time. We were growing in the relationship, but it wasn't easy.

I distinctly remember our going on a marriage retreat together. One of the exercises was for each of us to write down our top five needs in the marriage and to also write down what we thought were our mate's top five needs. I listed all five of Lisa's needs correctly, and I listed them in the proper order! She listed only 1 of my needs, and it was fourth on my list. Instead of her looking at my list apologetically or in surprise, she turned to me, fired away and said, "Those have never been your needs!" I said, "Those are my needs, but you're not paying attention. You better get locked in." And that was how you worked it with Lisa. You said what you needed to say, and then you let her figure out her own response, in her own timing.

No kidding, it took at least two years for me to convince her to go to the doctor to get some blood-work. She wouldn't take medication, and she was just living with a lot of pain. You could suggest, but you couldn't demand. She had to be the one to make the decision.

The blood-work revealed that she was carrying a strep infection that affected her bowel tract. Until she had the surgery to remove that infected part of her bowel, she was in misery. Once that was done, Lisa was able to properly metabolize food again, and she lost about 120 pounds in just over a year's time.

Also about that time, a job that I loved was slowly dissipating. I was soon to realize that it probably was for a bigger purpose that I could not ever have imagined. That was a tough season. A lot of problems just hung around.

My very close and good friend (who is a pastor) talks about how a husband and wife should pursue each other the way God intended. Your spouse is the single most important item in your life, and you pursue them to always make them feel this way. He says that you should feel that everything is always okay between the two of you. That allows for disagreements, discussions, or communication between the two of you to always be concentrated on the issue at hand. I felt this way in my interactions with Lisa! Everything between the two of us was always okay, because we were in it together. There was never a thought differently or otherwise on my part.

What have you learned the most in your life that Lisa taught you?

She was the consummate professional about her work. She had a consistency about how she prepared for her day. It was a system that helped her face every day prepared with energy and excitement. She loved everything about school: the social aspect, the kids, her principals, the special "something-something" and rolls the lunch ladies would cook and fix for her, her daily conversations with the lady that cleaned her room, and playing jokes on her OCD colleagues by moving things on their desk and in their room just to watch them put it back in the specific place. She loved decorating her room throughout the year as the seasons changed, sponsoring cheerleaders, and doing the jitterbug for the kids at school dances. She was a loud and proud independent Texas woman: big hair, big smile, big laugh, and big personality! When she laughed—you laughed. When she smiled—you smiled. Her students loved to come into her classroom and tell her stories. Lisa invested time with the students. I once asked my pastor friend, "Do you think Lisa knew me so well because she loved me, or because she wanted to know me because of her controlling personality issue?" He said, "Neither. She knew you because she spent TIME with you."

She helped me learn to manage time better (not that I do all the time). I have had to really work hard at it, but it's much improved.

She also helped me be more self-aware about my responses around people. I'm not a politically correct thinker—I will call people out on their BS, I just say what I'm thinking with a hard line of right and wrong, and my tone has to be softened. She'd coach me on those things often, "Bruce, you can't say it like that, people are sensitive." Or she'd say, "Bruce, you'll damage the kids if you handle them like that." She understood the needs of kids. She made sure the kids had consistent structure.

My kids and I laugh often about her way with people. We've learned that they loved Lisa—they only tolerated us!

I recently started a new work career. In the interview process with my division manager, I discovered that his workout partner is a guy I played baseball with at MCC. Before I was hired, I told him, "I bet you my job right now that when you tell him you interviewed me, he will say 'Bruce is a great guy—but man, you should have known Lisa!'" He called me two days later and said, "I owe you a job!"

What do you think you taught Lisa the most?

My dad has a phrase that I think applies here: "You've got to pay attention. There comes a time when everyone needs help." I am usually quick to lay down things that are important to me in order to help others who may have a need. That heart for servitude got me in trouble with her at times, especially if her priorities were being held up by my attention elsewhere. Over time, she began to appreciate and incorporate that kind of mentality into her own life. She loved Angel Tree at Christmas, which provided gifts to children who had a parent in prison. Every year she would pick out a student who needed financial help, and she would buy them school clothes. She was so proactive and had a real heart for helping the poor. She loved giving to the different missions and ministries in Baton Rouge that helped single teenage moms who are pregnant. She told me that her next venture was to work at a soup kitchen that served Thanksgiving and Christmas meals to the homeless. I'd like to think I helped her develop an appreciation for that kind of service.

We know that Lisa received serious injuries in December 2002 because of an automobile accident. What happened?

It was December 27th, and we were going as a family to south Texas to go deer hunting with her dad. As irony would have it, Lisa and her dad didn't have the greatest relationship. When her dad remarried after Lisa's mom passed away, he didn't tell his two daughters until after he was married. There were a lot of hurt feelings between them all. Her dad's new wife wasn't very receptive to Lisa and her sister being involved in his new life. It was a very difficult time. So when Lisa's dad called and invited us (and Lisa's sister) to the house in Three Rivers, it was a really big deal! We had been to my parent's house in Ft. Worth, and we were on our way to Three Rivers.

It was a beautiful day and the weather was perfect. Courtney (15) was driving to get some highway experience. Lisa was riding shotgun up front in the passenger's seat, Baron (12) was asleep in the middle seats, and I was sitting in the third row working on my day planner. As she was making a change from the right lane to the left lane, a van going about 90 mph blew past her on the left side of the Suburban. Courtney over-corrected twice, and the Suburban rolled 3.5 times. Lisa took a blow on the back of her head that caused trauma between the C2 and C3 vertebrae. The MRI showed that the blood that gathered in her spinal cord was about the shape and size of a black-eyed pea. It killed those nerves on the right side in her spinal cord.

She and I were flown by helicopter to University Hospital in San Antonio. They took Lisa one way and me another and stapled up the split on the back of my head. Courtney didn't have a scratch on her!

I probably won't know what happened to Baron until I get to heaven. When I crawled out of the Suburban after the roll, I'm counting heads, and I notice that Baron is in the median about 400 yards away, walking towards the Suburban and picking up articles that had flown out of the truck during the spin and roll. He doesn't know, and I do not know how he got out of that Suburban without a scratch on him! It's a miracle and a blessing that he has no idea! God must have just reached in, or his angels yanked Baron out of the Suburban before it got too rough. As I said, only God knows those details.

The people who rendered aid on the highway were awesome. God sent a medic who had just gotten back from Iraq to attend to my wounds. Baron was the one who noticed that my head was bleeding.

Once at the hospital, we (Lisa's sister Shelley and me) were not getting answers on Lisa's condition because they only had one doctor who handled spinal cord injuries. That doctor was skiing in Colorado for vacation. The staff was consumed with just stabilizing her until that doctor returned. The doctor returned early, and once she arrived on the scene, she took control of the situation immediately. She offered us a group of research facilities: of which one was in Houston (TIRR Memorial). I also remember another being Shepherd in Atlanta, as well as Boston (where Christopher Reeves received treatment) which were part of the research group. Texas Medical Center was much closer, and she was a Texan, so we opted for Houston. After being in San Antonio for 15 days, they flew Lisa in a medical airplane to Houston. She was at TIRR for 6 months—180 days. While she was getting her therapy and treatment, they were also training me how to take care of her.

What was Lisa's condition after the accident?

She was considered a C2 spinal-cord injury tetraplegia incomplete, a.k.a., quadriplegic.

What were her bodily capabilities?

She had lost all functional capabilities from the neck down. She could move her arm, but she couldn't utilize her hands or fingers in any way—same with her legs. She could move her legs, but couldn't do anything for herself. She was totally dependent for anything requiring dexterity. She drove her wheelchair using her head.

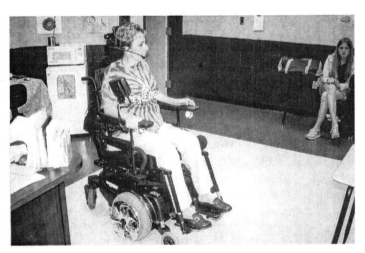

In June 2005, we went to Lisbon, Portugal, and she had adult stem-cell surgery. Dr. Carlos Lima was one of the finest doctors we had ever encountered. He had found a way to differentiate between smell mucosa and breathing mucosa in the sinuses. When you have a common cold, your stem cells die and regenerate in order for the cold to run it's course in your body. So they went into her nasal passages, harvested the smell regenerating mucosa from the breathing mucosa, cleaned out the scar tissue (the black-eyed pea between C2 and C3 which halted all the proper signals in her spinal cord), and repacked it. With therapy, those stem cells begin to conduit communication again. She had made amazing progress with her therapy until...

In February 2006, on Valentine's Day, Lisa had a raging yeast infection. Her OB/GYN had asked me to keep her legs open so her body could breath. It was diametrically opposed to the training I received at TIRR. After talking it through with Lisa, we decided that she'd prop up on her backside and cross her legs Indian-style. During the night, Lisa somehow kicked her heavy therapy boot off the bed (The boot kept her foot up and locked. It also stretched her Achilles to prevent what is known as "foot drop" and helped her walk on the Auto-Ambulator for therapy.) In that process, the weight of the boot spun her and simultaneously dragged her off the bed.

It had been a really cold day, and I allowed our cattle dogs in the house for the night. I gave Lisa her meds at 11:00 p.m. By 11:05 p.m., I was usually in bed asleep because the next morning started at 4:30 am. One of the dogs jumped on my bed and barked in my ear to wake me up. I looked and could see that Lisa wasn't in her bed. I got up to find her lying on the floor beside her bed, and I screamed out for Baron. She told me that she felt something had happened with her leg, and sure enough, it was broken. From that point on, she quit improving with her therapy. In fact, she began to digress.

That was emotionally very hard on me. I complied with what the OB/GYN doctor asked us to do, but it was totally contrary to how I had been trained. It went against my TIRR training, and it cost Lisa dearly. It took me a very long time to forgive myself, and I had several breakdowns. I never went against my TIRR training again.

How did she maintain her drive to keep on during all those years of therapy while attaining such limited progress?

It was difficult, but Lisa was motivated to get back to her teaching job. She was very focused on returning to the classroom. Everything she endured with therapy was so she could get back to work.

Lisa's principal had given Lisa her job back. Our sound guys from church fitted her with a microphone and installed speakers in her classroom. She was so pumped. But in July 2003, shortly after her getting that news that she had her job back, the Superintendent called her in for a meeting. He had taken some bad advice from an attorney and an assistant Superintendent. He said, "I can't have a woman in a wheel-chair teaching in our school system." Lisa immediately burst into tears. He had made his decision, and her safety was his voiced concern. It was a weak argument, but he wasn't budging. Once she got that news, living day to day was very difficult for her. She lost a lot of weight, and therapy became a real drag for her. During that season, my concern was keeping her alive. She was devastated! In her mind, she didn't have enough of a reason to live—only to endure the amount of physical pain she was dealing with on a daily basis.

In March 2004, the same Superintendent had gone to a conference where Christopher Reeve was the main speaker. Christopher and his wife Dana had started the Christopher Reeve Foundation. They had written to Lisa and requested information about her medical condition. We sent the Foundation the information about Lisa's status. Interestingly enough, Dana would use the material that was sent back to quiz Christopher in order to keep his mind sharp. He had read and memorized some of Lisa's information. After the conference, the Superintendent went up to introduce himself to Christopher. When he told Christopher where he was from, he said, "Ah. I know one of your teachers in that school." Christopher proceeds to tell the guy all about Lisa, her family, and the accident—the whole story. Christopher said, "Hire her back. Give her a reason to live." As a result, the Superintendent gave Lisa her job back. We lost a year of income because of that little episode, but it was the motivation she needed to keep steady with the therapy!

I need to say this here because it's so amazing. I gave up my career so I could take care of Lisa. Lisa didn't get her job back until the fall of 2004. Our church, Jefferson Baptist Church in Baton Rouge, Louisiana met our income and medical obligations. The church members gave over $98,000.00 from 2002 – 2009. The provision was nothing short of miraculous.

How long did she teach after she got her job back?

Until the day she died in August 2009.

What was the cause of Lisa's death?

Lisa was very prone to dehydration from medication and because spinal cord injury patients don't really sweat, it's easy for them to overheat and dehydrate. She had a stomach bug that resulted in a bad case of all night long diarrhea. After a ride to the hospital ER in the ambulance, I told the attending physician that she was a medication lightweight, and very susceptible to drugs. I told him that I was very concerned about her being severely dehydrated. I had previous experience with her, and I knew she needed fluids.

He elected to give her Dilaudid, which is a synthetic morphine, to help ease her pain. I went down to the nurse's station and told them that I wanted her off that medicine because it wasn't her normal meds. I said, "Call our doctor! Do whatever it takes, but get ahold of him." He showed up that next morning at the hospital very early. He told my son and I that she just needed to sleep off the affects of the medication, and he put her back on her regular meds.

It was the last day of the month, and I had to go home, pay some bills, get a shower, and take a short nap. So I left my son with Lisa while I went to do a few chores.

Not long after I left for the house, the phone rang, "Dad, you better get up here. Mom isn't doing very well." I rushed back as soon as I could. When I got to the room, I went over to hug and kiss her, and she was cold. She was gone.

Lisa wasn't on a monitor, but once the nurses realized we had a problem, they rushed in and asked me to step out of the room. I said, "Listen, she's gone. She's with the Lord. Don't get up on her and pound away. Let her be." With the dehydration, nothing in her system, and then the meds that were foreign to her, her heart simply raced out—it was too much.

There is a thing called "medication half-life." If you're given a medication and it causes death because of the side effects, there is a window of time called the "half-life" which determines how much of the drug is still in the blood stream when the death occurs. If it takes 12 hours to metabolize a drug, the half-life would be 6 hours. If death occurs within the first 6 hours, it is within the half-life. I knew that Lisa had responded negatively to the Dilaudid. I knew how her body handled different medications.

Did you have a conversation with a malpractice attorney?

Oh yeah. But because of the half-life definition and the fact that Lisa died after the window of time, we were told we didn't have a case. When I pushed the doctors about the half-life on the Dilaudid, she died 15 minutes outside of the half-life window.

How did Lisa handle her physical limitations emotionally?

She hated her limitations and the need for dependence on others. That was really frustrating for her. She ran through a wide-range of emotional spectrums—negative and positive. At times I could catch the brunt of her frustration. I believe it's fair to say there were moments of verbal abuse.

How did you handle her limitations emotionally?

I'm a pretty simple guy. I meant what I said when I said my marriage vows. I wasn't just standing up there for the hell of it. I made a promise. It was my job to take care of her. Yes, I loved her, but I also had a duty and responsibility to her. She was my wife.

My son used to make fun of me because of the roles I sometimes had to fulfill. We might be at Walmart looking for her make-up, and I'd antagonize my son because at least once a week he would tell me I was gay! "Baron, do you think your mom's mascara is brownish black or black?" He once said, "Dad, I know you have to do this stuff, but you don't have to like it!" **[laughing]** I'd shoot back, "Listen, I have to put the stuff on your mom. I might as well learn what she wants." This was the hand that was dealt. I just figured that if I had to get in touch with my feminine side, I might as well be good at it. It was just a part of it.

Let me tell you, it wasn't like dealing with an Alzheimer's patient. Her mind was plenty sharp, so I still had her. That part was still very much alive and well! If you got crossways with her, you'd also find out how sharp her tongue was. Communication was the only thing she had to blow off steam. If I was the target... I might have to just take the lashing. I knew she needed an outlet for her frustration. Shelley always said that I was Lisa's safe place to fall. I only really crossed her once in a tenuous situation, but it was a discipline issue that just had to be handled by a dad.

Lisa was a curve buster. People with her kind of injuries are normally on a ventilator. She willed herself off the vent dependency. God did bless her to live much longer than the statistics and what she was "medically" supposed to. It's a testimony of how tough she was. It was my job to help give her a life. It was my role, and I was glad to do it. I didn't question God, nor did I press him for answers. I just did what I needed to do.

I've had people suggest to me that I should have tried to get a job at TIRR after Lisa's death. I can't. There was a grace to serve my wife. I can't even think about doing those things on another person. I had to do more things with the female body than any guy should ever have to do, but that was my wife, and it had to be done. I did my tour.

So Bruce, are you genuinely going to be okay with this kind of disclosure about the communication patterns between you two— particularly the harsh stuff?

All of our intimate contacts, those who knew us well and were vested in our life, knew the struggles I was having with how Lisa could react in a verbal assault. This stuff won't be news to anyone who really knew us during that time. Many people were steadfast in their prayers for us. I understood her personal battle with the confinement. God gave me grace to withstand quite a bit.

So you just took the abuse?

Yes... mostly. Ninety percent of the time, I just absorbed it. Lisa's sister (Shelley) begged me and pleaded her case that I had to start looking Lisa in the eye and tell her, "You can't talk to me like that. If you want me to listen to your concerns, you'll have to change the way you talk to me." It took me many years to finally get that tough and firm with Lisa. Shelley was right, and she knew her sister well. A straightforward confrontation usually stopped whatever was going on. It could get extremely intense.

Honestly though, can you imagine the loss of control over your life? There was some misery, anger, and constant frustration in that for Lisa.

What kind of daily care did Lisa need from you?

Everything. I fed her, bathed her, transferred her in and out of bed and into her chair, washed her hair, brushed her teeth, put her make up on her, curled her hair, dressed her, gave her meds, and attended to her hygiene. She had a bowel program every other day that required attention, and I had to change her leg bag when needed. I did therapy on her twice a day, stretched her and massaged her, and took her to therapy after school. Basically, whatever she needed, I did it for her.

A typical day once she was back in the classroom started around 5:00 a.m. It was full-on work to get all those things done by 7:00 a.m. because she wanted to be in her classroom by 7:15 a.m. Once I got her into class, I helped her get the classroom ready for the kids. I'd leave the school around 8–8:30 a.m. Only then was there time for a cup of coffee and breakfast. I'd have a break to do what I wanted or needed to do until 3:00 p.m. I'd get her home, and the evening activities would fill in the rest of the day. It was usually the reversal of everything I had done for her that morning. Take her makeup off, etc. I slept hard at night **[laughing]**.

When you were around her, you had to pay attention. She couldn't make self-adjustments. She could drive her chair really well, but if she hit something, she might spasm or just need to be physically readjusted in her chair. That required me to pick her up and make the corrections. Many times I would have to go up to school and do this during the day—sometimes more than once a day.

Traveling also required another level of attention to make sure she was secure in the van. You just had to be alert. That could definitely be mentally grinding. If she needed something, it normally couldn't wait, it had to be attended to immediately.

*** *Bruce has graciously allowed us to publicize a video link that will give you more insight into their daily routine post-accident. Watch Bruce as he prepares Lisa for work:* http://youtu.be/FJ1cI0II4B4. *Patti and I know that it might not be easy for everyone to watch, but it is a very telling 52-minutes. Extremely sobering, yet very inspiring! -MDP-*

Generally, what was Lisa's response to your caretaking?

Her standard response was, "I'm so sorry that you have to do this," especially if it was the hard stuff. This strong, independent Texas woman was totally reduced to helpless confinement. She was grateful, and I knew it. She felt she was a burden to me. She wasn't, not even close.

To do all the things she needed was mentally tiring and time consuming, but they were not burdensome. She'd contact my friends and ask them to take me out or take me to play golf. She knew exactly what I was doing all around the house to take care of what was needed. That was a big part of her "thank you" to me.

How much of that overall burden did you shoulder by yourself?

All of it until she died. As I mentioned earlier, I gave up my career to take care of her. While Lisa was at TIRR Memorial in Houston for rehab, they were simultaneously training me to take care of her. We tried hiring help, but I was paying people and then having to train them how to take care of her at the same time. It was soon obvious that it was just a better fit for me to take care of Lisa.

Also, early on, Lisa was having separation anxiety. More than once, I had to cancel my work plans in order to fix some issue she was having. When she got anxious, it wasn't good. So again, it was another reason for me to just take care of her myself. I didn't have to wonder about the care she was getting. I knew she was being taken care of.

How well do you think you did under that stress?

I think I did a good job. I made it my commitment. We had the numbers early on about the potential of her longevity, and she was a curve buster. I knew that infections and disease could harm her. So I worked hard to keep her environment clean and sterile. I gave it my best shot.

What were your big "priorities" before the accident? How were those things affected by Lisa's condition?

Physical intimacy was a priority before the accident. That completely went away. Flexibility of schedule was also gone, because I needed to be no more than 5-10 minutes away from her at any given time. What she had going on, no matter what the situation, became the priority. Keeping her healthy and alive was the priority. Period.

Was there a point when you knew that your caretaking days were numbered?

I can only put my finger on one memory where I wondered, "What is it going to be like when she's gone?" But that was the only time I went there. I do remember that I was pretty beat up emotionally, tired, and out of gas at the time, but it was just a thought. It wasn't something I'd ever voice out loud.

Did you two ever talk about "your" future without Lisa in the picture?

All the time! That is the one thing that my closest friends didn't understand about us. Early on during the initial hospital stay after the accident, Lisa would communicate that she really wanted me to be able to see things from her perspective. She had definite ideas and instructions on how I was to handle the kids. She had instructions about what she wanted done with the house. I had a list of things that she wanted done. I made a lot of changes to the house after she died because she wanted them done. My friends thought I was nuts. I would always tell them, "You don't understand. She wanted this stuff done, and I made a promise."

She planned her own funeral basically. Talking through all those things were some of the sweetest conversations we ever had. She worked hard to express the emotional reasoning of why she wanted stuff done a certain way. There was some aspect of this particular conversation that happened almost every day. On the days when she was really angry with me about something, we couldn't have those discussions. But otherwise, it was in the mix somewhere.

Was remarriage ever a topic?

It was never discussed with me, but because of her personal experiences with her dad remarrying after her mother's death, she told my daughter, "I want you to be okay if your dad dates someone. There is no reason to be upset about it. I'm not certain that he'll ever remarry. He'll feel like he's cheating on me if he ever engages intimately with another woman. He might date, but I'm not sure he'll ever remarry." Courtney later told me about the conversation. There are some things you hate when you feel your mate is right **[laughing]**.

Looking back, how prepared were you to let her go?

Because of how she died, there wasn't really any preparation. We were still living life and doing everything we could to manage what health she had. I felt I had failed. I shouldn't have allowed her to be given the drug that I'm fairly certain took her life. I could be very combative when it came to her healthcare. I knew what she needed and how she was going to react to what she was being given. But, there was the same eerie peace during that ordeal in the hospital that I had experienced on the day when I let Courtney drive the Suburban. Those are the only two times I have felt that sensation. I don't think I was prepared because I wasn't in a place of letting her go. I had dedicated my life to her helping her live. There was no downturn. It was just over. I have always said, "It's easy to celebrate where she is, but that doesn't mean I don't miss her."

Was there an opportunity to say "goodbye" before her final sleep?

Lisa knew how much I loved her. I told her I loved her every day. I knew her wishes and desires. I feel those wishes were mostly comprised by her experience of losing her mother. Those wishes that she wanted from me were actually wishes that she never got from her mother. The fact that she entrusted me with those things was a sort of a healing "goodbye" for us. I feel she had a deeper purpose in conveying her desires.

So it's been almost 5 years since she passed. How are you doing?

The last two years have been the hardest. It's not been easy finding a rhythm in the job arena after taking so many years to attend to only Lisa's needs. Every memory is tied to my 30 years with her. There is a lot of identity in something like that. For me to get into a new season is going to require me to do something different than what I've ever done. I'm in my 50's now. It's not that easy to fire up again, and quite frankly, I've struggled a bit. I've heard "no" way too much. I couldn't get a job. I couldn't get a date. Confidence is sexy, but I lost my mojo. Depression was more active than happiness. God doesn't want you to live like that, but nothing was working. If nothing is working, you just want to find hideaway places—disengage from people and friends because you don't want to repeat telling the unsuccessful horror stories all the time. But currently, I have a new job, and I'm hoping for some good stuff to begin to happen soon. I'm just now mentally getting to the point of excitement for what God has in store for me in this new season of my life.

I'm not a jealous person, but I won't say that I haven't been envious of those who have found love again quickly after losing a spouse. It would be nice to occasionally not eat by myself. I've had a hard time. I have been turned down so many times for dates, it's ridiculous. So I quit asking. One of the reasons why I quit asking was I figured I needed to focus on work. God gave Adam a job to tend the garden before he ever gave him a mate. But I don't want to be an old-hardened guy because all I ever did was protect my heart. I know God's timing has to be right; it has to be his idea and I can trust that.

My daughter has said to me, "I don't care who you date, but I want to be able to pick out the one you pursue." My response was pretty normal I think, "What business is that of yours?" Out of the mouth of my kid came, "You can't pick a good one. Mom picked you, and you didn't have a choice." **[laughing]** I couldn't totally disagree with her.

I consider myself to be a solid stand up Christian guy, a quality person, and a man with good character. Sometimes it seems that Lisa was the only one who ever knew that or recognized it. It's been a bit confusing. I've wondered if anyone cares about those kinds of qualities in a man anymore.

Do you ever sense that Lisa is with you?

Yes. Every time I checked off one of her projects on my list, I felt an instant connection to her. I felt her with me back in 2010, when I returned to Grand

Junction, CO as a baseball coach. That place held a special connection for us both back when we were dating because my group of incoming freshman in '79 was the first class to ever take MCC baseball teams to the Junior College World Series for two consecutive years. I feel her with me when our kids are accomplishing some of the aspirations she had for them. It was heartbreaking for Courtney, but I felt her with me when Courtney's engagement broke off a couple weeks before the wedding in 2010. Lisa never felt that guy was the right guy for Courtney and had vehemently expressed it. I've wondered if Lisa might have elbowed Jesus to intervene in that situation **[laughing]**. Baron has since found his way into coaching, and Lisa always felt that was where he would find his greatest joy. The fact she knew us all like that is stabilizing and brings a certain level of peace. Her influence is still very active.

I can have a conversation with Shelley about the things going on in the kid's lives, and I can immediately sense Lisa in the mix because Shelley knew her sister so well. It may sound silly, but it feels good when that happens.I can celebrate that Lisa is with Jesus, but that doesn't mean that I don't miss her.

I have had people suggest I am still in love with my wife. I don't understand that thinking. I am not living my life through the rear view mirror. This interview forces me to go back in time and talk about someone I loved with all of my heart that was extremely important to my life for 30 years. But I am pressing on into a new season for where God needs me to be, and it's challenging! I am not sure that you could talk about my life without including the post-accident years of 2003-2009, but I do not want to be defined only by those years. I still have a lot of love to give and life to live.

Most marriage vows contain the words: "For better or for worse... in sickness and in health... until death do us part." Describe what those words might have meant to Bruce & Lisa.

I believe those words implied an implicit trust between Lisa and myself. We made a commitment to each other before God and witnesses when we said them June 7, 1986. We meant them when we said them. I said earlier that I'm a simple guy and that I meant what I said when I said my wedding vows. I loved Lisa. I gave my word which had my honor. Maybe it's true—I've heard it said before that you have to grow up together in life to really grasp what those words in the marriage vows mean. Obviously, I've told a story here that suggests we had to face some perils much different than others. But I know that we both felt blessed to have the other one chosen by God to live our lives together.

I have been given a huge heartfelt compliment from several men at church and good friends who told me that I set a high standard of how to love a woman. That meant a lot to me, but I wasn't looking for accolades, and it is actually hard for me to accept the compliment. I normally tend to just cut them off in mid-sentence because it was an honor for me to be her husband. There was never a thought that I was supposed to do anything different.

From the Newlyweds:

Were there times during the illness that you didn't think you could do it anymore?

No. I had tremendous support from my friends and my church. Lisa's dad helped us financially in tremendous ways. Because he had experienced so many of the same challenges with Lisa's mom (who died of Lupus), he was sensitive to helping with a lot of Lisa's needs. He knew, most times before I did, what I was going to need to take care of Lisa. He was usually ahead of us when a need arose.

He bought us a van for her wheelchair. He bought her a hot tub for her therapy. Mr. Smith was actually a huge inspiration to me because he was going through this for a second time in his life—first with his wife, and now with his daughter. I would ask how he accomplished the day to day tasks, and he would say, "I had great help from Nona" (Lisa's grandmother), which was different from me being out there by myself.

Shelley was a legitimate strength to me as well. She was there for her sister and in the foxhole with me. I was motivated to never let her down. I couldn't bear to think that Mr. Smith or Shelley might be disappointed by my actions. It would have devastated me. They held me accountable with their influence. I can honestly say that all I ever wanted was for Shelley and her dad to be proud of me.

We learned first-hand that people were actually being blessed by helping us. As weird as it seems, that's not an easy lesson to learn. Pride can get in the way. Sometimes in order for God to get his way and for everyone to be blessed, you have to let people do what is on their heart to do. I had to learn how to receive help and accept a gift. Our friends and our church blew us away! They had our back—you could feel their prayers, and it was quite remarkable. I had friends like John Conine and Terry Dixon that prayed for me and called me every day. Mentors like Ridley Smart, Bro. French, Tom Allen, Eddie Campbell, and Jeff Gould kept me focused and on track. Friends like Ron and Sandra Willett or Mike and Susie Chaisson, who would drop whatever they were doing to fix, repair, build, or assist in anything for Lisa or my children. My two closest friends, Tiger Edwards and Dennis Meyers, kept a finger on the pulse of activity for answers solving a multitude of stress levels. Plus many others that served willingly when God placed it on their heart.

If my spouse were just diagnosed with a terminal condition, what advice would you give me?

Be selective about your doctors. Make sure you're comfortable with all aspects of that doctor's practice and manner. Don't just automatically succumb to what you're being told. Get a second opinion if you're not settled on what you're hearing. If you're paying attention, you'll know the difference between the good doctors and those who are just making a living. There is a big difference. Those dedicated to patient care and what was best for Lisa stood apart from the rest. It was obvious.

How did your mate's condition affect your normal intimacy patterns as a couple?

Lisa was one of the bravest women I have ever known. She lost all sensations from the neck down. The new "normal" intimacy pattern was "no sexual intimacy"—post-accident. It just wasn't possible. She felt nothing, and you couldn't put her in a position to risk hurting her.

She came to me one time after the accident and said, "I want you to listen to me very closely. I've talked to someone about this, and I want you to consider it." I had no idea where she was going with the conversation. "I know somebody who will have sex and make love to you... and I want you to do it." I said to her, "Absolutely, 100 percent, that will not happen! This is not up for discussion." Of course she pushed back, "Listen to me! You serve me constantly by doing all these things...," and I interrupted her and said, "Why don't you just kiss me to the best of your ability, and how about we let the rest be between me and the Lord?" Honestly, the only way I can even remotely explain it is to say that God took all those impulses away from me during that time period. But how brave was she? Have you ever heard of anything like that?

How did you handle those changes?

I've mentioned that God really helped me deal with the abruptness by which all those changes happened. I was naïve and was just trying to handle all issues coming at me—the kid's schedule, Lisa's progress, therapy, insurance coverage, financial responsibility, and coordinating responsibilities of those trying to help—just attempting to function day to day, hour to hour, minute by minute. I discovered the obvious later. I had zero control over the long term condition of her progress, so I focused on handling the "right now" and what I could control. I didn't tarry too long to fret about any long-term effect. There was always something that needed immediate attention. I just prayed daily for the healing of her injury, and I let God do the rest.

It was Shelley that took me for a walk, grabbed my hand, and looked me in the eye and said, "I've done the research Bruce. The extent of Lisa's injury is going to require your constant attention. You need to face reality, wake up, and realize this is going to be a whipping and a 24-hour fire drill. This will not be easy; you have to be ready, and you have to be trained."

Were you two still able to play together during your mate's decline?

Oh man did we! That woman liked to go. That van really allowed us the freedom to go and do, and we went and did a lot. She had a mall speed on her chair that required us to almost jog to keep up with her. She was still mobile and eager to be on the move. If she wanted to be some place for whatever event, we'd attempt it. Baron's football games, baseball games in Omaha, vacation in Disneyworld, church, shopping, or whatever—girlfriend could roll [**laughing**].

We'd go in that big van, but she didn't like anyone driving but me. It got to where she could be comfortable with Baron driving, but I was pretty much delegated to all the driving chores. Anyone else behind the wheel stressed her out.

How did you find joy together when so much time and emotion was filled with the disability? How did you avoid not focusing on the bad all the time?

She was alive. Her brain worked. We could communicate. I still had her. We were still team with the kids and in our marriage. We were a functioning family. We were focused on what she could do, not on what she couldn't do.

One time a friend came to see her while she was in the hospital. When that person left the room, Lisa shot me a look and said in a heated military vernacular, "Do not let anybody come into this room that has pity in their eyes. If I see pity, I'm going to give you the nod, and I want them out of this room. I will not tolerate pity around me." That right there set the tone for our approach. So to answer your questions, we focused on what we could do, not on what she couldn't do.

Could she be stubborn? Yes. Could she be difficult? Yes. Did it take her a while to make up her mind on things? Oh, hell yes! Was it always easy living with her? No. There were times she was verbally abusive towards me. She was demanding and had standards she expected to be met and would ride hurt on you in every aspect without a consideration of please or thank you when they were not achieved. But Lisa was alive, she was my wife, and I loved her like crazy and would do anything for her.

What was the dominant emotion during your season of caretaking with your mate—as compared to your emotional state now?

I'm not as fatigued mentally or physically now. That's probably the biggest difference; my emotional stability is probably much more secured now than it was back then. She could be thanking me one moment for what I was doing for her, and then she'd rip into me the next. I took a lot of verbal headshots through all of that. That was much more difficult than any other frustration I might have been feeling. You just never knew what kind of reaction you were going to get from that head strong woman.

What's the one piece of advice you'd give someone just starting out in marriage?

Live within your means. You don't have to have the biggest and the best starting out. Grow slowly as you acquire assets. Pay as you have the cash. You'll be happier if you can stay out from under the burden of too much debt. Plus, as I stated earlier, going through the mud together in the lean early years is the fun part.

What's the best thing a husband can do for his wife every day?

Listen to her. If you'll listen to her, you can find out what she's afraid of. You'll know what she's worried about. You'll hear where she is insecure and stressed. That's where a man's strength can be most appreciated. Moving towards her fears pays big dividends. But most men won't listen. We minimalize what we don't want to be bothered with.

A mother of three former students (Lisa taught all of the kids more than once) said to me recently that she always admired how powerfully confidant Lisa always was in the classroom. She so admired that about her.

I called Shelley and said, "Isn't it interesting that because of that woman's observation of Lisa being powerfully confident professionally in the classroom, she just assumed that Lisa's confidence trickled over into every aspect of her life? Oh contraire! Nobody was better at holding a grudge. She had a master's degree in worry. Lisa could fret over the smallest of things, and she could be anxious when she felt like she was losing control. She never ever admitted she was wrong, and she could be so hard headed about something you'd think she was wearing a football helmet! Then she would want me to hold her at the end of the day and ask me to pray for her, asking God to forgive her of all of her shortcomings." Shelley responded by saying, "That's why you were her safe place to fall."

Unless a man listens to how his wife speaks, he'll never know what she really needs or what is truly important to her.

What's the best thing a wife can do for her husband every day?

A little bit of encouragement can do wonders for a man's self esteem. Loving words from a woman can melt a man. Complaining about all of the world's deficiencies can deflate a man. If she'll watch her words, make them encouraging, letting him know that she believes in him, she can help him run the race he's supposed to run! Positive, affirming, loving words are a source of life in a man's head and heart. He's got to have at least one person in his corner.

What one piece of advice you would give to a newly engaged couple?

I have more than one thought for that question. Understand that marriage is work where both spouses give 100% all of the time, not some of the time 50-50, but all of the time 100%. Marriage is a covenant relationship, not a contractual relationship. Covenant means to come together—to be bound together. A covenant is intended by God to be a lifelong relationship of unconditional love, reconciliation, sexual purity, or I like to think of it as a life well spent. Contractual is to negotiate an agreement or to compromise. That's how a business is run, that's not how a marriage operates.

A man thinks if he does something special today that he has earned enough brownie points to use later that weekend. But with a woman, all points end at midnight! What you did today has zero effect on what you get to do tomorrow! Thus, God didn't design us to negotiate and compromise.

My pastor friend says, "If two people agree all the time... one of them is insignificant" **[laughing].** You have to have conflict resolution skills, an ability to listen, and an ability to express your feelings and opinions openly with respect in order to keep your goals and priorities for your family moving in the right direction. My pastor friend also says, "When a situation or conflict occurs, the mature one of the two will always be the first to say, "I'm sorry. I was wrong. Please forgive me."

My Dad's name is Vachel. I always think of his words of wisdom my brothers and I call: Vachel-isms. I've already referred to a couple earlier in this conversation.

1) Always tell the truth—that way you don't have to remember what your lies were.
2) Not "if," but "when" you make a mistake—admit it, correct it, and ask the other one's forgiveness.

TRUST. I believe that today's social media, cell phones, and instant access to one another produces an incredible lack of trust. I hear young people say, "Oh, so and so won't let me do this or wouldn't like it if I did that." Are you kidding me? Freedom is what made America great. God gave you a brain to utilize and a free will! So use it, and make good decisions. You have to trust your spouse and pray that she or he will make a good decision.

Embrace an older couple as mentors. You need the wisdom, and they'll have some to give. It might be that you don't have all the answers for growing your marriage. Have some humility and ask for help when you need it.

What are your most important memories of your marriage?

Our first date, our wedding, and the birth of each of our children. I remember the look on her face when I told her that we needed to move from Texas to Louisiana for my job. I knew she was going to fight me like a panther, but it had to be done. I remember the day we beat Roger Clemens, who was pitching for San Jacinto, in order to go to the Jr. College World Series in Grand Junction in 1981. It was so hot and humid that day. I lost 18 pounds in that game. Lisa hated sweat and was totally grossed out by anyone that had sweat on their body. After we won that game, the stands emptied onto the field for a celebration. Lisa grabbed me in pure joy to hug and kiss me, totally oblivious to the drenching sweat on my uniform [laughing]. I remember when she was finally starting to wake up at the hospital in Houston after the accident. Again, I remember the look on her face as she was trying to understand what had happened to her as a result of the accident. I was the one who explained everything to her.

Knowing all that you know now, what would you have done differently in your marriage?

I think I would have insisted that we get some education very early about finances and how it affects a marriage. We needed training on how to budget. I didn't understand the destructive power of mismanaged credit. There is no blame here, but it needed to be different.

I also think I should have taken a firmer stance in the home on things that I didn't necessarily agree with. I totally believe in the power of female intuition. I've seen where it's kept me and my family out of a lot of trouble. But sometimes a Dad's "no" just needs to be the final answer. Not all the time, and not in every case, but that influence definitely needs to be in place, respected, and heard.

Do you still think that marriage is a great idea?

Yes I do. After being single the past 5 years, it seems that there is a definite "vulnerability" in singleness that I never felt while married. I feel exposed to all kinds of craziness out there. Being inside of a healthy marriage protects you from all that nonsense—if you allow the protection.

I agree with the Biblical and theological reasons for marriage, and my experience with Lisa affirms the benefits of the institution. How two individuals can become one and develop growing together as lovers and friends is a magnificent idea! It's a great idea! It was God's idea—so why wouldn't it be great?

Any final words of advice for married couples of all ages?

Honor and respect one another. Be willing to seek counsel and wisdom when you need it. Share in the leadership, physical, and daily work and function of the home. Trust each other. Understand that unity of the two of you as one, with one heartbeat, is a mighty force. Enjoy every moment with the passion and emotion you feel; smile, laugh, and cry. Time is short and precious! Pay attention. LISTEN. Allow your mate to know your heart. Agree together to make your spouse your number one priority.

In memory of
Lisa Smith Cotharn
April 29, 1961 – August 31, 2009

Lawanna

Introduction

Her home is hidden from the road but, once you saunter down the winding path to the house, you drop into an overwhelming presence that says, "rest." April in Georgia is magic. The azalea, dogwood, and magnolia blooms can overload your senses in a heartbeat. In that setting, we enjoyed a perfect afternoon with Lawanna McKinney Busby St. Clair, a superb host, the consummate Southern lady and one classy woman.

When we arrived, she was waiting on the front porch, as you would expect. The white wicker furniture begged for us to sit a spell. Iced tea was served and we connected again with our dear friend as the cardinals fluttered and sang about in the woods. It was perfect. A clear sky and a warm day — a sacred space if there ever was one.

Our histories are somewhat intertwined. Lawanna's late husband, Dave Busby, pretty much single-handedly got me kicked out of a church I pastored back in the early 1990s. It genuinely wasn't his fault, but that little twisted guy turned that place inside out in a matter of a few short days. Dark clouds rose with lots of heavy thunder. Not everyone in church liked the freedom Busby was spewing in those days. Honestly, I must confess that he was one of the most radical influences upon my own spiritual journey of any man I have ever known. Jesus and the Holy Spirit had rocked my world. Busby was on the short list after that. He was one of the dearest friends I have ever had. I loved him with all of my heart.

Every guy that was in Southern Baptist youth ministry in Texas from 1985 to 1997 knew Busby. This guy's ministry profoundly affected thousands upon thousands of ministers and kids. He was real and authentic (rare among ministers) and he was passionate. You had to love him. He made you love him. You were helpless not to love him. His legacy is still very much alive.

Behind this powerful little man, there was a strong woman of equal passion and purpose. A woman who knew her role as her man chased the things of God. It took them both to pull it off. We have asked her to tell the story. It's not widely known, so we feel that we have been given a gift. You'll understand why, soon enough. Hold on. Strap in.

From the surreal surroundings of a land that is birthing spring, we move to the howling and icy winds of the Minnesota winter. A different kind of wonderland — a frozen tundra only fit for the strong and hardy soul. Two kids came together to face those winds — determined to live, focused to love and forged forever in the divine dance of life and death. And the music plays on, and on, and on.

It is a distinct honor and privilege to present to you Lawanna. -MDP-

Tell us about how you two met and fell in love?

I first met Dave when our respective Baptist Church youth groups went on a hayride together in October of 1963. I was 12 years old and had just entered 7th grade. Dave was in 8th grade. Dave and I happened to be seated on the hay wagon, and I don't remember anything else about the night or about him, and I'm sure he didn't remember anything either. I tell everyone that I must have made a huge impression on him because he asked me out again seven years later!

So seven years later when I was a freshman in college and he was a sophomore, I came home for spring break. I had just broken up with a boyfriend that I thought was not a good guy, only because anytime I was stronger than the man I was dating (even at 18 years old), I was smart enough to figure out that was a real bad idea. This guy was weak and small-minded. So I broke up with him and just left him in the dust. He happened to be an acquaintance of Dave, so he went to Dave and said, "How about you take Lawanna McKinney out and get her to like you. Then, after she likes you, maybe you could dump her? That would be the best retribution that I could think of." So Dave did. He took me out on a dare from this guy. Sparks and chemistry flew from the very first moment we were together. We often laughed about how this guy's plan backfired. So that is how I met him.

We began to date some, but I went back to college, and so did he. The love letters were frequent and passionate. I have all of them to this day. By late spring we were in love—star-eyed, cross-eyed, sparks flying, and chemistry—you name it. That summer, we happened to be in a touring musical group together, so we were together a lot, and that really cemented our relationship. By fall, I transferred schools to go to his university just to be with him. So that took care of our sophomore and junior years, and then we married the following September.

Was it love at first sight?

Yes, but not when we were 12 years old. **[laughing]** Dave and I had a special connection straight away. I dearly loved being around his family, and he loved being around mine. We did a lot of family dating—camping trips, water ski days, combined family picnics, and Easter Sunday dinners, things like that. That was an integral part of our dating experience, being with our families. I happened to hit it off with his family, and he loved mine, which created a strong connection for us as well.

When Dave and I became engaged, his wonderful Mother, whom I cherished, wrote us a letter. She wanted us to see God's work in Dave's life. On May 21, 1971, she penned, "The Lord has impressed me to write down for you all of the facts concerning your illnesses from your birth to show you just how much God really loves you. I don't want you to miss seeing the hand of God on your physical life. You should not be here. But God clearly has a special purpose and plan for your life." For the next eleven pages, she painstakingly chronicles all his 'mysterious' bouts of illness. "From the first day of your life, you had a cough," she continued. Dates, times, doctors, medicines, etc. We were both keenly impacted by it, and I will keep it forever. That was the beginning of a lifetime of thanking God for each day Dave was alive.

When were you married? Where?

We were married in Alta Loma Baptist Church on September 10, 1971, in Madison, Tennessee.

How long were you and Dave married?

We were married 26 years in September of 1997. He died in December of that year.

What was the first year of your marriage like?

I think we were that storybook marriage that first year. We moved to Orlando, Florida because that is where his job took him.

What was going on down there?

He was a youth pastor in a church. We left both of our families, and that was probably a good breakaway for us. It helped us to focus and turn in towards each other. By doing so, we found out who each other was. We set up housekeeping in a little two bedroom rented house on Orange Avenue in Orlando and lived there for 2 years. I would say that first year was pretty idyllic. We were discovering each other and finding out more and more about ourselves. Because Dave was an extreme extrovert, we had lots of friends and lots of activities going on.

When did Dava [daughter] come along?

Six years after we got married, in June of 1977.

How differently were you both raised?

We were raised very similarly. Both of us were conservative, from the South, and grew up in Southern Baptist churches. We had both parents in the home with multiple siblings. We had a lot of external things that were completely identical. Given that as a background, you would think that whatever might surface, we could work it out, whatever it may be. Surprisingly enough, about three years into our marriage, we discovered how very different we were. One of those differences was in personality. I am an introvert, even though I may not sound like it right now. However, I have learned to become more of an extrovert, largely through Dave's influence. People energized Dave. The more the merrier. He never got tired of people, never got tired of being around people, never wearied of others—they fueled him. So by personality, we were different. But as the years progressed, we both moved toward the middle of each other's personalities.

Another distinctive difference was that David Eugene Busby was the most secure man I had ever met! And by secure I mean, he just walked into a room and anticipated a positive environment. He wasn't cocky; he just exuded confidence and energy. He was secure, and it never occurred to him that interaction with other people would be negative. I, on the other hand, came from a shame-based background, which was entirely different from his. My background said, "Walk into a room and prove that you have a reason to live, and then we will decide if we will accept you." So we had extreme differences in our personalities.

So do you think his dealing with disabilities was a part of that confidence and assuming that everyone liked him, or did he really just not care if everyone liked him or not?

Dave came to appreciate his own sense of self and worth by struggling every day. Yes, he cared what others thought of him, but he grew into an acceptance of himself day by day. Physical disease and weakness forced his life-struggle, and he had to decide to give in or move on. In the midst of that, however, he was taught to face and deal with life's disappointments. Let me explain.

Dave was born in December of 1950. When he was six months old, his brother and sister brought the poliovirus home from school, and Dave contracted it. It didn't affect either of his siblings, but it did affect Dave. He was temporarily paralyzed in both legs and only learned to walk after several surgical procedures and leg braces. Then he was a sickly child—always coughing, constantly riddled with fevers, pneumonia, bronchitis, and all varieties of respiratory ailments. In 1950, simple salt tests (commonly called the 'sweat test' for determining cystic fibrosis) were not routine. It was a very rare disease. Most children born with CF died in infancy, and many of those babies wouldn't even go home from the hospital. So he made it, but he was this very sickly child.

However, Dave's father, Ray, determined very early on that to give in or give up was not an option. Instead, he instituted a 'we live by faith not by fact' attitude. He saw Dave's resilience and passion to live and was careful to reinforce that every day. So if that is all you know and that is all you got, then the parent is free to say to a six year old, "Dave, take the trash out," because the trash needs to be taken out. Or, "Dave, make your bed," because the bed needs to be made, or "Get yourself ready for school." There was no preferential treatment. Consequently, when he went to school and he got bullied, and he did, especially on his Little League baseball team, his Father would tell him, "Well son, that is life. Life is hard. So buddy, you are going to have to deal with it because when you get out into the real world, you have to go for it." Dave built on his own sense of normalcy.

As Dave grew, he began to develop an ability to accept himself. It took him about 10 years to really realize that he was different. He had very thin legs with atrophied muscles, and he looked funny in shorts. But by the time he was in high school, he was playing on the tennis team, and he wore shorts. So he was learning. It wasn't that he didn't care. He did care. But he learned that he had to go deeper than being embarrassed by skinny legs because skinny legs could not define who he was. But make no mistake about it. The process was arduous.

Early on, what were some of your toughest challenges as a couple?

Boy, I want to be completely honest here and not romanticize, but I will say the first years of marriage, Dave and I had a special relationship that always brought us back home. We were each other's home base. So whatever the conflict was, it never took us where we could not come home to each other, to home plate. With that being said, we argued over everything the first two or three years, from where he should put things in our room, to what he liked or didn't like to eat, whom should we have over, or who is going to pay the bills. Because we were so young and everyone told us we married so young, we decided we'd just have to raise each other and finish growing up together.

We realized we had made a commitment to be married. If we were truly going to be married, that was going to require us to be truly intimate. And intimacy, as we figured out, cost us a lot—a lot of arguing, a lot of late night talks, and a lot of tears. That forced us to weave our way back to find home plate—over and over again. We held on to home base as we worked out the knots and kinks in the ropes that held us together. There was a lot of costly intimacy, but it built and secured our devotion to one another.

I knew that Dave was devoted to me, and I was surely devoted to him from the very beginning. I couldn't wait to get married. Marriage meant the mutual and constant exchange of our souls—sounds romantic, right? But what that came to mean in the following years became profound to us both.

What were your shared goals and ambitions?

Initially, mine was to just be his wife and to take care of him. That is all I thought about and all I cared about. When we were first married, Dave had had a particularly dramatic experience with Jesus. His faith came alive as he pursued the heart of God. I think the heart of God pursued him in a palpable way. It so entranced him that he never got over it. So when we got married, that was the stage we were on.

He wanted then, as a goal, to reach people who seemed to be "anesthetized" in their spiritual journey. For whatever reason, their faith had become nothing more than a glossed over, go to church, sit there, and get through it stupor. He would say, "No, no, no, it's a relationship! It's more than you're experiencing!" So he began to have that goal of reaching people who were anesthetized in their faith. He grew up in the church, and so did I. It was just something you did. We both had a common faith, but it wasn't all consuming. But once he had that encounter with the presence and grace of God, it changed him. He yearned for other people to have that same passion, and he devoted his life to it. I did too, because I was convinced that to live in this kind of freedom was life changing.

We wanted to have children some day. We wanted to be close to our families. We wanted to leave an imprint of some sort on this world. It was important to us to live in integrity and authenticity. We knew how imperfect we were, but what we did and how it affected the greater good was important to us.

So when did he start traveling?

He traveled before we got married with a guy named Barry Westbrook. Barry had that same kind of fire, so that is why we moved to Orlando. Barry's headquartered there. A year or so after we married, he went on staff at a local church.

So as the marriage began to develop and mature, what did "normal" look like for Dave & Lawanna's relationship?

We had a significant event that happened in 1976. Dave got an extreme case of what we thought was the flu. That year, a flu epidemic swept Nashville, and he was one of its victims. I was being the perfect wife and nursing him, giving him aspirin, taking care of him, thinking he would be better in the morning. But he didn't get better. He got worse and worse. Finally, he ended up in Vanderbilt hospital, the premiere hospital in Tennessee. Doctors could not find out what was wrong with him. "You have the flu, you have bronchitis, you have this and that, but we don't know systemically what is wrong with you." One morning, a young intern doctor walked into Dave's room just as Dave coughed. The intern's head whipped around toward Dave and he said, "You sound just like my daughter. My daughter has cystic fibrosis. Have you been tested for cystic fibrosis?" And Dave said, "I don't know." So they gave him the standard sweat test.

Had he been coughing all the time?

Yes, all the time.

So what did they think it was, bronchitis, or something else?

Pneumonia. His lungs were full of junk. They would give him rounds of antibiotics, but he still coughed... and coughed... and coughed. Yet he never got better. He was in the hospital about 12 days by then, and he should have been getting better because he was on high-powered antibiotic drugs. When that young intern made his rounds and heard Dave cough, it sounded unique and familiar to him.

They did the test and then told Dave that he had CF. It was a moment of revelation because every doctor had erroneously diagnosed his health issues. Honestly, I don't think it had ever occurred to the medical community that a man who was in his twenties would be a cystic fibrosis survivor.

A team of doctors called a conference in our hospital room and basically said, "We didn't look for CF because no one your age has survived this long with CF." At this time Dave was 26 years old. "We know of no one this old with CF, but you do have it, and there isn't a darn thing we can do for you, so go home and die." We checked out of the hospital that day, reeling from the news. That was also the day I found out that I was pregnant with Dava. So it was the ying and yang of life—all at once.

You know how Richard Rohr talks about life being up and down, ying and yang? This was like the ultimate, "Yay! Oh wait... no! How do you do that? What do we do?" So we went home, and in the quietness of our home we asked, "How do we do this?" And clearly life and death are in the dance together. And how do we bow and dip in this dance? How do we live to die and yet have life in me (Lawanna pregnant)?

We both cried a lot for the next week or two. We didn't say anything to our families about either my pregnancy or his death sentence. We just needed some time to absorb it. Once we did, I clearly remember the morning that Dave got up and at the breakfast table he announced, "I tell you what we are going to do. Here's the plan. We are going to live life, not dreading death or mourning the fact that we have only been married a few years. We are not going to live like I am dying right now." So we had this big ceremony, he and I, where both of us declared that we were going to live. We had talks late into the night where I clung to him saying, "Please don't die, please don't die, I'm pregnant." Those late night talks went on and on, into the late hours of the night. You know the kind—they leave you undone and unwound, but force a fork in the road. That is the decision we made, but we had to make that decision every day... every single day.

That is when we both came to that moment—resolved that we are going to move forward and live. Yes, we are going to trust God. Yes, we are going to do whatever is necessary to take care of ourselves—especially Dave. By then we were already under the care of pulmonary specialists. Doctors had automatically enrolled him in all these medical studies because he was "old" for a CF patient. He was a bit of a novelty to them. We advised the doctors to get their research elsewhere and opted out of their studies. We didn't want CF to be our daily focus for life—it had already consumed enough.

But the questions were ever present: "Will he make it long enough to see this baby born?" "How am I going to make it if he doesn't?" "What will I do?" "Is Lawanna going to have enough to survive on if I die soon?" And all those kind of questions were depressing. So we had to make a choice. *We choose life. We choose life! We choose life!* Every day in our household was a day of rejoicing on some level. I don't mean kick up your heels and do a 'happy dance.' We chose to go to that place in our heart that says, "God, I am so glad to be alive today. Thank you for this breath." And that began a journey of rich and honest gratitude. "I liked seeing the dragonfly that came by our window today," "I haven't been sick with pneumonia in two whole months now," "I am so glad I have my husband today." We chose, at some point in each day, to embrace the fact that he was alive! I can't tell you how important that was to us. Every day.

We loved each other deeply, sincerely, passionately, and completely, but it just didn't look like it looks on your wedding day. Instead it looked like, "Do I need to take you to Vanderbilt again because I see that you can't breathe?" That's what love looks like when you are six years into marriage and he is dying of CF. And then, when he catches me bent over the kitchen sink in tears because I had just gone to that dark place, he comes up behind me and says, "It's going to be okay." That's what commitment and love look like in that moment. It isn't the hot sex right there or the stars on a romantic evening, it's the nitty-gritty at that point.

What part of your life with Dave was the most rewarding for you?

Seeing him choose life every day in the face of death. That was the most rewarding for me. We walked that path every single day for over 21 years. We were married 26 years, but 21 of those years we knew that he had a pending death sentence. When he drew his last breath in my arms, I patted him on the chest and said, "You have taught me how to live. Now you have just taught me how to die." Of course that affected me. You cannot watch someone go to the brink of death dozens of times, see him choose life every single day, and then see him embrace death with such dignity and not be affected by that.

What did Dave teach you? Obviously we know that he taught you how to choose life, but what were the other things that he had going on in his life that taught you? What became a part of your personality—an extension of him—still in you?

Well that is a good question because you know how people say dogs and owners start to look alike after a few years? Well I think couples do that too, and I hope my life reflects Dave's spirit on many levels. As I watched Dave, I saw a host of things that were imitable and winsome. For most of our lives, I took the pictures, ran the ministry details, and sat in the audience. As time went by, I realized that I am a keen observer of people. And as I observed Dave, I saw how much of his life he gave away. "If you give something away... what do you get in return?" That was my real question. I saw how Dave got ten-fold in return.

Dave didn't do things *for* a return. He just loved people. But as I watched him interact, I saw this compelling return. Dave became rich in relationships. Even now, some 16 years after his death, the most oft repeated memory others tell me about starts with, "I always felt important when I spoke with him—I had his full attention."

Practically, he had a unique way and style. He gave full eye contact when he talked to people, and so do I. He focused. He concentrated. He remembered names, first names, last names, children's names. He loved people and he taught me that it is people that matter.

He also knew to drink deeply from the well of laughter. Don't take yourself seriously and always look for the laugh. In fact, he often laughed so hard that he ended up coughing uncontrollably. It was always worth it.

What do you think you taught him the most?

Servanthood. He would say that I taught him how to serve other people. He gave his life away for other people, but he didn't know how to serve people in the little things of life, and he would say he learned that from me.

So we know the two big things that he battled, CF and polio. As best as you can, would you give us a view of Dave's complicated medical history?

Dave struggled with post-polio syndrome beginning at the age of 35. Post-polio syndrome occurs years after polio has taken its toll. Basically, it's severe pain and aching in the limbs that polio initially affected. For Dave, that was both legs. There was nothing to do for it except to massage his legs. At age 40, he developed diabetes. That meant an entirely new regimen of diabetic medication and nutrition. He also had pancreatic attacks and the pain associated with that since his pancreas was about 90 percent dysfunctional due to CF. At each meal, Dave took multiple pancreatic tablets to assist in the digestion of his food. He also developed an enlarged heart 2 ½ times the size of a normal heart.

What was his lung capacity when he got the diagnosis of CF?

I don't recall. It was probably in the high 70th percentile. However, by the time he was 45 years old, it was reduced to 7 percent. Imagine inhaling a 100 percent breath, but only enjoying 7 percent of it. That was what it was like for a person with CF. His energy was quickly consumed by his perpetual cough. As he aged, his lungs became riddled with all the fibers that looked like intricately woven spider webs. The lowest sections of the lungs began to die. When he coughed, he would often expel a piece of his lung. It was bad the last two years of his life—most distressing for us both.

His daily regiment included taking about 50-60 pancreas tablets, and taking four, one-hour breathing treatments in order to open up enough space in his lungs so he could function. That meant dealing with all the tubes and three nebulizers. Then there was the all-important vest. Invented by his pulmonologist, this equipment allowed him to expel the thick mucous in his lungs and was vital to his survival. There was an almost perpetual round of various combinations of antibiotics, and as a result, he developed numerous complications from them. Eventually, his body became resistant to all of them.

It was a constant revolving door of hospital stays. If his lung capacity dropped to a certain percentage and his white cell count rose to a certain number, he would be hospitalized for what the doctors called a "tune-up." Sometimes, even when he did not feel that bad, his doctors would say, "Your numbers are spiking. You are going to feel bad soon." Sure enough, within 3 or 4 days he would be really ill with high fevers. He would stay in the hospital a week, two weeks, three weeks, four weeks—getting a "tune-up" which consisted of a BiPAP machine and 6 breathing treatments a day. If his weight dropped below 135 pounds, he would be hospitalized to gain weight. During those hospital stays, we would never know the outcome. We wouldn't know if he was coming home or not.

Sometimes he would respond well to treatment and sometimes... not so well. Toward the end, he was hospitalized about 3 times a year for almost a month. Until about the year 2000, CF was housed entirely in the pediatrics ward. Patients just didn't live to adulthood. When we went to the hospital, we were in rooms with drawings of giraffes and elephants on the walls. Every time we would see his doctor, who was the father of The Vest System, we sat on child-sized stools, surrounded by children's artwork. "What are we doing here?" [laughing]

(Here is a description of Dave's compression vest from the product website: The Vest® System uses a technology called High Frequency Chest Wall Oscillation (HFCWO). The Vest® System has an inflatable garment connected by Air Hoses to an Air Pulse Generator. During therapy, the inflatable garment inflates and deflates rapidly, applying gentle pressure to the chest wall. This works to loosen and thin mucus and to move it toward the larger airways, where it can be cleared by coughing or suctioning.)

When he got really sick and entered the shadows, how did he handle his complications emotionally?

'Going into the shadow' is a descriptive phrase for it. Only the person who has been *in* the shadow can come *out* of that darkness and live in the light with any real depth. Dave embraced the shadow when it overtook him. Sometimes that's what shadows do. When he needed to go into that place of retreat in order to gain perspective, he just embraced it. He let the shadow fulfill its purpose. He knew it would pass, yet he was keenly aware of reality.

Dave kept a journal on a regular basis. I have all of them. He made statements like: "God, what are you doing?" "What am I doing here?" "I'm scared I'm going to die in here." "This time I do not know if I can make it." At other times, he'd write about how much he hated the weakness that CF brought. "I hate having CF. I hate every breathing treatment. There is nothing I like about any of it, and God, while I'm on the subject, I'm kind of pissed off at you too." He was completely honest and embraced it all. He had to. We had to. Some days would be better than others.

It didn't happen often, but sometimes he'd move into depression about having CF. Little things could trigger it. We were living in Edina, MN, and our house had a very tiny lawn. He loved to mow that grass in straight lines. He insisted, and that was his deal. Then came the spring when it was too much. He came into the house and said, "I can't do it anymore." He went into the bedroom, lay down on the bed, and grieved. That is what CF does to a person. It nibbles you to death.

That is how he did it. He wrote in his journal, he fussed and cussed, he embraced, he was honest, and he kept moving forward. Somehow he grabbed the heart of God in the whole bloody process, and he was thoroughly convinced God was embracing him along the way. In fact, Dave told me more than once that if he had it to do all over again, he would ask for CF. "Cystic fibrosis," he said, "is a master teacher." To this day, that completely staggers me.

How did you handle his complications emotionally?

I was fearful, because I thought that his illness, coupled with bouts of loss and grief, would be enough to deter him from embracing life. I was afraid he'd let go of life and just move toward death. He worked so hard to live. But it would have been easier to let go and move toward death. I was very fearful of that.

David Johnson was Dave's best friend. Pastor at Church of the Open Door, [crying] Johnson became a tremendous resource of encouragement and validation for Dave. The affirmation of one man to another to be strong and know it, even when all the externals were fading, was a real gift to my Dave. And although I've told David this many times, I doubt he really knows what a gift to he was to Dave.

Dave had influence with lots and lots of ministry people, but when he'd come home to crash, Johnson was always there for him. Dave was facing a long protracted death. He needed the strength of his friends. I too had a wide assortment of friends who were holding my arms up. Our friends were amazing for us. Real friends. Friends like the ones who went into the Garden of Gethsemane with Jesus were with us.

Dave would often say to me, "My biggest temptation is to make you my source." That was my temptation also. He'd say, "I cannot pull on you for life. You have no key to life. I do not either. If I make you my source, our marriage will be dysfunctional." So when we would see each other leaning into one another during a time of great neediness, it would always lead us back to that truth. We can't be each other's source. We can be a resource, but certainly not the source.

Had I had the key to life, I wouldn't have let Dave die. But it wasn't up to me. Keeping all that straight in our head and heart allowed me to say things like: "I don't want you to die, but I know you're going to. I just want you to know that you've been the best resource in my life. You are not my life, and I will live after you're gone." He'd say, "I can't believe I'm going to die and leave you all alone in that big old bed." He was thinking about me, but he knew he didn't have the key to life either.

So when he went into the hospital that final time, was there a moment of communication when you both acknowledged the seriousness of the complications to each other?

Yes we did. That's where we were different from a lot of couples. People die all the time from sudden and tragic events. The opportunity for that kind of moment doesn't happen for them. We had been at death's door many times. The time I had to process with Dave was the biggest gift of his death. Let me grab my journal. I think it will answer your question best.

(The following is from Lawanna's journal. She read this aloud to Patti and I. She has graciously agreed to include this intimate material in this interview.)

There were giraffes and elephants on the walls of the diminutive pediatric office we sat in with miniature chairs and tables. My mind wandered for the hundredth time, "Why won't they bring cystic fibrosis out of Peds and into the adult ward? After all, adult cystics are living longer lives now—way beyond childhood." Perhaps seeing those juvenile images really reminded me that Dave was a walking miracle and every day another gift. When will the miracle run out?

I see his face fall into that familiar dismay when he was told, "You must come into the ward again. You are dangerously ill. We'll do everything in our power, but you will have to fight fiercely with us over the next six weeks." Six weeks! Another six weeks after a month at Abbott and three weeks of home nurses and IVs! The doctors leave the room to arrange a bed and set up his treatments. We cry together softly, carefully. Almost a mourn. "I can't do this again, Lawanna. I'm just too worn out." I put my arms around him and cry. Somehow, we allow the system to automatically process us through the details. "You'll need your red card. I'll call for wheelchair assistance to help you find your room. We'll order the PICC line."

On and on the orders fly until I find myself in the chair next to his bed. It's all too familiar... all too scary. I must leave him alone while I go home to gather his clothes and medical equipment. Only God knows what fears filtered through his head while I was gone. Lifting and loading the equipment into the back of the Jeep, I can barely see for the tears. I can't cry right now! I have to remember his meds. His bible. His briefcase. It's Christmas, and I am so afraid.

I make calls on the cell phone to Bonnie, Lynn, Dava, and Bev: "He's back in. This time for six weeks." Details fly through my head like bullets: Don't forget to inform his folks. Stop and get cash. I'm almost out of gas. Call Northwest Airlines and get another leave.

Finding a parking space in the ramp, I wind my way through the three-block tunnel, my heels clicking to the beat of my prayer, "Please don't let him die." The same old prayer each time he is ill. The cacophony of that beat bouncing off the walls crescendos in my head until I want to burst into hysterical crying. Faster and faster I walk. I have to get to Dave. Once I'm with him, I find him calm, but glad to see me. What a comfort we are to each other during these times. Our tears aren't scary to each other, and neither are the fear-filled comments of "I don't want you to die. I need you." Rather, they are affirmations of the intensity of our love and utter helpless dependence on God. This thing is way too big for us.

His room is changed. Oxygen in use, a respiratory board is in place, along with a BiPAP machine, IV, and more equipment... nine machines in all. I unpack his clothes and "set up" his room. Bible and briefcase are by the bed. Underwear and pants in the cramped little drawers. His shaving kit is by the sink. There is a TV with a VCR in it. The room overlooks the Mississippi River. It is an unusually warm December day but overcast and gray. Just like me.

Then we begin all the treatments and discussions with the doctors. Test after test. Does he have the dreaded pseudomonas cepacia at infiltrate levels? Are the lobes affected? What is his white count? What is the magic combination of antibiotics, and at what levels are they safe? How many daily calories will it take to sustain him? And so our journey begins. Endless days of treatments, long hours at the hospital, phone call after phone call. "I don't know," rolls off my tongue almost hourly.

My days turn into this endless adventure, getting smaller and smaller until all I know is the hospital and Dave. Focused, tunneled, we both begin rehearsing our lives together. Ups. Downs. Dava and Charlie [our daughter and son-in-law]. We offer forgiveness and grace to one another for any imagined or real offense. We recite the wonderful 26 years together. "Remember that time..." and Dave utters his favorite movie quote, "It's been quite a party Woodrow." I caress his continually sweating body. "He's working too hard to stay alive," I think. It was never like this before. Dave and Bonnie [Johnson] go to Vegas for a short trip. I am terrified that Dave will die before they return, but decide not to say anything to them for fear they would cancel their trip. I can't be certain of anything.

It is clear to us both that he is not getting any better. On Saturday (December 13), I am at home for a bit. My brother Dewayne calls from Nashville, and I burst into tears. He decides to come up the next day, and I am comforted by his gesture. We begin a ritual that lasts until the day of Dave's death. I stay all night until 6:30am. Dewayne relieves me, I go home, shower and sleep for about two hours, make calls, etc., and return to the hospital. He is there every day, on time. I find that after staring intently at the oxygen levels and Dave all night, Dewayne is a welcome sight. I had the doctors there at least once each night. He gets worse at night. I am convinced he will die with me there, alone, at night.

Wednesday morning. Dewayne had just gotten to the hospital. I came home. Standing in the shower, there is a burst of Dave's body scent when the water cascades over me. How much longer can I breathe in his smell? Clutching the faucets, I wail.

Just after I climbed into bed, Dewayne calls. "Sis, he needs you. He is pretty bad. I think you are winning the war and losing the patient. I'm sending Lynn [best friend] to pick you up. Don't drive here alone." Lynn and I chat on the way down. What can this mean? The implications are just too big.

Entering his room, I find Dave on his stomach, his favorite sleeping position. I whisper to Dewayne, "Is he asleep?" Dave answers, "Is that my lovers voice?" Now comes the talk I always dreaded. "Yes, Honey. It's me." Dave then utters the words, "Honey, would you think me a quitter if I just went on to be with the Lord?" Fast as lightning, God gave me the next sentence, "Honey, you aren't quitting. You are finishing. It's ok with me if you discontinue all treatment. I will talk to Mary Jo (Dave's doctor's assistant.)" Dave had already talked to Mary Jo about his wishes.

Dave's doctor corners me in the hall and berates me for this decision. Dewayne stands at my side. Lynn appears for the last 15 minutes of the discussion and is internally incensed at the doctor's attitude. Calm, carefully worded phrases roll off my tongue, and I am absolute. He will not shame me out of this. But he tries. "It is almost assisted suicide. I cannot go along with it. You are wrong to give up. He may get better." For an hour he persists. But I am steadfast and unmovable. Dewayne is amazed at my demeanor and impressed that I didn't 'whack that guy on the head'. It would have cost me too much emotion. I needed to save it for Dave. The doctor circles back around to ask for my forgiveness and apologizes profusely. I am surprised that he did that. He offers me a hug and his big hand extends toward me in a 'please forgive me' gesture. I do. What's the difference? I would have sided with Dave regardless of the doctor's response.

Lynn and I begin to throw out every piece of medical equipment except for the IV, which we will use later for the Demerol if needed. I take inordinate pleasure in ridding the room of those devices, and I'm not really sure why. I make that room a home now, for this is where he will die. We both know it now, and it is certainly no secret.

And so the death journey begins. Dewayne and I carry him to the shower for his last time. He is so light that it is an effortless task. Dewayne shaves him as he has each day. I take particular joy in helping Dave feel clean. He enjoys that feeling. What a small thing he asks of life now—to be clean. He falls asleep for a solid eight hours, at complete peace, on his stomach. When he awakens, he begins seeing people, telling them goodbye, blessing them—hugging them. Over and over I watch this ritual. Then night falls. "Are you afraid to die, Dad?" Dava asks. "I was... but, not now. I'm ready."

Once again, I put on his lounging pants and one of his t-shirts, crawl into bed with him, and we begin our talks. Soft, compelling, long, and fragile talks—as if handling something precious. Our marriage. I sing again and again to him. Early in the morning he falls into a restful sleep. But I don't go home this time. I simply will not let him die without me by his side. Friends come and go. Family and intimate friends from Texas and Arkansas call. More goodbyes. My senses are keen and razor sharp, even though I haven't had much sleep. I notice everything, hear each noise, watch the oxygen levels, feel his pulse, and count his respirations. I even hear the phones at the nurse's station. The rubber sound of tennis shoes on the linoleum floor, the smell of the food trays, and the looks on the faces of the staff as they come and go are permanently imbedded and vivid in my mind.

I don't know how long this process will last. Another long day turns into a long night. He keeps asking 'Can I go now? Is it time to go now?' I'm not even sure who he is talking to—me, or the Lord. But I assure him that indeed, he can go whenever he is ready.

I am just sure he will die that night. We continue our talks, and I keep singing. After each song, he whispers endearments to me. I keep a close eye on the oxygen monitor and his respirations. Without even noticing it, I try to take the same breaths he does, but I can't—it's too slow.

I have never seen death before, and I'm not sure what to look for. At 3:00 am, I stop singing and he doesn't whisper his love in return. "Dave? Dave? Can you hear me?" The narcosis coma has begun. I pace the room for ten minutes, my heart racing. Once, he rose up on his elbows and draws in a deep, shuddering breath. I'm sure he has died. But he lays down again and breathes more evenly.

Later in the morning when Lynn gets there, she and I give Dave his 'burial' bath. Up until now, he still slept on his stomach. This time, we carefully bathe, shave, and dress him. His nurse helps us change his sheets. As I turn him, his eyes flicker. "Dave!

Oh honey, can you hear me?" But when I look into his eyes, he is not there. I fall over his feet, kissing them and crying. Is he already with Jesus, but his body is barely functioning? It doesn't matter. I can't keep my hands off my fine warrior. He will be there soon. God, I can't imagine what he is about to experience.

David Johnson (Dave's best friend and pastor) reads Dave a piece about heaven. As he does, Dave begins to struggle into an upright position as if reaching forward for someone or something. "Where are you going, Honey?" Because his breathing is so labored, I am convinced he is in pain, and I order more Demerol. But he wasn't in pain. He was in death.

Reaching heavenward with his arm outstretched, he collapses back into my arms. Of course I am convinced he was meeting the Lord and grasping for the very Person for whom he had passionately lived—his Savior.

I never knew that death was a step-by-step process. Since I have never seen anyone die, I was novice, inexperienced—naive. The doctor steps into the room just a few moments prior to Dave's death. Soon, he announces that there is no heartbeat. My love is still at last. Dave's body is covered in a fine sheen of sweat. It is clear he worked hard doing death. His heart stopped before his breathing. Prayers and tears out loud. Then quiet.

We gather in a circle with the doctor and his nurse for a final prayer. I kiss him a final time and leave the room. Our good-byes were said. He taught me how to live and how to die. I only hope I learned my lessons well.

So yes, we had those deep and compelling talks—at least a hundred times—but that was the last one. I don't let many people read that... so use it with caution.

{Mike} It's sacred. I promise we'll take good care of it.
Thank You.

What kind of daily care did Dave need from you?

He did his own mixing of medications and did his breathing treatments entirely by himself. He would just disappear downstairs and handle his business. My job was to keep the machines functioning, sterilize all the equipment, and get all the meds in order after a UPS shipment. Before he got The Vest, I had to give him his treatments by hand. I had to cup my hands and pound his back with concussive blows. Unless I heard it pop, it wasn't working. That is what broke loose the mucus in his lungs, and then he could expel it. I did that for 30 minutes—four times a day until he got his Vest.

Generally, what was Dave's response to your caretaking?

These routines were so engrained in our life. [to Mike] It would be like your response when Patti does the laundry. Sure she did the laundry. That is what she does. It was normal, and it was a team effort. It took a village to keep Dave alive, and I was just one player on the team. He appreciated it and thanked me, as you'd thank Patti for doing the laundry. We grew into that process. It didn't happen over night. We did what needed to be done when it was needed.

How much of that overall burden did you shoulder by yourself? For how long?

At the daily care level, no one else was involved. It was just Dave and I. We tried to keep life as normal as possible for Dava, our daughter. I'm sure she had bucket loads of fear and anxiety. She'd see the meds arrive and know the treatments were happening. Equipment was everywhere. The hoses would hang in the laundry room after being sterilized. There was a wheelchair, and she'd push him around in that, but the daily care we tried to shield her from those routines. We wanted her to have as much of a normal existence as possible.

Dava was introverted, and I'm sure if you had a discussion with her, she would reveal much about the pending fears she had about her dad. But she didn't ask too many questions, so we didn't really tell her much. We would have answered any question, but it was probably all too obvious. She saw everything. She knew he was sick. We never practiced a 'don't ask, don't tell' policy—we were honest but didn't want to make his health the focus of each day.

How well do you think you did under that stress?

I did very well in crisis and poorly in day to day. When it took extreme action because of some extreme condition with Dave... I'd be on it. Boom!

Done. Strong and focused. But in the everyday thing, hearing that relentless cough, sometimes I wanted to run screaming in the night! Dave coughed all night—every night of his life. It's not an exaggeration. When he'd lie down, the mucus would settle in his lungs. There would be times when I'd get exasperated, "Would you please stop that? We need to get some sleep." I'd get cranky because I couldn't get the sleep I needed. But, you go on. What else can you do?

Where did you find your strength and courage?

A lot of it I found through Dave. He was the one who was dealing with it the most, and I was the secondary party. He would have said that I had the hardest part because I had to live with the reality that my mate was going to die before me. But the bigger truth was that God was my source. Dave knew that, and I knew that. So no matter what it took in life and death, we had an end. That end was in Christ and in our faith. That sustained us through all the small steps we took along the way. It wasn't miraculous or magical. Every single day we realigned ourselves in the truth that God was in control, and I'm not. I didn't pick the day I was born, nor will I pick the day I die. So what makes me think I can control everything else in between? So we embraced it and kept on walking. That was a big word for us: embracing. Not give up, but embrace whatever we were given as we moved forward. Because it was hard didn't grant us permission to check out and quit. We held it in our arms and walked through the hardship.

Did you two have any goals about big things he wanted to stay alive for?

We thought he might make it to age 50. There was nothing magical about that number. We just thought it would be great if he could live to age 50. Dava had married in July, and Dave died in December. He would often say, "I know I won't live to see my grandkids," and he didn't. Every birthday, he'd be amazed he made it another year.

On his 47th birthday, we went to the Edina Country Club with a couple of our board members. He was very sick and running a high fever. He thanked everyone for his birthday lunch, and then said to the board, "I don't know how much longer I can continue doing this. Can you guys help me figure this out? My schedule is totally packed for 1998 and some things are already scheduled for 1999. Do you think I should start cancelling events? I need your input and advice." That is what we talked about on his birthday. It was December 7th. Dave went into the hospital on the 9th. He died 10 days later.

By September that year, we knew he was spiraling downhill towards death. We had just become empty nesters. We were like newlyweds again. Dava had married in July, and we had some of the summer together. He was traveling as usual, but he usually tried to take September off and stay home. So we felt like two kids again. Then he took a turn for the worse in October and spent that month at Abbott Northwestern Hospital.

What were your big "priorities" before he took his final turn for the worse? How were those things affected by the illness?

We were living the same. He was still traveling and even had a speaking event in San Antonio, TX in early October. We didn't really change one thing as far as priorities go. We just kept doing life. Every single day... doing life. We were closer to death than we had ever been, but we weren't watching it or altering anything because of it. The choice was always to live. Waiting around to die would have just been too grievous an experience.

Did you two ever talk about "your" future without Dave in the picture?

Every single time he went into the hospital, we had topics that we would rehearse. There wasn't a list, but the same things would resurface. Dave was adamant that I should remarry. I'd poo-poo that, show my disgust at such a ridiculous notion, and insist that the discussion go away. I'd almost get angry with him for taking me there. "Don't tell me that anymore," I'd respond. Then we'd talk about Dava, and he'd share his perceived regrets about what kind of father he had aspired to be or what kind of grandfather he wished he could be to her children. These topics would surface often.

Then we'd always get around to the big topic. Every time I'd say, "I wish I knew how you felt on the inside." He'd always reply, "I wish you could too, because you can't understand how hard this is. It's a real piece of work." And then he'd eventually say, "I'm glad you will walk with me to the door of my pain, but I've got to leave you there. You're not invited in—there is only so far you can accompany me." That's how he would say it. "Honey, I appreciate everything you do for me, your sympathy and empathy, but there is only so far you can go. I have to go the distance on my own." So the last time at the hospital he said to me, "You're going to walk me to death's door right?" And I said, "Every step of the way, and if God will let me, I'll come with you." He'd say, "Nah, you got stuff to do around here," and things like that. But that is where we went. We talked about bearing one another's burdens, but there was a limit to the care. He had to do the death part alone. He would get this far-away look and seemed like he had left my company because it was so hard, and then he'd refocus and dial back in. I'd say, "You left me, didn't you?" and he'd say, "Yeah, I did." Because he knew that was a battle that would require all of his strength. We talked about that every single time.

Was there a point when you knew that your caretaking days were numbered?

Not really. I was working to make him as comfortable as possible—much too busy to think about it. Playing his music, dimming the lights, changing sheets, bathing him—anything I could to help. I physically held him for his last few breaths.

When did it finally sink in that your remaining time with Dave was near?

I did have a moment of knowing that we were not going home together this time. I've heard that life and death are partners in a dance. I felt that as I danced that dance of death with Dave, I thought I might die too, but I also realized how much death is like life. I felt the same way on the day that my daughter was born as I felt on the day my husband died. It was something enormous, surreal, so big and supernatural. I was acutely aware of how similar it felt. The emotions were different, but the presence of God in it all was the same.

I knew this was the end of a man who had lived well. I had been privileged to walk with him for 26 years. He had convinced me, and I was personally convinced, that I would live, but I didn't think I'd want to. I knew it was going to hurt. I had questions about whether or not I could do it, but I got through it. I wouldn't have missed a moment of any of it.

I wouldn't want to portray that any of this was magical or whimsical. It was hard, and it felt huge. HUGE! God's spirit hovered on us during those days. I'm still in awe of it. It's so difficult to describe. Overwhelming in fact.

Looking back, how prepared were you to let him go?

All the way prepared... and none of the way prepared. We had said our goodbyes. We had done everything that we could physically do, but when Dave died it shocked me so much that I wanted to die. It wasn't out of depression, but more that I was calling out to not be left behind. I was as prepared as anyone could be, but totally unprepared at the same time.

I took comfort in three words written by Dave in the margin of his Bible: 'SEE THIS, LAWANNA!' The verse reads: "For David, after he had served the purpose of God in his own generation, fell asleep…"(Acts 13:36). It was Dave's personal message to me.

Was there an opportunity to say "goodbye" before his final sleep?

Yes. I've mentioned those soft, compelling talks that went late into the night. Around 2:00 am, when the words had all run out, I'd sing to him *It Is Well With My Soul*. After I'd finish, he'd pat my leg and say, "Keep singing, honey." Later in the early morning, when I'd sing and he was no longer patting my leg, I knew he had moved into that narcosis coma.

So it's been 16 years since he passed. How are you doing?

[crying] This has been emotional today to take this journey into memory. I want to say again, "Why are you leaving me? How dare you leave me! It hurts like hell. How could you do this to me? Don't go. Please don't go!" That's how it is. And then on the other side, God has taken massive care of me. I cherish and honor Dave's memory. Yet, I did not stop living (even though I wanted to). I went on to embrace life. It's the thing in my life that I'm most proud of. I lived after Dave died. It's the singular thing that I'm proud of. I kept living. I kept breathing. It is exactly what he wanted for me.

Do you ever sense that Dave is with you?

That's not the first time I've been asked that question. Multiple times actually. My initial thoughts about that were that I don't have a zip code in heaven. [laughing] He's dead, I'm alive, and we don't talk like that anymore. Sounds rather callous, but I faced reality. It would really bother me when people asked. As time went on, I finally caught the gist of what people were really asking me. I think they wanted to know if he consumed my thoughts—he did. I've never really felt that he was trying to give me a download or a message. But what does happen from time to time is that certain smells and memories evoke strong emotions that suggest his presence. That's happened countless times. It could be listening to a song on the radio, or when I would see God moving in a particular way. And I've even had dreams that have Dave in them, but I see them as more symbolic and not literal. The symbols are prophetically being used to convey understanding about stuff in my life.

Honestly, because we had so much closure in our marriage, I've never felt that anything was left undone or unsaid. We laid it all out there. There was nothing more to resolve or left to agitate reoccurring regret. I understand that isn't so for everyone, but I did have that as a gift. I'm very grateful for that. So, no, I don't hear from Dave like that. I hear from him if I read his journals or listen to his old sermons. I have memories. Every. Single. Day.

Most marriage vows contain the words: "For better or for worse... in sickness and in health... until death do us part." Describe what those words might have meant to Dave & Lawanna.

For better or worse was the same. For us, the worse was that he had CF, but the better was that we were fighting together for him to live. It meant some lean times physically for him, and financially for us. But behind the worse was always the better—because he was alive.

Sickness and in health was every single day. He was always sick, and on some days he was in health. He was systemically ill, but it could be amazingly well. He'd throw back his head and laugh so deep and so loud, or preach a message that would exhaust normal men, and you'd have to remind yourself that they guy had a disease that was eating up his life. In fact, David Johnson used to tease him all the time that he was faking... being a phony... coughing to get attention. "You're lying to us all just to get sympathy. I'll die before you do." **[laughing]** Dave would laugh so hard you'd think he might pass out. He could be so strong for such a sick man.

There is no death that will ever part Dave and I. I am happily remarried for 14 years now. Yet, even remarriage did not part Dave and I. I still have 26 years of life, experience, memory, impact, and influence that are still a part of who I am. We haven't parted, and the older I get, the more like him I become. I'm fine with that. I hope I grow up to be just like him.

From the Newlyweds:

Were there times during the illness that you didn't think you could do it anymore?

A lot. There were a lot of those times. But thinking you can't do it anymore, and then turning around and doing the best you can for the next crisis, is not the same thing. I thought about it a lot. But I always went into action mode when I was supposed to be in action mode.

If my spouse were just diagnosed with a terminal illness, what advice would you give me?

You're going to need to go home and figure out how to do life from a source bigger than you or your mate. You have to figure out that you are not in charge. Life doesn't owe you anything. You are not the most important part of life. The picture is much bigger than you can see, and you are going to have to figure out your small role—the down deep—the invisible part of life.

How did your mate's condition affect your normal intimacy patterns as a couple?

When Dave would be in the hospital for months at a time because of CF, there would be long periods of abstinence. As soon as he'd get home, we'd resume our normal intimacy patterns, which were fantastic. Dave was a very passionate man for everything. Whether it was eating a bowl of cornflakes or making love to me, he was extremely passionate. His long stays in the hospital were about the only time we were really interrupted.

How did you handle those changes emotionally?

During his times in the hospital, honestly, I didn't think about sex, and neither did Dave. We were extremely tethered emotionally. If he was in the hospital, the man was really sick. Coming home was always a celebration! The times that were hardest were when he was feeling well but would be on a preaching tour and might be gone 2-3 weeks in Texas preaching youth camps. He'd come home, drop his bags, and put his hands on me! [laughing] I'd say, "Hold on buster! How about we shake hands first!" How about saying, "hello" or "how are you" before you start taking my clothes off?" [laughing] He eventually learned that a little romancing was a good dance step on the front side of all that passion.

Were you two still able to play together during your mate's decline?

Yes, but not as vigorously as we always had. Dave had been active. He went snow skiing, played tennis, swimming, water skiing... he and I did all kinds of things, but eventually most of that was all systematically picked off by cystic fibrosis. A ride around the block in a wheelchair was now the activity, and that was plenty good. We were out, and we were together. Thank you very much.

How did you find joy together when so much time and emotion was filled with the illness, disability, and disease? How did you avoid not focusing on the bad all the time?

You've heard of the glass half-full or glass half-empty analogy? {YES} I'm not sure that people think like that... so black or white all the time. Dave was definitely a glass half-full guy. I was more glass half-empty processor. But we both had seasons of sorrow and joy and seasons of fullness and sorrow. So we poured into each other and reminded ourselves that many things had changed, but there were still much cause for rejoicing. Maybe skiing was out of the question, but a ride around the block was still feasible! Awesome! We did walk with sorrow. But by pouring into each other, we were never consumed by sorrow.

What was the dominant emotion during your season of caretaking with your mate—as compared to your emotional state now?

Life is the same. I no longer have to sterilize Dave's tubes, order meds, cope with hospitals, but my life is just as busy now as it ever was back then. My husband [Barry St. Clair – www.reach-out.org] flies in and out, all over the world, we have a ministry to run, and I have duties as a wife, a mother, and a grandmother. Life has filled in the gaps. I don't do caretaking like I did, but now the demands of my caretaking look different.

What I went through with Dave taught me a lot about fear. I'm a person who is easily startled. Come up from behind me without my being aware—it gets a reaction. Sometimes more than you might want. But I don't live in day-to-day fear. The fear of Dave dying was pretty big for me. After he DID die, I examined fear from a whole different perspective. I lived in this constant agitation of *I hope he doesn't die, when is he going to die, and don't leave me here alone.* The truth was simple. He was going to die, and he eventually did die. After that, all of the fear is removed because it's already actually happened. Go from the front around to the backside of it and you can see it for what it really is. What I learned is that it was horrible for me to lose him, but I did live and I continued to have a life.

It reduces your fear of the future. You go through the fire and realize it didn't burn you up. I was a 46 year-old widow. I had very few job skills and very little job history. My job had been to take care of Dave. I didn't have a resume, nor did I have a huge financial portfolio. Most people would be terrified in that situation. I wasn't worried in the least. I had been to the door of death with my mate. I lived, and he went through, but I continued to breathe after Dave didn't. I saw most everything much different after all of that. It diminished fear and took away the power of that fear that had so tormented me. I faced the grizzly. It was bad, horrible in fact, but I'm still here.

What's the one piece of advice you'd give someone just starting out in marriage?

Realize that there is a higher purpose and role for you to play other than just your marriage. No doubt, your marriage is important. It needs to be important. Your being a healthy and whole individual is vital and important to the overall health of your marriage. There is very little you can do to fix your mate. So do what you can with yourself. That might be what is jamming up the works.

What's the best thing a husband can do for his wife every day?

Stop trying to be the all-encompassing source of well-being. Be a resource, and I'm not talking about bringing her flowers and all of that stuff, which is totally fine, but just try to be present... AND stop trying to fix everything, for crying out loud!

What's the best thing a wife can do for her husband every day?

Present to him a whole and healthy person. Broken marriages are usually about broken people who won't do the work. We think externals will repair things.

What one pieces of advice you would give to a newly engaged couple?

Wait, and wait, and wait. [laughing] Disclose as much as possible about yourself prior to marriage. As much as you know... as you can. Too many people haven't really paid attention to themselves, so they can't really articulate these kinds of things. If intimacy really means: In-To-Me-See—then become that person. Disclose, and expect disclosure from the one you love.

Knowing all that you know now, what would you have done differently in your marriage?

Nothing. Not a thing. I wouldn't pick a different course. Dave helped me grow up on the inside. I'm still reaping what he taught me. Most of the healthy stuff in me is because of his influence. I could say something stupid or immature, and he'd turn around with that crooked grin of his and ask, "Really? Get over that." He could do that. He could challenge me to grow up. It helped me immensely.

Do you still think that marriage is a great idea?

I've been married 14 years since Dave died. As I age, I can totally affirm that it is a great idea. We need someone with us in order to finish the journey. Having a good resource in our life that will call attention to our shadow-side, our dark spots, and our up-side is vital to our growth! You just don't get that if you live alone with 10 cats in your house and no one ever says, "Hey, we need to examine what's going on here." I'm 63 years old now, and I'll say something and Barry will say, "Really? You want to go there? That's a bit immature don't you think?" See, that's what a healthy marriage does. We all need an accountability relationship. Marriage is perfect for that.

Any final words of advice for married couples of all ages?

Do not expect your mate to meet all your expectations. That would be tantamount to (a Dave Busby quote): having two ticks and no dog. You can't be each other's source.

In Memory of
David Eugene Busby
December 7, 1950 – December 19, 1997
www.davebusby.com

Jordan

Introduction

Are you familiar with the term "church planter?" It might not be something that you hear every day, but you can probably figure out what it means rather easily. A church planter is a person who either starts a church in a community or village where there is usually no church of any kind, or there is an opportunity to add to the variety of churches already in existence in an area. If you need to picture Johnny Appleseed or Lewis and Clark as an archetype, go ahead—that works just fine.

Church planters are a different kind of animal. These people start with a seed of desire that ultimately morphs and grows into a raging conviction. It's the conviction that really drives them. Once they believe that the task is of divine origin, it's usually game on. Most church plants start as one or two people. Sometimes it's just a couple of close friends or a husband and wife who have sensed the call and are compelled to birth the thing that started in their heart.

From what I know by experience, church planters are courageous, unflinching, convinced, focused, driven, hopeful, extremely tough, and often moved by forces beyond logic and conventional wisdom. It's the stuff that causes highly educated men and reasonable women (and visa-versa) to forgo their professional day jobs in order to dive headlong from their sensible perch into a frothy puddle of hope and potential. Yes, in every sense of the word, they are kamikaze pioneers.

As Jordan Lawrence Rice was standing on his tower, looking down at that tiny wet speck on the grooved streets of Harlem, where did he find the right stuff to muster such a leap? Yes, God had spoken, but it would take something more than his own confidence. We would all need more wouldn't we? Jordan needed help to bend his knees and spring forth with all of his might, and that would require a sacred influence from his past. There was another voice on his tower, and that voice carried a steady weight of hope. The story of Jordan and Danielle Rice is not totally hidden from the world. One day while doing some online research about cancer, I came across a video that was produced by the ABC News affiliate in New York. I was deeply moved by the video! The story was about how two people found each other after both had lost their spouse while still in their twenties. Jordan Rice lost his wife Danielle to cancer within 2 years of their being married, and Jessica Jackson lost her husband Jarronn in a motorcycle accident just a couple months after they were married. Jordan and Jessica, the young widower and widow, met, fell in love and remarried in 2013.

Possibly at another time Patti and I will try to capture the Jessica & Jarronn story, but for this project, we really wanted to tap into Jordan and Danielle. It took a bit of digging to find Jordan, but we eventually made contact and he graciously agreed to spend some time with me for a conversation. Honestly,

I have to say that this young man was a rock during the interview. All those qualities of the church planter that I mentioned beforehand became evident as we looked back into his season of love, joy, and pain while battling his newlywed's cancer. I was blown away by his maturity concerning priorities and what he gleaned from his short time with Danielle.

It seems that Jordan firmly faced the shadow of death and embraced the healing work of God in his life. The man has something to say. It's an incredible story and I feel very honored to have been entrusted with something so precious. Please open your heart and allow this planter to touch you with his seeds of life. Thank you Jordan. You're a prince. –MDP-

Tell us about how you two met and fell in love?

We met in 2006. We were both active on a bunch of different message boards. We also had a lot of friends in common. I was in school in Baltimore, and I was going back and forth to Washington D.C. to see friends on a regular basis. Danielle was living in D.C. at the time. She and I were talking back and forth online, and I invited her to come visit my church in Baltimore. We went to church and then out to eat after the service. We had a really great time together. After that, the nightly phone calls could go to 2:00 a.m. I knew very early that there was something very special about Danielle. We laughed a lot. Our views on life aligned. Our views on God and faith aligned. So there was a strong connection very quickly.

One of us was traveling every weekend to the other's place, and we did that for about a year and a half. We hit it pretty hard and fast. We became inseparable. Within a couple of months of hanging with Danielle, I knew she wasn't someone that I could just set aside. I saw things in Danielle that I had never seen with another person. I was completely settled that I could spend the rest of my life with her. Once I moved into a reckless abandonment about having her, I realized just how much I loved her. I went for it with guns blazing! I put myself in vulnerable situations to lock her up.

Danielle was teaching school, so when the summer came, she subleased an apartment in Baltimore to be near me.

Was it love at first sight?

Pretty much. I knew I wanted to pursue her from the beginning. I don't know if I believe in love at first sight, but there was definitely a strong attraction at first sight. I remember thinking soon after I met her, "I'm going to marry this woman." I was very interested the first day.

When and where were you married?

We were married in Baltimore on August 22, 2009. The wedding was at the Morgan State University campus. There were about 150 people in attendance. Danielle wanted a big shindig, so we went all out. It was bigger than what I wanted, but hey, happy wife—happy life. [laughing]

How long were you and Danielle married?

Twenty months (ten months before she got sick, and ten months after she got sick).

What was the first ten months of your marriage like?

Overall it was great! We had a lot of fun together. The warning is always that the first year is the hardest, but that wasn't so for us. Both of us had been abstinent before we were married, so there weren't many arguments that you couldn't cure by getting naked. **[laughing]**

How differently were you both raised?

We were raised very differently. My parents have been married for 37 years. My parents are attorneys—both professionals, both very spiritual, and I grew up in circles very different from Danielle's. Her parents split up when she was about 5 years old. She grew up in a single-parent environment and was shuffled back and forth with a grandparent. She moved around quite a bit. Her mom wasn't a religious person, so Danielle didn't really have much of a spiritual background. Danielle was the first person in her family to go to college. I was the fourth or fifth generation in my family to get an education.

In the early months of your marriage what were some of your toughest challenges as a couple?

There was a definite hiccup early on. Danielle's mother has severe mental and emotional issues. She's bi-polar and also suffers with drug addiction. Her mother would meddle in our marriage a little bit. That was the one big blip in our relationship that caused an argument that lasted more than a night. Her mom wanted control over Danielle. Danielle was paying all of her mother's bills, so it was creating a lot of problems. Once I showed up on the scene, I wasn't having any of that. Danielle was basically paying for her mother to be a drug addict. She had no disabilities, she could work, but she just didn't want to change. Her mom knew what to say to set Danielle off, so she'd pit us against each other. It would get nasty around the holidays. Our first Christmas together was a little tense. Her mom wanted us to come to D.C. for Christmas, but she was violent and verbally abusive to everyone around her. So we stayed home together.

Danielle's father did begin to show up much later in her life and he had a positive effect, but the relationship with her mom was definitely toxic on our marriage.

What were your shared goals and ambitions for your future?

Danielle was one of the big reasons why I planted this church in New York (www. renaissancenyc.com). I was practicing law at the time of our marriage. I had a heart to do ministry and plant a church. She was the impetus behind that vision. She and I had attended a church planting conference and on the drive home from that conference Danielle said, "Go ahead and say it." "Say what?" "Go ahead and say it!" "Say what?" "You want to move into the city and plant a church don't you?" I said, "Absolutely!" She never flinched, "Then, that's what we're going to do." Danielle was much more confrontational than I am... in a good way. I normally try to avoid conflict issues. She said, "Hey, just tell your parents that you're leaving the law firm to do what you want to do." Obviously, it wasn't going to be that simple for me, but she was immediately in my corner for us to plant a church together.

So as the marriage began to develop, what did "normal" look like for Jordan and Danielle's relationship?

We did have a few connection issues. She was an introvert and I'm an extrovert on steroids. I knew what those words meant, but I had no idea of how much work it would require from both of us to make our relationship life giving to each other. I always wanted to be out, or have friends over, or have people around. Danielle very much so wanted it to be her and me. Her love language was quality time. Mine was words of affirmation, which explains why I always wanted so many people around. It took some conversations on how to respect one another's desires. I feel it took us at least six months to respect our differences in this area. I think we felt we could change each other. Once we figured out that we couldn't have it our way all the time, we began to click together. I finally realized that we couldn't have people over five nights a week. She realized that we couldn't veg on the couch and watch T.V. every night either. Once we made those adjustments, things smoothed out.

What part of your life with Danielle was the most rewarding for you?

That's a great question. Danielle might have been the most loyal personality that I have ever known. She was an extremely safe place for me. I never had to worry about confidentiality with her. I felt I could be totally vulnerable with her. I could tell her anything about myself. Because I was a little brother, I always had to entertain people and do the dance to make people laugh. But with Danielle, I could be fully me. I didn't have to perform at any level, and she accepted me like that. In the best sense of the word, she was my best friend.

What did Danielle teach you?

Certainly she taught me not to be afraid of conflict. I did have a fear of disappointing my parents, but Danielle brought another perspective, "Wouldn't your parents be disappointed if they found out that you spent your life doing something that you didn't really want to do?" I had to consent to that truth. Right before she got sick, I told my parents that I was going to make a career shift to plant the church.

Danielle was tough as nails. Nails are like cotton candy compared to Danielle's personality. She was not in denial about her sickness, but she was resolved. That can be good or bad as far as digging in goes, but she taught me not to fear. When Danielle was first diagnosed, we went into a room together alone. I asked everyone to just give us a few minutes together to process the news. We were just told that she had an incurable cancer. So we held each other and wept. Finally, Danielle said, "Either God is going to heal me or I'm going to soon be in heaven, but either way it's a win-win situation." She was fearful and she definitely didn't want to die, but that's how brave she was. Very brave.

I still think about it all quite a bit: the sovereignty of God and how His plans are accomplished in our life. Whether I have a cancer in my body or I'm called to plant a church, it still requires courage to face our fears of the unknown. If His plan is being accomplished through me, it's a win. Knowing that God is sovereign and good requires resolve.

What do you think you taught her the most?

I think I passed to her a good picture of what love looks like. Her dad situation had been very negative. She had some good boyfriend relationships and some of those guys had been kind to her. But, I showed her what commitment looked like. I did the things I told her I was going to do for her. I kept my word. She questioned the integrity of men, but I did help her to see that a man could have integrity towards her. By the time we were married, I feel sure she had rested in that truth. Not to say that I hadn't disappointed her in some way, but overall she knew how much I valued loving her.

When did Danielle's medical complications begin to surface?

She had been nauseous in the middle of the night for a couple days. Even though she was on birth control, we thought that maybe she might be pregnant. So she took a pregnancy test, and it came back negative. The symptoms continued, so she went to see the doctor, and he prescribed some medicine because there was a virus circulating at a time. She took the medicine and felt better for about a week, but then she started throwing up violently one night, and I took her to the hospital. They did another pregnancy test, which was negative, but they discovered that she had fluid around her heart. They admitted her, and we were nervous about it, but the doctors said not to worry about it too much. The plan was to give her some steroids to reduce the inflammation. For the next five days while in the hospital, her condition just got worse. Danielle ended up in ICU. Her resting heart rate was around 140. She was in danger of cardiac tamponade. That's when the fluid pressure around your heart is so great, there is danger of crushing the heart. The doctors informed us that they needed to do a pericardiectomy in order to relieve the pressure around her heart. They assured us that the procedure was simple and quick (about 40 minutes), and there was no reason to be alarmed. The moved her to Columbia Presbyterian Hospital and did the surgery that evening.

Danielle was afraid, because we had no idea what was causing the problem. Once they anesthetized her, her blood pressure bottomed out. So what was to be a minor surgery with a small incision under her breast became a major life saving surgery that required them to crack open her chest and spread her rib cage. The surgery lasted three hours. Once the surgeon came out, he said, "Mr. Rice, please take a seat." I thought she had died on the table. My knees buckled. I was super terrified. He said that she was stable and in recovery, but he had no idea of what caused her issue. The lab had her tissues, and they were running tests to see if they could get an answer. The preliminary test didn't show cancer, but the doctor insisted that we had to wait for further results.

I had been online to research all of her symptoms. Every time I searched, I got back the results of some kind of rare heart cancer. The doctors were not saying it was cancer, so I didn't want to go there in my mind. It was scary enough as it was. On the fifth day after the surgery, our cardiologist woke me up. I was sleeping outside of her room in the hallway. He said, "Jordan, I'm going to shoot straight with you. It's the worst news. Danielle has a rare form of cancer inside of her heart." We didn't tell her immediately because they wanted to triple check the results. Once it was confirmed, the cardiologist didn't want to break the news to her. He wanted the oncologist to talk to her, because he knew we'd have a lot of questions about treatment.

Once the oncologist arrived, he shot straight as a laser. "The cancer is called primary cardiac angiosarcoma. There is no cure. We'll try to do everything that we can, but there is no known cure, and it is almost always fatal." We asked about life expectancy, but he told us that he didn't like to give a timeline because people respond differently to the treatment. Then he reiterated again that it's almost always fatal. In my own research, I had found a story of a young boy who had a six-year remission. He acknowledged the possibility, but he didn't want to project false hope. I was pissed off, but the kindest thing that he did for us was to tell us the truth.

There are about twenty cases a year of this kind of cancer in America. Half of the people who have this cancer die before they know they have it. Yeah, it's pretty brutal.

What was the progression of the illness?

That surgery was on June 10, 2010. We found out that she had the cancer on the 15th. Even though she was still in the cardiothoracic ICU, she started on chemo immediately. So not only was she trying to rehab from surgery, the chemo was taking effect. Once she was moved out of ICU, it was a major victory for us. She got her own room, and I could now sleep in the same room with her. That was great, because I had been sleeping in the hallway outside of her room. I also had a place to shower now. I was basically cleaning up in the sink about every third day when she was in ICU. It was genuinely nerve wracking because you never really knew what to expect. Danielle was nervous and never really wanted me to be away from her side, so I was with her 24/7.

She was 26 years old. I was 28 years old. We had been married for 10 months. The hospital staff felt bad for us, so they moved her to the wing of the hospital where they put President Bill Clinton after his heart surgery. It was the regular hospital room rate plus $900 a night. They put us in that wing for free. It was like the most luxurious hospital wing in the world. It was like a nice hotel! There was a bed for me in that room, and the food was regular restaurant food. It wasn't cafeteria food. I'd check out all the menus and order really nice meals. All of that was because they didn't think Danielle was going to make it for very much longer.

She started improving, but took a turn for the worse in late June. Danielle had a lot of pain in her esophagus. We thought that maybe the cancer had spread somehow, but she only had a fungal infection. When they did that test, they realized that the tumor in her heart had started to shrink. By the first week of July, she was feeling better, and she got released from the hospital. A week later, she went back to the hospital to do another round of chemo. On July 27th, she had her first MRI since the diagnosis. It was then that they told us that they couldn't see the tumor anymore. I remember driving that day on the Brooklyn Queens Expressway and thought I'd wreck my car because I was so happy. I could hardly believe what I was hearing. Everything was turning. She was getting stronger, her appetite was back, and she was gaining a little weight. She lost her hair with the chemo. They were giving her the Doxorubicin, a.k.a., the red devil chemo. She took the anti-nausea stuff, but depending upon what day it was, she might throw up all day regardless.

By October 5th, she was told that she was in remission. Every time we went to the hospital in October and November, she had different medical teams drop by to do their examination. The doctors could barely believe it. Our doctor would tell us not to pop the champagne just yet, but things were looking promising. I took her to North Carolina for Thanksgiving with her dad. It was a huge trip for her. She was feeling good and was able to eat. It felt like things were normal again. When we got home, she started getting the paperwork back together to go back to her job of teaching. She wanted to be back at work in January.

On December 30th, we had a birthday party for Danielle to celebrate her 27th birthday. She did not feel well that day. She was struggling to breathe, and I just blamed it on a medicine change or asthma. Deep down, I suspected that we had a deeper problem. By January 7, 2011, she was still not feeling very good. I called the doctor, and he asked her to come back in. They did a test, and we found out that cancer was back. It wasn't like it had been, but it was enough to get everyone's attention again.

In November and December, they had been giving her Doxil, which is a lower dosage and form of Doxorubicin, but it was supposed to be safer on the heart—less effective, but safer. Doxorubicin had a ten-dose limit for a lifetime. After ten doses, it supposedly loosens the elasticity of your heart. At that point, she had only had eight rounds of Doxorubicin. So in January and February, they put her back on Doxorubicin and got the tumor to shrink a little bit. They were adding other experimental drugs along the way. By April 1, she was really struggling to breath. So we took Danielle back to the doctor, and he told me privately that he didn't think she'd make it through April. So he went to her room and told her, "Danielle, we tried. You've really fought this cancer, but this is it. There is nothing more we can do." So we entered a discussion about hospice versus treatment. I remember that the Physicians Assistant stayed in the room and wept with us. It was probably the worst moment of my life. I'm holding her and I knew she wasn't going to make it. It was the worst April Fool's joke ever.

Danielle hated hospitals. Someone was poking at her all the time. So my last gift to her was to take her home. She had a fentanyl patch, so her pain was well managed. I had promised I wouldn't allow her to feel the pain, and I would take her to the hospital if the pain became unbearable. She was scared, so I wouldn't leave her. The last three weeks we were at home. She was on oxygen, and that helped her so much. She was really sick, but comfortable.

On the morning of April 23rd, she woke me up to tell me that God had told her that she was going to die that evening. I asked her, "Do you even know where you are, or what day it is?" I thought she might be delirious. I'll never forget it. She was in a full body sweat (Danielle didn't sweat. She was always cold.) The window was cracked because she wanted it cold in the room. She put her forehead against mine and said, "God told me that I am going to die today." I asked, "Where are you?" She replied, "I'm at Centre Avenue," which is where our apartment was. So I rushed her to the hospital, and when I pulled in front of the Emergency Room doors, she stopped breathing. I left the car running, but got her out of the car as quickly as I could and took her inside, all the while screaming. I watched them cut her clothes off and go to work. They did resuscitate her and put her in the MICU. I called all my family and her mother. I wanted to give everyone a chance to say their goodbyes. Her blood pressure was on the way down, and I was told that as it dropped, her heart would just stop beating. That is exactly what happened. Danielle died about 10:00 p.m. that night.

It had been ridiculously depressing all that day. The lighting in the waiting area was dim, her room was depressing, and it was cloudy and rainy all day. Danielle was never coherent that day. After about 11:00 a.m. she didn't respond to any kind of stimulus.

How did she handle her complications emotionally?

She went to therapy. Honestly, we cried a lot. Probably every day we cried. Danielle didn't really like for me to see her crying. She was not in denial, but there was a lot of disbelief. She had to work through a lot of grief to move into acceptance. It wasn't all depressing. She thought she was making the turn and doing well.

How did you handle her complications emotionally?

It was a rollercoaster. I was convinced she was going to die. Then I was convinced she was going to beat it. And then I was convinced she was going to die again. I was in therapy also trying to process the data. I was definitely in denial. That kind of stuff doesn't happen to people like us. People in their twenties don't get cancer. There are billions of twenty year olds, and we're not supposed to be sick. It was a crazy rollercoaster for sure. I was super angry for a couple years. Angry at God. Angry at my friends. Just angry with everybody.

Was there a moment of communication when you both acknowledged the seriousness of the complications to each other?

Yeah, on April 1st, in the hospital. When she first got diagnosed, we talked quite a bit about our future. I'd ask her, "How do I honor you with my life?" It was also a time to talk straight about what we were facing—what she was facing. We were staring at the end of her life. It was a swift kick in the nuts.

What kind of daily care did Danielle need from you?

From August to December 2010, not much really. I went to the store for her nonstop and took care of the chores she needed, but she was mobile and doing most things for herself. I was able to go back to work a little bit. She was pretty self-sufficient physically, but emotionally she didn't want to be alone. I think she was afraid of being alone in her thoughts. She needed me to either distract her or encourage her. Every waking moment I tried to be with her. I didn't know how much longer I'd have her. I tried to cherish every moment.

Generally, what was Danielle's response to your caretaking?

Very positive. It was great. We laughed a lot and really enjoyed one another. We watched a lot of stupid T.V. shows together.

How much of that overall burden did you shoulder by yourself?

Most of it. She didn't want a lot of people seeing her in a bad condition. My brother took a lot of my cases for me. He was working 80 hours a week so I could be with Danielle. That was the kind of support I had. My family was there. My parents dropped by every single day to bring stuff, make food, and help us clean. When I'd take Danielle to the hospital, we'd return home to a clean apartment. Someone cleaned the place while we were gone. It happened any time we'd leave the apartment. That's the kind of support we had.

How well do you think you did under that stress?

Good for the most part. I can think of a lot of days that it wasn't so good. I called her cardiologist one day because I was having chest pains. I thought I was having a heart attack. He said, "Jordan, I can diagnose you over the phone—its just stress." Some days I was very stressed out.

I remember one day that she didn't eat very much, and that was a problem to me because I figured about the only control that we had in this whole ordeal was how much she ate. I would obsess on how much she would eat. "Did you drink your two Ensures this morning?" If she didn't feel like eating, she wouldn't eat, and I'd meltdown about it. "You have to try. You need your strength. This is for your health." I just needed to have control of something. I was working the logic: "If she eats, she gets the nutrients. If she gets the nutrients, then she'll live." I knew she could have eaten ten pounds of spinach a day and not much would have changed, but doing nothing was too painful.

Where did you find your strength and courage?

There is an A.W. Tozer quote that says, "Let a man commit himself to doing the will of God and he is instantly free." I remember reading that quote and being blown away. So many things, especially Danielle's condition, burdened me, but it wasn't within my power to control any of it. The freedom I needed was only to be found in relinquishing my control. My strength came from releasing the false sense of control that I was carrying.

Also, my support system really moved around me in pretty radical ways. Friends from Baltimore would drive up to see Danielle for just 30 minutes. Someone who will drive 6 hours only to stay for 30 minutes is pretty great. My family and friends really encouraged me. Philip Yancy's book, *Where is God When It Hurts* really helped me. That might have been the best thing I read in that season. There were a lot of prayers lifted on our behalf. With all that said, I was still terrified.

What were your big "priorities" before you found out that Danielle was sick? How were those things affected by the illness?

My focus was my career. I wanted to build up my client base and make more money. Once my heart shifted towards church planting, I hoped to position myself in a good place in order to do research and learn. I wanted to glean from a church-planting network. Those were the two big ones.

Was there a point when you knew that your caretaking days were numbered?

Yeah, April 1, 2011. That was when I knew. It was crushing, yet sobering at the same time. I knew that we couldn't sustain the pace we'd been on for previous 10 months. Initially, I felt guilty for being tired—much the same way that I felt guilty after she died for feeling relieved. I was relieved because Danielle was in so much pain, and relieved for myself because I was living in a nightmare.

How was Danielle processing her physical decline?

It was hard. She was always slim. She took a lot of chastisement from my family because she could eat whatever she wanted and remain slim. Fried chicken, root beer float—it didn't matter. She wouldn't gain a single pound. She wore a size 0 or 2. Before Danielle got sick, if she gained a couple pounds, it was cause for celebration. That kind of metabolism does not lend itself well to chemo. She probably weighed 80 pounds when she died. Skin and bones.

She pretty much ignored her physical decline. She wouldn't look at herself in the mirror. She never saw herself bald. Danielle would always put her bandana on before she'd go into the bathroom. I saw her bald plenty of times, but she wouldn't walk in front of a mirror bald.

Did you two ever talk about "your" future without Danielle in the picture?

After she was first diagnosed, she'd tell me that she wanted me to remarry and have kids. That was very freeing for me. Not that I wanted to hear it at the time, but it was helpful. We talked about her funeral and what she might want and whom she might want to speak at her funeral. I asked her many questions about what she wanted. Danielle wrote it all down in one of her journals.

What was going on in your head and heart during the few final days with Danielle?

Supreme anger. I said I wanted to plant a church for God, and this is how I'm repaid? He lets me watch my wife die a slow and miserable death. I tried to hide it, but I doubt I did that well. I'd vacillate between faith and anger. One day I'd think, Jesus you died and the world collapsed for the disciples, but you ARE the resurrection, so I can't put you inside of a box that makes much sense to me right now.

Looking back, how prepared were you to let her go?

I wasn't prepared. Every day I would have said, "Tomorrow!" I really was very tired, but I would have done it for the next decade. I definitely wasn't ready to let her go.

Was there an opportunity to say "goodbye" before her final sleep?

Yes. Not as satisfactorily as I would have liked. A picturesque moment would have been better, but we had the talks a thousand times. April 1st, we had a definitive conversation, but it wasn't like that on the day she died. She did try to thank me early on the morning that she died, but I told her that she didn't have to thank me for anything. We cried a bit, and then I put her in the car and took her to the hospital.

So it's been almost 4 years since she passed. How are you doing?

Great! I'm really doing good. I still have some reoccurring issues, especially with the church plant. It's like I have a fear that when things are going well, I need to prepare myself for the walls to come crashing down again. I'm sure I've still got a lot of wounds and scars from that journey with Danielle. Especially when she moved into remission and was feeling so much better. I mustered faith to believe that the world was good again. It was short lived.

For about six months after she died, the only way I could think of Danielle was "cancer Danielle." We had been together for almost five years, but I couldn't get past those horrible images of what cancer did to her. All the bad stuff was so heavy on my mind and heart. It was baldness, and chemo, and throwing up, and every bad side effect she had. It was the staff cutting her clothes off to try to save her and her final moments in ICU. Once that fog started to lift, I was able to start moving forward and dream again. I stopped seeing myself as a widower, stopped feeling sorry for myself, and resolved to man up and do life again. That is what she had asked me to do in the first place. It was time to live again. She wasn't coming back.

I found love again! A year and a half after Danielle died, I spoke at a church and went out with some friends who mentioned a woman named Jessica. I said, "Who is Jessica?" They said, "You need to know Jessica!" To rewind a bit, Danielle and I were at a couple's retreat and heard a story of a woman named Jessica who lost her husband in a motorcycle accident in August, 2009. Danielle and I talked about it later that evening, and she went on and on about how horrible that must have been for Jessica. After Danielle died, someone had sent me a link to Jessica's blog, but I hadn't followed through. So after that evening with my friends, I went home, found the link in one of my Facebook messages, and pretty much read every entry on her blog and cried. My immediate thought was that she'd be a cool person to know. So I reached out to Jessica on Facebook and apologized for the random friend request. I wrote to her that her name had come up in a conversation at lunch with some friends. She responded, and we started talking online. We had a lot in common, and I was very intrigued by her. After about two week of talking, I reached out to my friends again to ask if she had a boyfriend. She didn't, so I lied and made up a reason to be in D.C., and told her I was going to be in town. If she could connect, that would be great, but if not... no big deal.

We did get together and talked in a bar for about five hours. We sat there and cried as we told each other the whole raw and uncut version. I remember looking at Jessica that night while thinking, if Danielle was in my shoes, I'd want someone like myself to either pursue her or leave her alone. I wouldn't want anyone to string her along. To me, that would have been the most disrespectful thing I could have done. Later that night, after I had dropped her off, I sent her a text and asked about meeting again the next night. I immediately knew she was great. I didn't really know anything other than what she had already told me. I didn't know about her politics or social views, but she felt very compatible to me. The next night, we went out and we talked for six hours. After that night, my mind was blown. I thought she was absolutely incredible. The next day, I told her that I didn't know what had just happened, but that we needed to explore our potential together. She agreed!

I had some women friends that I was spending time with, but I immediately told them that I was moving into something exclusive with Jessica, and they were all very supportive of my decision. Within two months, I felt certain that we were definitely going to get married. Jessica and I are probably a lot more compatible than Danielle and I were, in general. I was a widower, and Jessica was a widow, but the compatibility had more to do with our personality types.

We started our premarital counseling within five months of dating. When we took our premarital communication assessment, the counselor asked if we had taken the test together instead of separately. She declared that we were probably the most compatible couple she had ever counseled with. She said, "I really don't have anything to tell you." It was like we had the green light to go forward. The counselor's only advice was for us to not get married until we had our first good fight. We've been married about a year, and we haven't really had that fight yet. It's not perfect around here, but there might be some strong conversations about my doing the dishes. [chuckle]

{Mike} I've seen the pictures of those two women you've married. How did you get such beautiful women to marry you?

[laughing] I don't know man. I pulled the upset twice!

Do you ever sense that Danielle is with you?

Not really. Not in the sense of an angel or something like that.

Most marriage vows contain the words: "For better or for worse... in sickness and in health... until death do us part." Describe what those words might have meant to Jordan and Danielle.

We had become one person. Her pain was my pain. Those vows mean that you commit yourself to your mate for their comfort, their safety, and their betterment, at whatever cost to me. Love always costs something. The real love does. Maybe not the emotional feeling, but the act of love always costs something. For better or for worse meant cleaning up after Danielle when she couldn't make it to the bathroom. It meant brushing her teeth. It meant carrying her to and from the bathtub. It meant sleeping in a chair in the hospital for months at a time. It meant taking a shower once every couple of weeks. It meant waking up in the middle of the night only to realize that you were weeping in your sleep. It meant hiding your tears because it was too painful for her to see. When your spouse suffers—you suffer. There is no separation when it comes to pain.

In sickness and in health means that sometimes people get sick, and sometimes they even die. You are the spouse. You are the last line of defense. You committed and you're obligated to fulfill your role. If the doctors had told me that Danielle and I were a perfect match for a heart transplant, I would have gladly done a John Q, pulled the trigger, and given her my heart. Gladly. It wasn't an option, but those were my thoughts. Gladly.

From the Newlyweds:

Were there times during the illness that you didn't think you could do it anymore?

Yes. Several times I had questions about my ability to continue, especially when I was having chest pains. I never hoped that she would die, but only that she would get better. We lived with a lot of desperation. I had patches of my own hair that were falling out. It still hasn't grown back in some places on my head. The stress was unbearable. I had never been through anything that was as stressful as that.

If my spouse were just diagnosed with a terminal illness, what advice would you give me?

Take it one minute at a time. Don't project what tomorrow is going to be like, or what the next 5 years are going to be like, because most likely you are going to be dead wrong. You can't fathom, good or bad, how things are going to turn out, or what things will be like.

I remember that in March, 2011, we knew she was going to die, but it wasn't yet imminent. It was raining like crazy outside, and we turned the T.V. off and lay in bed to listen to the rain. We laughed and talked, and it was one of the sweetest moments that she and I had ever experienced. It was also one of the most intimate moments that we had ever had as a couple. It was truly a beautiful thing, but if you worried about tomorrow, you'd miss out on moments like that. Be kind to yourself and really embrace what is happening right now.

How did your mate's condition affect your normal intimacy patterns as a couple?

It shut it down. Once we got the diagnosis of her cancer, we probably had sex twice. We were active newlyweds, but it took her months to recover from the heart surgery, and the chemo had really affected her drive and desire for sex. When we went there, it was all about the oneness with your partner. The focus wasn't on climax. It was the oneness. That was what mattered, and it was fantastic.

How did you handle those changes?

I felt I was gracious. I didn't put pressure on Danielle for much of anything. I knew that sex was going to be difficult for her, so I just put it out of my mind. I didn't marry her to have sex. I have no complaints about sex in a marriage, and it's a great component, but marriage is so much bigger than that. I didn't have an expectation so it was cool.

Were you two still able to play together during your mate's decline?

Yeah, definitely. We spent most of our time at home laughing and joking and dancing in our apartment. As we moved closer to the end, playing took on much more subtle forms. She liked me without a beard, so I'd shave it and wake her up. Danielle slept a lot during the day, so she'd see that my beard was gone, and she'd grab my face and give me a couple kisses on my cheeks, and then go back to sleep. She was too ill to do too much.

How did you find joy together when so much time and emotion was filled with the disease? How did you avoid not focusing on the bad all the time?

Knowing that she had an expiration date (and we all do) caused me to just enjoy everything that I was able to do for her or with her. I loved her hugs. I ate up when she said, "I love you." I would hang on those words.

I wouldn't allow myself to be buried in my phone or ... [laughing] before she was sick; there were arguments about my involvement with fantasy basketball. I'd be at the computer for hours. I put all that away. I didn't care about those things anymore. It so narrowed my focus so I could appreciate what I actually had with Danielle. So when the center of your focus says, "I love you," man that's a good moment.

What was the dominant emotion during your season of caretaking with your mate—as compared to your emotional state now?

Anger versus acceptance. It took me a very long time to accept: it is what it is, and it's not going to change. I also had to accept: God is God, and I'm not. That definitely settles some dust. [laughing]

What's the one piece of advice you'd give someone just starting out in marriage?

I could think of about 30 pieces of advice, but I'll try to give you one. You will be happiest when you're loving your spouse. Whatever it takes, love your spouse. We usually default to a form of romantic love because we make love about how we feel. That is a selfish thing because we make their existence to serve us. They exist to make us feel good or wanted or desired. That is not loving them—that is us loving ourselves. The greatest joy and health for yourself is to love your spouse for their benefit. I'm not perfect, and I'm not trying to portray that image of myself, but selfish is making love about me. Doing the difficult things that are necessary for your spouse... that's love. Not what makes you feel good.

What's the best thing a husband can do for his wife every day?

Do the dishes. [chuckle] Doing the dishes could mean a lot of different things. In our household in New York, nobody had a dishwasher. So, doing the dishes is a chore. To wash by hand, to dry, and to put up the dishes requires time and patience. In my house, my wife hates doing the dishes. She actually feels loved when I do the dishes. And I know that, so I do the dishes. The most loving thing I can do for her is to do the dishes. Roses, candy, and cards doesn't do it for her. She feels loved when that sink is empty of dishes. So do the dishes.

What's the best thing a wife can do for her husband every day?

Listen to what he actually wants. I'm very comfortable in admitting that I do not understand the female brain. But because most women are smarter than men, they believe that they can get to the bottom of what a man wants and totally ignore the surface levels of what a man says he wants. I'm not a complicated person, and most men aren't either, so listen to what we're saying. It might be what we really want.

What one piece of advice you would give to a newly engaged couple?

Take all your ideas of marriage that you gathered from romantic comedies, put them in a blender, let it run for 10 minutes, and then throw them all away. [laughing] Sprinkle them like the ashes of a burnt corpse. Your spouse will absolutely disappoint you if that is your expectation. Then you're going to have to make a decision on whether or not you're going to remain true to the promise of love that you made.

That's pretty wise for such a young man.

I've lived some life man. I'm potty trained. Danielle put a lot of work into potty training me. [laughing]

What are your most important memories of your marriage?

Our honeymoon. I was in paradise with the person that I loved more than anything. I have a video of us on the beach ordering Jerk Burgers, and we didn't have a frik'n care in the world. One night we went to Boston for Valentine's Day. We were in a restaurant at the top of a tall building there. You could see the whole city from up there. I remember looking at her, and she was beautiful that night. I told her that I loved her, and she broke out in this girlish giggle. Man, it was magic. People and beauty surrounded us, but we were alone in that moment.

Knowing all that you know now, what would you have done differently in your marriage?

I would have listened more early on in our marriage. I'm a better listener now, but early on I might only hear what she said just in order to respond. I didn't really listen, tune in my ears, and hear her heart. I would have worked harder to learn who she was. I could have explored more concerning the things that made her happy or sad. Danielle was a fascinating person, but I didn't really start digging until after we found out she was sick, then I was playing catch up until it wasn't possible any longer. I would have stopped trying to fix everything and entered her concerns with her.

What did you learn about your spouse that caused you to love her even more?

Danielle loved God. Even though she was afraid, she had a real faith that inspires me to this day. She loved me very deeply. My current wife didn't get to have the conversations with her husband that I had with Danielle. He died tragically in an accident. She didn't get to hear all the wishes that he might have wanted to share with her. Danielle knew exactly what I needed to hear at almost every point of her illness. She had a firm grasp on what I needed.

Do you still think that marriage is a great idea?

Marriage is the best idea. It's fantastic. Marriage is like a vacuum: if you use it right, it's great! If you don't use it right, you'll think it's a dumb invention. If you use it for what it's intended for, you'll love it. I'm a huge proponent of marriage when it's done the right way.

If your goal in getting married is to find someone to make you feel special or good all the time, then I'd suggest you reconsider. Those things are byproducts of two lives lived in the service of the other.

Any final words of advice for married couples of all ages?

Have fun today. Stop worrying about all the things that consume you with fear. Do the right things, and you'll move in the right direction. Have fun. Smile. Don't put off being present with your spouse today. Don't take that for granted.

In Memory of
Dannielle Wikia Willams Rice
December 30, 1983 – April 23, 2011

Marcy

Introduction

It's the classic 50's teeny-bopper, sock hop romp: a poor kid out of South Arkansas, dressed in his dazzling soldier's uniform, meets and ultimately wins the heart of a small Central Texas beauty, who charms, yet withdraws, and eventually succumbs to the love they both were meant to have. That's pretty close to how it all started and continued for almost 57 years. Two kids who fell in love and stayed in love for a really long time.

Patti and I find great joy in presenting to you Marcelaine Chamblee Paschall's story. This is my mother. She's one of our favorite people, so bear with us if we're unabashedly proud of this woman, and very honored to portray some of the life she lived with her man.

Joe and Marcy moved to McGregor in 1957 and never left. They raised, educated, and married off three children, who gave them seven grandchildren and nine great grandchildren (currently). A visit to Jokey and Marmie's house meant fun, food, a "Jokey drink," always music, and lots and lots of love.

For over 50 years, my dad tirelessly built and serviced a successful insurance and real estate business in McGregor, Texas. He might have been one of the most knowledgeable agents to ever work in both fields. The man had game, and the city of McGregor owes him a huge debt of gratitude for his never-quit mentality, and his positive hope for change and growth in that little village. Marcy poured herself into stoking the home fires until the kids were grown and then she inherited her mother's cosmetics and floral business, which still bears her mother's name. Marcy was proof that some apples don't fall too far from the tree. All of those businesses have now been sold. Things have drastically changed. Time has marched on.

Patti and I caught up with Mom in her home on a rainy afternoon. She talked. We listened. We cried. She cried. We said "Thank You" one more time. There's stuff here for all of us to learn. Thanks mom... we love you! –MDP-

Can you tell us about how you two met and fell in love?

I went to the Milk Bucket one night, which was a local burger joint where kids could dance and hang out, and Joe was sitting there with a big cast on his foot. He was a soldier at Fort Hood, and he played football for the base. He had broken his foot and had come into town for some R&R with a buddy. I had been to a pageant at my High School and was all dressed up with lots of rhinestones and costume jewelry. I had gone home to change, but I had left my ring on. His first words to me were, "Is that ring real?" and I said smugly, "Of course." He was really looking at it, because it was a big piece of glass that was about the size of a large grape. I noticed him a couple more times when he visited from Fort Hood with his friend. His friend was dating a McGregor girl.

Was it love at first sight?

No, because I had a boyfriend at the time.

When did the love story begin?

Well, he dated my best friend first. At one point, my boyfriend and I had a spat, and we split up. I was sitting at the Dairyland, which was the other burger joint on the other side of town, with my friend, and Joe walked in. He came over to where we were and sat down with us. We were sitting there having a Coke and fries—it was all we ever ate in that place. He told us he was headed out on bivouac and said to me, "I need you to do something for me." I said, "What?" He said, "Look after Janet for me." Joe told me later that was his "in" with me. It was his way of starting a conversation. Well, it flew all over me that he had asked me to do that—that he would think about her and not think about me. He then left with the guy who had given him a ride, because he didn't have a car. He had never owned a car. When we were leaving, my friend said to me, "I think I would be after him," and I said, "I think I will." That was in December 1955. Once he came back, he dated Janet a couple more times, but nothing serious. By that time, I was dating another boy, and we even double dated a couple of times with Joe and Janet.

So in the Spring, I was at a slumber party, and a bunch of us girls had walked down to Dairyland. There was a group of boys that were going to give us a ride back to the house. It was a 2-door car, so all of us girls piled in the back seat, and all the guys squeezed in the front. Back in those days, you could do that. So when we started to get out, one of the guys said, and I don't think it was Joe, "Okay, everybody has to give us boys a good night kiss." So the love story started when I leaned over and kissed Joe. That is when I fell in love with him. That very minute! He was a good kisser, I might add! **[laughing]** So we had a date the next night and several more afterwards until my boyfriend came sniffing back and broke us up—which I knew broke Joe's heart.

So he went to Arkansas on leave, and I wrote him a letter and apologized to him. He didn't write me back, so I didn't know if he was going to have anything to do with me or not. Joe was coming back into Waco on the train, and his friend Donny was going to go pick him up. I talked Donny into letting me be the one to go get him. When Joe got off that train and saw me, he smiled real big, and that was pretty much it. We were together after that.

When were you married? Where?

I picked him up at the train depot in August, and we married 3 months later. We were married in Texarkana, because his parents couldn't come to McGregor because they had an old car. Joe's sister said she would help get his parents to the wedding if we could do it closer to Arkansas. His sister knew someone who knew the Pastor at the First Baptist Church in Texarkana. We were married about 5:00pm on a Sunday, November 4, 1956.

How long were you and Joe married?

We were married 56 ½ years.

What was the first year of your marriage like?

Oh my, the first year was like a fog. We moved so many times, and we were just trying to get our footing. It was wild and hard because he was gone a lot and the baby (Mike) was on the way. When we got married, he was still in the service, and he would leave before sunrise and be gone all day. We had moved to McGregor because I wanted to finish High School. It was a temporary arrangement, and we were living with my parents. Once he got out of the service, we moved to Arkansas so Joe could go to school. He and I lived with his parents for a while because he was still gone all the time. We finally got an apartment in Monticello, and he was playing basketball at the University of Arkansas Monticello, and again he was still gone all the time, traveling with the team to tournaments and games. At the end of that semester, he got a job. We decided to move to Pine Bluff and settled in an apartment there. And then a little package came along in June 1957 (Mike), and we tried to make it work living in Pine Bluff, but it was hard.

Around July 4th, we took the baby for a visit to McGregor to see my parents. I stayed two weeks in McGregor, and Joe had to go back to work and close out the apartment in Arkansas. All kind of rumors went around McGregor that we had separated. Not true. But after two weeks, we did not like being apart, so I went back to Arkansas and moved in with his parents again. Joe had a summer construction job building the new paper mill. The dream was that we'd move to Fayetteville in the fall of '57 so he could play basketball and start Law School at the University of Arkansas.

You mentioned a consternation?

During those days, my Dad (a used car salesman) had made a deal with Joe. He had given him cars to drive during his time in college. If Joe could sell the car at a profit, then he could keep the extra money. That was my Dad's way of helping us to make some extra cash, plus provide us with a car. Daddy had given Joe a Studebaker to drive, and a family member in Arkansas asked to borrow the car and then wrecked it. The family member couldn't afford to fix the car. Joe went to his own Dad and talked to him about it. Joe's Dad told him that family was the most important thing. At that moment, Joe gave up on his dream of going back to school. It was very difficult for him, but he knew that it wasn't in his future at that time. So Joe told me to call my Mom and Dad to come get us. They were there the next day to get us, and they were so excited. I was happy too... much more than Joe.

My parents moved us to McGregor, this time pulling the wrecked car and our few belongings back to Texas. This happened at the end of August. Joe soon got a job with the National Life Insurance Company. That job eventually led to much bigger things for us. We rented a little house on Fillmore Street and have been in McGregor ever since. It was a crazy first year. By the end of the year, another baby was on the way.

How differently were you both raised?

Oh goodness—like daylight and dark. There was a world of difference. I was an only child. I was the apple of my parent's eye, but both of my parents worked outside of the home. Each had their own business. I was a latch key kid before we called it that. Back in the 40-50's, it was pretty rare for a woman to work outside of the home. I was adventuresome enough that I was a pistol, and there's no question about that. I had a hard time sitting still. There was so much going on out there that I wanted to experience. It took both of my parents to keep at least one eye on me at all times [laughing].

On the other hand, Joe had a lot of responsibility for a whole lot of people at an early age. He was one of five kids, the oldest boy, and was called on for finances when he was still very young. He used to tell me that he remembered picking blackberries with his mom as a small child. He raised rabbits and sold them to the market because his father was just gone all the time and money was tight. His dad had left a bad home situation when he was 13 years old. Home, or anything to do with home, was not a good memory for his dad. So he was basically absent and not a source of family stability. So Joe was called on to take up the slack when he was a little boy.

I lived in the middle of a small town. I had access to movies, music, burgers, and most of the modern comforts afforded to two working parents. Joe barely had any of those things. Going to church or visiting his grandparents was about all the social exposure he got. Those people lived deep in the piney woods. His mother would slick down their hair, polish them up, and they walked miles to church or miles to school. So there was a world of difference in how we were raised.

We had very different world-views and ways we processed things. Naturally, he was going to look at things totally different from me. And we squared off pretty regularly over stuff. Some of it was because I was a woman and he was a man, but how we were raised factored into most everything.

What were your shared goals and ambitions starting out?

Joe's ambition was to get a better job than just collecting nickels and dimes from the people who had bought small life insurance policies—to gain more knowledge and be the best provider he could be. My job was to be home with my babies, and there was never any discussion for me to get a job. My ambition was to provide a home for my family. Joe never finished college and talked about going back to school, but he knew that was impossible. He wanted the best for us, so that is when we bought our first house on 9th Street. He was focused on taking care of his family. We lived in that house for 7 years. Then we found out that we were expecting our 3rd child, and that is when we built the house I am still living in today. I've been in this home 50 years.

So as the marriage began to develop and mature, what did "normal" look like for Joe & Marcy's relationship?

Normal was busy. It was ok because we worked hard to make it good, despite how busy we all were. We had our problems like everyone, but we remained steady and in love. We were both happy with each other, we loved our kids, we loved our families, we had a lot of friends that we were crazy about. We regularly attended church and were very involved with our friends in Sunday School. We still dated often and made that a priority. We communicated well. It wasn't perfect, but it worked for us.

Joe was working a lot of hours, and sometimes I resented that, but when you own your own real estate and insurance business, it's not a 9 to 5 job. You worked until stuff got finished. He'd be on the phone all day and then still have a ton of paperwork that had to be done after business hours. Joe was adamant about the kids having a college education, we had 3 kids who were growing up, so he was burning the candle at both ends. I was trying to keep up with their crazy schedules, make all the ball games and school events, and keep a home in order. It was never boring. It was full of activity every day. But even with all of that, we made time for each other. It was important to us.

What part of your life with Joe was the most rewarding for you?

Our whole life was rewarding. Spending time with Joe is all I ever really cared about. We loved being together and having fun. I was married to my best friend. I had three perfect children, and I had a beautiful home. I didn't want a lot of stuff. I just wanted to be with Joe.

What have you learned the most in your life that Joe taught you?

A lot. He was a lot of things I wasn't. Patience! Religion! He was the one that insisted on us joining a church. He grew up as a true believer in a very spiritual home. Also, he taught me about the grace of God, pure love, and the power of forgiveness! He was so smart about so many things, and he was my go to person about everything. I don't think I realized how smart he was until after I matured. It's too bad that he didn't get to finish college, but he never complained about it.

When did Joe's medical complications begin to surface?

The first time we had any kind of real problem was in 1972. He was 34 years old. We had gone to dinner with some friends and he was sitting there eating and just tipped over, face down into his plate. It scared the crap out of all of us! He was non-responsive, so we took him to the hospital. He started waking up on the way to the hospital, and they kept him overnight for observation. He was diagnosed with high-cholesterol and high-blood pressure. He was under stress, slightly over weight, and he was smoking 2 packs of cigarettes a day. That is when we started watching his diet. He started exercising and finally stopped smoking at the age of 40. Mike was going to college at the University of Arkansas in Fayetteville. Joe said he couldn't afford out of state tuition and cigarettes at the same time. So he quit. Cold turkey.

Was there a progression to the medical issues?

Yes, he had a triple-by-pass surgery in 1992. He also had terrible allergies. He coughed constantly. Most of the focus for the next 20 years after the bypass was managing his diet, managing his stress, and paying attention to his heart related issues. Joe's dad died at age 62 with a heart attack. He knew his cardio genetics were not the best.

So towards the end, when Joe started declining, what happened?

The first real change was probably around 2009. I started noticing little things that were strange for him. Once, he was driving and he went into a fog like he couldn't hear me. I think at that time he was probably having TIA's. This happened a few more times after that. Then in May of 2011, he passed out while talking to a customer on a business call and hit his head on the concrete floor. He didn't slouch to the ground when he fell. Joe's eyes rolled to the back of his head, and he fell like a fallen tree backwards. While he was in the hospital, he had an MRI and they discovered numerous problems.

He had a clogged carotid artery, a bleed in his head, he was in atrial flutter, and he had an Anterior Aortic Aneurism. They couldn't decide if the fall had caused the bleeding in his head, or if the bleeding was caused by a stroke. So between May 26 and September 26, 2011, he had two major surgeries (repaired the carotid and the AAA) and three ablations trying to fix the A-fib. That was a brutal summer for him. It was obvious that all that had taken a major toll on him.

Did his cardio issues take his life?

No. After those surgeries, Joe was definitely talking less and less. His speech was getting harder to understand. We tried speech therapy, but it didn't seem to help. He fell a lot. He would do strange things. He seemed to be disoriented and lost. He was having a hard time swallowing. He would cough uncontrollably (especially when he was eating). The doctors were diagnosing him with dementia, and they had him on strong heart medicine. They finally did take him off some of the heart meds, and we had a pretty good spring.

Later that summer we had a checkup with our cardiologist, and he was not happy with Joe's progress. He finally sent us to M.D. Anderson in Houston to see a neurologist. This was August of 2012. Basically, the neurologist told him it was still after-effects of the strokes. I still wasn't pleased with the diagnosis. The rest of 2012 he was still deteriorating. He was falling a lot, talking less and less, and steadily losing weight.

I took him on a trip up into the Ozarks to see the fall foliage, and he never said 5 words. He enjoyed the trip, but I think he was miserable, not feeling well. He wanted to see a show in Branson, but he couldn't stay. He was anxious, he slept a lot, he would try to do things and couldn't and would give up. That wasn't like him at all.

The doctor in Houston did tell him not to drive on the freeway or in traffic, but he could drive to work and back. One day he was going to go to the office, and we lost him. (We live in a community of 4,500 people. His office was less than a half-mile from our home. He'd been driving to work for over 50 years.) I couldn't find him. I feared he drove to Waco. I finally found his car at the post office. He had driven to the post office and when he came out, he had forgotten that he had driven his car, and he walked home. I knew then he didn't need to drive anymore.

I wanted to fix Joe, and I couldn't. I wanted answers to what was going on with him. I was getting none. But I didn't give up.

Did you finally get a diagnosis that made sense to you before he passed?

Yes! We finally went back to Houston in April 2013, and the same neurologist did a series of tests on him that they hadn't done the first time they met with him. The young intern doctor working with the neurologist is the one who actually diagnosed Joe with Progressive Bulbar Palsy (It's a part of the ALS family). We knew nothing about the disease, but after researching it, we were absolutely certain it was the right diagnosis. There is no cure, and it runs its course in about 3 years. It drastically attacked Joe's speech and his ability to swallow and properly use his tongue.

The neurologist suggested we put in a feeding tube. The doctor said it very nonchalantly—like you can do this and live a perfectly normal life. Days later, we saw a gastrologist, and he recommended the same thing. But after all the information had been explained to Joe, he adamantly said, "NO!" He didn't say much, but he had "NO!" down pretty good **[laughing]**. He was wasting away at that time and couldn't eat without violent coughing. And when he did eat, he couldn't keep anything down. The disease had been shutting down his speech and swallowing capabilities for a long time. The disease had run its course. But I finally had an answer. I finally knew what was wrong with him. He passed away 10 days later.

How did he handle his complications emotionally?

He never complained. Not one time. With time, I could see a small decline. He never got back to where he was before the surgeries. It was pretty much down hill since then. He did get upset at one doctor who suggested he had dementia, and Joe shot back, *"There is nothing wrong with my mind."*

How did you handle his complications emotionally?

Mostly angry. Especially at the doctors and the lack of answers. They wouldn't address him. They would only talk to me. We couldn't get a good diagnosis.

Was there a moment of communication when you both acknowledge the seriousness of Joe's complications to each other?

We had gotten the diagnosis of Progressive Bulbar Palsy on a Wednesday. We went home, and on Friday night, he started choking; I had to call 911, and the EMT's took him to the hospital. They admitted him and ran more tests on him over the weekend. The doctors ordered a barium swallow test and discovered that nothing he was attempting to swallow was making it into his stomach. Everything was going into his lungs. Later that day a nurse came in to Joe's room and posted orders that he was no longer to ingest food or water by mouth. So I sat down, and I told him, "You are very sick honey, and I am so sorry. They are telling us that when you eat or drink, it makes you worse." He just looked at me and never tried to say a word.

Do you think he understood what you were saying?

I don't really know. I think so. He never asked me a question. That next morning a young doctor told us that there were no good options. He confirmed that the feeding tube was a miserable idea for Joe. He recommended we meet with the hospice reps and take him home. Mike came in later that night from running errands, and Joe grabbed his hand and said very clearly, "Take me home." I'm pretty sure he knew the score of the situation.

What kind of daily care did Joe need from you?

He needed me to be more patient. I wasn't mad at him. I was mad at the situation. I think that is a lesson that needs to be taught early on. Your frustration is so enormous at the whole situation and all the changes and all the things he was going through—physically and emotionally, too. I had to manage his meds and stay with him at all times. I wouldn't leave him.

One of the hardest things was trying to find things he could eat because he just kept losing weight. I had no idea of his swallowing issues. Even at that point, I never thought he wasn't going to always be here. I wouldn't go there. Even after he came home from the hospital with hospice, I wouldn't go there in my mind.

Generally, what was Joe's response to your caretaking?

He just tolerated me for the most part [laughing]. I think he was grateful. As I said, he got to where he couldn't verbalize anything. He knew that I knew he was grateful. He didn't have to say anything to me.

How much of that overall burden did you shoulder by yourself?

I didn't. My kids were always there, maybe not hands on all the time, but emotionally.

How well do you think you did under that stress?

I didn't have the patience that I wish I could have had. Not with him, but at the situation.

Where did you find your strength and courage?

From within. I wouldn't go to a place that was dark. I couldn't dwell on how bad it was. You just had to jump in there and take care of it. I think I was angry at God at that time, so I don't think I was pulling any strength from Him, but I'm sure I was getting more than I thought. I was asking God, "How can you let this happen to us?" and I'm not sure I'm still not asking that question, but I'm sure I was pulling more strength from there than I knew.

What were your big "priorities" before you found out your spouse was sick? How were those things affected by the illness?

Well, for him to retire, and for us to travel the world. We went to a lot of gorgeous places during our marriage. We were going to spend our kid's inheritance. We did go on a cruise to the Caribbean in November 2011, and in 2012 we went up into Arkansas and Missouri. We just wanted to be together. The travel and adventure wasn't the point anymore as his decline was advancing.

Was there a point when you knew that your caretaking days were numbered?

Yes, when they told him he couldn't have anything else to eat or drink. But I didn't expect it to happen so fast.

How was Joe processing his decline?

The only thing I ever heard him say, and he had to struggle to say it, he was lying on the couch a couple days before our last trip to Houston and he said, "I'm tired." I think he was waiting on the end. He slept a lot, and I'm glad. But he never talked about it.

Did you two ever talk about "your" future without Joe in the picture?

No. Never.

What was going on in your head and heart during the few final days with Joe?

That's tough. Too many different emotions going on right now. Just a sec [crying]. I didn't want him suffering anymore because I knew he didn't want to live that way. But I couldn't think about living without him.

Looking back, how prepared were you to let him go?

Well, I'm still not prepared to let him go, and it's been almost a year. I wasn't prepared at all. But I knew it was coming, and I am just so thankful that all my kids were here, and that helped a lot.

Was there an opportunity to say "goodbye" before his final sleep?

No.

So it's been 11 months since he passed. How are you doing?

About the same. I'm sure I'm stronger, but I kind of went backwards for a while, so now maybe I'm just catching up again. I don't know. I miss him just as much today as I did then. I wouldn't want him back like he was either. So I'm doing as well as I can.

Do you ever sense that Joe is with you?

Yes I do. His influence is a part of who I am now. When people ask me to do stuff, I sometimes respond based on how I know Joe would want me to respond. I talk to him, say "good morning" every day. It's not a constant conversation **[giggle]**, but you know what I mean. I can hear certain music or hear a phrase that instantly pops his presence in me. One little thing can trigger it. The problem is that it won't stay. It disappears as quickly as it comes.

Most marriage vows contain the words: "For better or for worse... in sickness and in health... until death do us part." Describe what those words might have meant to Joe & Marcy.

Mine did! For better or worse meant we enjoyed the good times and got through the bad times. In sickness and in health—that's kind of self-explanatory, because I don't know how someone could leave someone and not stay with them, or stick them somewhere after 56 years and not take care of them. I don't understand that. His favorite saying to me was, "you are my mate." He would say laughingly, "Come on mate," and that was who I was to him. I was his mate.

We were kids. We grew up together. When you grow up together, you learn life's hard knocks together. He had been through some hard knocks, but I hadn't. I lived a charmed life. But he didn't.

From the Newlyweds:

Were there times during the illness that you didn't think you could do it anymore?

For the most part, no! But a couple of times... maybe [laughing]. One time, Joe was having some problems and he wanted some Milk of Magnesia. So I went to the store to get him some and gave him a dose when I got back. Well sometime during the night he got thirsty, I guess, and he drank the whole bottle [laughing]. He stopped up two toilets and used 17 rolls of toilet paper. I was about to lose it, and so was my son who was outside trying to clean out the sewer line. We had to move to a hotel and spend the night until the plumber could get out to the house and clean out the sewer the line. In that incident, I wanted to quit (laughing). Seriously though, deep down, I would have never thought about abandoning him.

If my spouse were just diagnosed with a terminal illness, what advice would you give me?

Get all the facts. It helps to know what you are dealing with. People can handle most things if they just know the facts. The unknown is so scary. Then, have the compassion that you need to have for the things they can't help.

How did your mate's condition affect your normal intimacy patterns as a couple?

Well, the fact that he could not talk or eat drastically cut into all of that. Because a lot of our intimate time together was around meal times and date nights to eat out.

How did you handle those changes?

With a lot of sadness. I tried to keep planning times together, but he just couldn't do it anymore.

Were you two still able to play together during your mate's decline?

No.

How did you find joy together when so much time and emotion was filled with the illness and disease?

Well, I finally got what I wanted. I got to spend all my time with him. It took a long time to get it, but I finally got it [crying]. Just being with him and helping him through it meant the world to me.

How did you avoid not focusing on the bad all the time?

Well, I learned a long time ago that the bad things that you don't want to deal with you put it in a box and you put the box on a shelf and you only take that box down when you have to deal with it, because if you sit and deal with things all the time, it's not good. It doesn't solve anything, and it only weakens you and prevents you from helping them in other ways. So the things I didn't want to deal with were right up there on that shelf. I think people that dwell and dwell and dwell on it have a harder time getting through it. And… I still tried to plan things for us to do. It might just be a ride in the country, but at least we were together. You just can't give up. You have to keep trying to help them.

What was the dominant emotion during your season of caretaking with your mate—as compared to your emotional state now?

Deep sadness for something lost, but thankful for what you have. A lot of people didn't have what I had. But… I'm still sad.

What's the one piece of advice you'd give someone just starting out in marriage?

This is what I told both of my granddaughters: It's not a perfect world, and if you try to make it one, it won't work out. And… don't stay mad. You have to forgive!

What's the best thing a husband can do for his wife every day?

Tell her he loves her, AND show it. Don't just tell her.

What's the best thing a wife can do for her husband every day?

Same thing.

What is the main advice you would give to a newly engaged couple?

Just keep making sure you are making the right decision. It's never too late to back out. Marriage is hard work, even with someone you're in love with. If you are not willing to work—rethink your decision.

What are your most important memories of your marriage?

Oh wow, I have lots of them. The love! The happiness! I don't dwell on the bad stuff. Joe and I fought a lot [laughing]. We had some big fights, but they we never bigger than the love.

What did you learn about your spouse that caused you to love him/her even more?

He was a loving person and a caring person. He cared for so many people!

Do you still think that marriage is a great idea?

Yes I do. You need someone to call your own. Because you aren't going to always have your mother, and you aren't going to always have your father, and I was an only child, so I didn't have a brother or a sister. But… I had one person.

As I said earlier, he was my "go to" person, and everyone needs someone in their life to help them get through all the stuff.

Was Joe that to you?

Yes! That doesn't ever mean you never get mad or frustrated, but if you have the person that you love most in the world walking beside you—there's nothing better than that!

What else was Joe to you?

Provider, lover, confident—foot warmer at night **[laughing]**. My everything!

Any final words of advice for married couples of all ages?

Work together! Love them more than you love yourself! Forgive easily! They have to be number one!

I'm not sure young people know how to do that today. My generation was different. There's a big gap! This generation is about me, me, me! I was an only child, but I wasn't raised that way—where it was all about me. It's an every day struggle to keep all that in balance, and it took us a while to get it, but we did. We were so young! We grew up together and went along with the flow. It was awesome.

In memory of
Joseph Donald Paschall
August 31, 1936 – April 26, 2013

George

Introduction

The distinguished English gentleman that you're about to meet is my friend George Robert Gilbart-Smith. After graduating from Cambridge University in 1965, George moved to Tonbridge and never really left his profession, church, or village. That tells you something about the man if you're paying attention.

If you were to meet George at church or some other social function—possibly an academic environment—it would be very easy for us Yanks to profile the man as overly educated, rigidly proper, and maybe even wound a bit too tight. As tempting as it would be to draw those conclusions, nothing could be further from the truth. I submit to you that the man is truly brilliant, he is consummately mannered, and he does carry himself in a seriousness that is quite noticeable—but there is another side.

I met George in Toronto back in 1994. I was there to explore and experience the spiritual renewal that was happening at a church in Toronto. My first exposure to this distinguished gentleman was... ummm... different. Picture in your mind a man lying on the floor, on his back, with shirttail out, hair disheveled, kicking the floor with the back of his heels in amazing rapidity, while thrusting his right arm into the air in a repeated jousting motion. It wasn't over quickly. It went on for a while. Surely some spiritual dragon was meeting its demise, and I doubled over in laughter at the sight, but I just couldn't turn my head away. I knew that God was working on the man. He kicked so hard that he broke the heel on one of the shoes! Yeah, that was George—so, so much for the "stiff and starched" assessment.

The next morning while at breakfast with an Elder from my church, George and his traveling companion approached our table, and a genuine friendship began. It has remained in force ever since. I've been in George's home many times. He's been in mine. My wife and daughters have also experienced Gilbart-Smith hospitality. We all felt the same thing: Love-is-in-the-house!

As personable and loving as George is, he didn't build that foundation of love alone. There was another influence. As Einstein is to relativity—so was the sweet Alison Bewes Gilbart-Smith to my esteemed friend. Alison was the perpetual effervescent sunshine on his life. She had an ease about her that put you at rest. Alison was grace with skin. Those piercing eyes and a soft grin that formed easily upon her pretty face just made you feel good when you were around her. She seemed to always say enough, without saying a lot. Not many people in this world are blessed with that kind of presence. Alison had it, and it was very good medicine.

When Alison was so sick, Patti and I regularly got the updates via email from George. We were very honored to be included and counted as friends while Alison and George forged their battle against her cancer. George has graciously consented to share the details of their story.

As with all of these stories, there is so much to glean, IF we're paying attention. George lays it out with unflinching clarity, and it's truly a privilege to ponder the astounding courage in these details. I am so proud and grateful for my British friend! You did real good mate! Real good!

Read on, and you'll understand why soon enough! Thanks for taking the time to meet George. –MDP-

Tell us about how you two met and fell in love?

I came to teach math at a boy's preparatory boarding school in Tonbridge, in 1965. When I arrived, I was just amazed at the commitment of many of my colleagues in that school community. I really prayed to the Lord about this, I didn't have a girlfriend at the time, and I was 22 years of age. I felt God was saying, "George, if you get any kind of invitation to go outside of the school community, accept it—however hard it is." One day, towards the end of my first year of teaching at the school, I received an invitation to go to the 21st birthday party of a friend. So I came out of school at 6:00 p.m., took a shower or a bath, got into my smartest dinner jacket, and drove for one hour up to London. I parked right outside of Westminster Abbey, which you could do in those days—you'd get a ticket now—and I walked to the Galleon Club on Totland Street, which was just around the corner from Westminster Abbey.

So I went downstairs and found myself seated at a table that consisted entirely of young men who I knew well. We were having a good time talking, when another friend dropped by and asked me to come along and meet some of the guests from All Souls Church - Langham Place (a large evangelical church in the heart of London). I was sat down opposite of one of the most beautiful girls I had ever looked at. That was Alison. We had a really good time conversing, and our first dance was a Scottish reel called The Gay Gordons. By the end of that first evening, having had such a lovely time together, I had to get into my car at 1:00 a.m. and drive back to Tonbridge; it was 2:00 a.m. when I got home. I graded papers until 5:00 a.m., promptly got into bed, and was at school at 9:00 that morning. I knew that going to that party would be costly, but as a result, I met my wife.

You could hope that things went smoothly from there, but they didn't because we were both so busy. We promised to meet again, but we didn't see each other for another six months, and it was only after yet another two months that we began dating regularly. We got off to a somewhat slow start, but nevertheless we were engaged within a year and a half of meeting each other and married a year after the engagement. It was a long engagement because Alison had to finish her nurse's training.

Was it love at first sight?

I think it was for Alison. In fact, she was reputed to have said to one of her best friends, "If I don't marry that guy, I'm going to remain single for the rest of my life." I regard that a bit too flattering towards me. I think had I been madly in love at first sight I would have been a bit more persistent, and it wouldn't have been six months until our next encounter. I fell in love with Alison when we met that third time. I came home from that time with her really in love like never before.

When and where were you married? Where?

We were married in All Soul's Church - Langham Place, December 28, 1968.

How long were you and Alison married?

Just under 34 years.

What was the first year of your marriage like?

I would describe the first six months as "almost traumatic." That is to say, I was so busy! Unless you've been in that particular situation, it's hard to imagine how busy I actually was. I know there are young people today who work so hard that it's hard to build a marriage. The difficulty for Alison was that she was taken away from a student nurse and a church environment where she had many friends, and dumped in a new place with no friends. I was very busy with the school, being gone most of the day. She was trying to get some part-time nursing work, but was unable to arrange it with hours compatible for her to be able to see me. Part-time work usually meant weekends for her, and weekends were about the only time I would be home from school. She eventually did get some work, but very little. Alison was very bored in that environment, and there was I working non-stop for days on end. There was very little time for each other during that first year of marriage. It was really tough. Those were not our expectations. Unless we had been very committed to each other and the Lord, I'm not too sure we would have gotten through that season and remained as a couple.

Actually, we laughed a lot about our lack of time together. Our sense of humor may have saved the day on that one. It was no fairytale that is for sure. It was a big test for us.

How differently were you both raised?

We were raised in a very similar way, that is to say that we both came from middle-class/upper middle-class British families. There was definitely a code about how those kinds of families operated and raised kids. The difference was that Alison was born and raised in East Africa. I was born in the UK, but my family was a service family. My father was in the Royal Air Force, and I was used to moving frequently, per my father's assignments. Alison was used to staying in one place for a long time. She spent nearly her entire childhood in one town in Tanzania, East Africa.

The climate in England was very different from where Alison grew up. At age 11, she came to school in England, but her first extended stay was for her nurse's training. She found it very difficult to adjust to the climate in England.

If you grow up in the tropics, you're used to consistently long days year round, not late evenings and early mornings during the summer months and the total opposite in the winter. During the winter months it's totally dark here at 4:00 p.m., and light doesn't reappear until 8:00 a.m. It took Alison a while to adjust to those differences, and she was still adjusting when I met her.

Early on, what were some of your toughest challenges as a couple?

Interestingly enough, we never really planned our children. [chuckling] They kind of just happened. We were both comfortable with committing that part of our relationship into the Lord's hands, and were happy with the results. Evidently we were both very fertile [chuckling], and Pete arrived 18 months after we were married. You could say that Pete was planned by Alison, Rosemary came 20 months after that, and was planned by me, and Michael was definitely planned by God. Our initial intention was to have two children then a gap before having two more. The gap didn't happen, so nor did the fourth child. As the children arrived, sharing the upbringing was a real problem. Alison had finally settled into the environment and had made many friends, yet I was still giving an immense amount of my time to the school, and I was conscious that I was somewhat of an absentee husband and father. Because I wasn't available a lot of the time when Alison felt she needed me, obviously, that became a challenge for the marriage.

You were asking about the toughest challenges? We had three children in four years!

That's a lot of dirty diapers.

You're telling me. I took Alison out for dinner one evening after Michael was finally out of diapers during the day (she continued for a short period to put diapers on him in the evening, just in case something went wrong at night). I said to her, "You have now washed, (in those days by hand, because you didn't have those lovely disposable diapers), fifteen thousand diapers. It is time that we have a nice dinner." When we got home after dinner, the babysitter said, "I think you'll find that Mike has a dirty diaper." [laughing] We might have celebrated a wee bit too early. [laughing]

Was Alison still trying to work with all that going on?

Once she was pregnant with Pete, she didn't try to work again. It was a tough first pregnancy. But after Pete was born, she was very content and fulfilled in being a full-time mother. It did challenge us financially, but it was definitely the right course for us, and our children.

She didn't go back to nursing until after all the children left home, when Michael left for college in 1992. She retrained as a nurse and was fortunate to get licensed in a fast-track course that didn't require another four-year degree in nursing.

What were your shared goals and ambitions?

First, we both wanted to be firm and true with the Lord. Second, we were fully committed to each other. Third, we were both fully committed to family. And fourth, I was fully committed to my job and providing for my family. By that time, I was looking to be promoted, maybe the head of my department, or in a boarding school, to become a House Master (with a responsibility for 50 to 60 boy boarders). I didn't become a House Master, but I did acquire the Chair of the Math Department.

We were living life one day at a time. We had our hands full with our own responsibilities, and we were happy and content doing what we were doing. I don't remember ever sitting down with Alison to discuss a game plan. The game just happened.

So as the marriage began to develop and mature, what did "normal" look like for George & Alison's relationship?

I want to be careful about how I answer this question. I may have whitewashed in my mind what actually happened in the light of what happened to Alison, but I can say, absolutely and firmly, that we hardly ever had a strong word of anger with each other. We only had about one or two arguments the whole time that we were married. It was a very harmonious relationship. I believe it was partly due to our upbringing. Both of us came from very stable homes. I never saw my parents arguing, and neither did Alison see that with her parents. We didn't argue. We did discuss, and we certainly had differences of opinion, but we never got heated over any of it.

I became more tactile as we matured. I began to appreciate things like cuddling and so on. Previously, I was a bit too much of the British middle-class gentleman, with not enough affection for Alison's needs. Alison was very affectionate, and it took me a while to learn that affection translated to moral support for her. I learned to add a hug with kind or loving words.

It was part of my attraction to her. I remember thinking, before I met Alison, that I wanted a woman who wouldn't mind me telling her that I love her two hundred times a day! My hope was that she'd say the same back to me, and mean it. We had that from day one. In terms of spoken affection, we were intimate immediately. The physical affection side of companionship (I'm talking about hugging, not sex) took me a little longer to develop.

Once the kids were gone, we enjoyed a great season together. Alison wasn't looking forward to an "empty nest," particularly Michael leaving our home. He was a very warm and loving kid. Before he left, she and I discussed what was going to happen once he did leave. Alison's big goal was to be retrained as a nurse. Once she was back into nursing, her attitude became very upbeat and positive. It really allowed us, because we were both so fulfilled, to enjoy the kids being gone. We saw and enjoyed them a lot, but we thought it was delightful to have "us" time, really for the first time ever in our marriage. At last, I was able to give her the time and energy she'd deserved all along.

What part of your life with Alison was the most rewarding for you?

The last part—quite definitely the last part was the most rewarding. It's when she meant the most to me. Not that she wasn't always important, but the eight and a half years prior to her getting sick were the best for us as a couple. That's when our relationship went deep. It meant so much to me. I finally had time for the relationship, in addition to having time for my job. I had just stepped down as department head and didn't take on any other responsibilities in school. That gave me much more time for home and marriage.

What have you learned the most in your life that Alison taught you?

Fun. She taught me that you could be Christian and still have fun. Being Christian when I married Alison was pretty serious business. It was a case of keeping all the rules, making all the meetings, attending worship, and smiling through it all. I don't think I was a legalistic Christian, but there was always danger in keeping everything square with the "right and wrong" thoughts, instead of being free in the Lord, and being governed by relationship instead of regulations.

Alison really freed me spiritually and emotionally. Her sense of fun really attracted me and kept me buoyant through our entire marriage. I had a sense of humor, but it wasn't integrated into my spiritual life. She helped shape and form my personality. She brought out the real me. How she saw it, considering the shape I was in when we met, is beyond me. [laughing] I'm not sure I would have wanted to marry me back in those days.

What do you think you taught her the most?

Possibly focus. Honing her mind into the things of the Spirit and faith. Let me backtrack a bit. When we were engaged, she knew that I was much more charismatic in my spiritual expression. She had been brought up with a very anti-charismatic posture. This was a bit of a stumbling block with her decision process when weighing if she was going to marry me or not. She decided she'd marry me anyway, but the net result was that I kept my charismatic side to myself for many years. Eventually, as Alison began to be "awakened" into that spiritual arena, she'd say, "Why didn't you tell me all of this before? Why did you keep this a secret?" [laughing] I'd respond, "You thought about breaking off our engagement because I spoke in tongues! Do you remember that?" I think she'd possibly say that I helped her warm to going deeper with the Spirit.

Also, I think she appreciated, as difficult as this is to say, my unselfishness and my sense of humor. I was always concerned for her directly, no matter what the situation was that she faced. I could become very upset with myself when I didn't have the time to be there for her when she faced certain challenges. I believe those would be the two features of me that she found most engaging.

When did Alison's medical complications begin to surface?

She had gynecological complications in the late 80's, which culminated in her having a hysterectomy in 1989. I'm not sure what the practice is in the States, but in the UK, a total hysterectomy now involves also removing the ovaries. In those days, they left the ovaries behind, and they put Alison on hormone replacement therapy. She really struggled because of various allergies that plagued her because of the hormones.

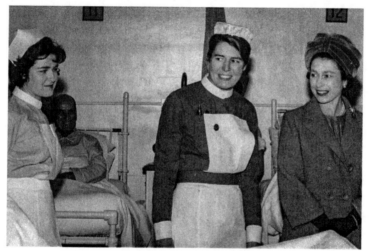

The Queen's visit 1966

As far as the cancer goes, she began to suffer with internal pains that she believed to be her ovaries, around Christmas 2000. Early the next year, because of our medical system in the UK, she couldn't get in to see our family physician, but one of the other doctors in the general practice diagnosed her with cystitis (a urinary problem). Alison was a nurse, and she knew enough about herself to know it was a gynecological issue—not a urinary issue. She was reasonably convinced that she had ovarian cyst.

So the doctor put her on antibiotics, but Alison knew that she'd suffer for it if she took the drugs, so she decided not to take them. Soon thereafter the pain went away, and she did nothing more about the issue for a couple months. In March 2001, she began to have serious pains and problems with her bowel.

So she went back to the general practice again. This time she saw a different doctor, but again not our own doctor. He diagnosed her with constipation, and prescribed medication accordingly. At this point, Alison was in lots of pain.

Two weeks later, she was still very constipated—the treatment hadn't done her any good—and she went back to the doctor again. He prescribed another two weeks of meds for the constipation. Three days in, she went back to the general practice for a second opinion, still unable to see our family doctor, and that doctor basically said, "Do as you're told. My colleague gave you a treatment, so get on with taking the treatment."

I wasn't with her at these appointments. I wouldn't have taken those responses for an answer had I been there. The following weekend was really hard on Alison, so I told her, "This is nonsense. We are going to see our own doctor right away on Monday!" On Monday I rang the doctor's office and we got in to see our doctor. He took one look at her and sent her to see the specialist. At 9:15 p.m., we saw the specialist, and he informed her she wasn't to go home, but report immediately to the hospital for tests. They conducted scans, x-rays, and other tests the next morning.

After the tests, Alison was diagnosed with stage four ovarian cancer. The specialist reported to me that she had multiple total obstructions in her bowel and gave her a maximum of two weeks to live. He suggested that he could remove the obstructions and reattach the bowel in order to keep her comfortable during her remaining time alive, but added that chemotherapy would be her only hope of extending her life by attacking the cancer. So they put her on chemotherapy immediately.

I made contact with a large number of friends via email, soliciting prayer for Alison, in hopes that she would respond well to the chemotherapy. As Alison's condition developed, whole churches started praying for Alison; eventually there were about 2000 people on six continents praying regularly for her. The immediate results were nothing short of miraculous. Her cancer count shrank to one thirtieth of its original level. It gave her another lease of life. It didn't grant her long life, but it allowed Alison enough time to meet two additional grandchildren who were born after her diagnosis and see them through to their first birthdays.

Alison started the chemo in March 2001 and she died November 2002. The last two months, there was no more treatment. The doctors had exhausted all their options. So she had 18 months of treatment for the cancer. The doctors did remove some of the bowel in August 2001, but from the end of the first round of chemo the cancer numbers started a dramatic rise.

In February 2002, she faced a decision about whether or not she was going to continue with the chemo. So she asked my advice. Had I answered, my advice would have been that we just accept what seemed to be inevitable—coming to terms with Alison leaving us, and our family dealing with that loss. But I said to her, "I'm really sorry, but this just has to be your decision. I can't make this decision for you, and I wouldn't want you to ever feel that I advised you to make the wrong decision." So she decided to soldier on and continue with various chemo treatments until September 2002. By then it was clear that nothing more could be done.

At that point, I did take her to another top specialist in London, just to make sure, and he reviewed her x-rays and looked at her charts, and agreed that there was nothing more that could be done. She died two months later.

Was there a progression to what the illness did to Alison?

What it did to her body was much different from what it did to her person. The cancer basically took over her body and ate away her strength and form. Alison was always very slim, with a petite figure. Her tummy became very large, with an increased waistline. The pain control was quite good, but sadly she was allergic to most all of the common painkillers. It was a real medical challenge to keep her out of pain.

She had anaphylactic reactions to two of the chemos. With that, she'd swell up like a balloon and be unable to breathe. When she first went in to see the doctors, she was violently ill. How she managed any functionality in that condition is beyond my understanding. The whole of the next 18 months she was on a tightrope between constipation and sickness, and there was a constant battle to get her blood count high enough for her next round of treatment. She went into the hospital in mid-March 2001, and came out in the middle of May. She had the operation in August and was somewhat normal until November 2001. Even during that time her energy levels were extremely low. After November 2001, until she died, she needed help with everything she did.

Once we were told in September 2002 that there wasn't any more the doctors could do, she got a daily visit from a District nurse. She also had a syringe driver regulating her pain meds, administered by hospice. This allowed her to stay at home, and she didn't have to go back to the hospital, but she did need constant care.

So she died at home?

Yes. Alison's mother, who lived in Bristol, was due to visit on Sunday, November the 24th. Alison had gotten very ill the previous Sunday-Monday, and things were moving downhill quickly, and by Friday, the doctor came to the house and I inquired about how much time we had left with Alison. He assured me that there was plenty of time for all the family to make their visits. "Don't worry about it. It takes time," was his advice.

I personally believe that Alison was physically refusing to die until she could see her mother. So she saw her mother, her sister, and our daughter Rosemary on Sunday, November 24th. Alison's sister drove her mother back to Bristol, and Rosemary followed them both to Bristol on a pre-scheduled visit, not knowing she wouldn't see her mother again. As it turned out, though, it was wonderful that she was able to be with her aunt and grandmother to share their grief.

On Monday, November 25th, the hospice matron dropped by the house and pulled me downstairs to tell me that in her estimation Alison was within hours of her end. I reported to her that information was very different from what the doctor had told me on Friday. She said, "Well, okay, but that's what my experience is telling me." By early afternoon, the doctor showed up and I told him what the matron had told me earlier that morning. He was in total agreement with her assessment.

So I then proceeded to call Peter and Michael to come to the house. Michael was able to come at once with Hannah his wife, and Peter came later in the day. I told them, "This may be the first of 15 false alarms, but this is what was said." Peter, Michael, and I were in the house with Alison when she died at 11:00 p.m.

How did she handle her complications emotionally?

Amazingly! But you have to bear in mind that she was being prayed for by that huge number of people from all over the world. I was sending emails twice a week with updates on her condition. I asked her how she felt about my asking for all this prayer on her behalf. Alison acknowledged that it was against her instincts, because she was a fairly private person, and it wasn't her way to spread around the details of her medical complications. But she did see the value in people having factual information, and not just being asked to pray in some vague sense. So she was good with the emails being sent out and often contributed to them herself.

I never expected to see such an example of courage by Alison as she faced her prolonged illness. Her conduct through that time was simply amazing. I could only hope that I could weather such a challenge with that much grace and courage. Her example was quite incredible.

How did you handle her complications emotionally?

When she went into the hospital the first time, once we knew that we were dealing with cancer, I felt as if I were walking on a cliff's edge in darkness. I couldn't see where that cliff's edge was, but I knew it was close. At that point, I thought I might lose Alison within weeks. I feared that would be all the time I had left with her. If she had died that soon, it would have been a massive shock to the family, and myself. I have friends who have lost their spouse in car accidents and such the like. I have been through that kind of bereavement. I lost my father at age 11 in an airplane crash. With that being said, I tapped in very quickly to how precious every day was. What I went through with my dad helped prepare me for Alison's situation.

I probably handled it by keeping myself busy, and that wasn't difficult because there was so much to do, and by spending as much time as possible with her. By this time I had retired from the school. I now had the time that I needed to attend to Alison. I needed to be with her for myself, she needed me to be with her, and we were able to have the time we both needed. When in the hospital, I was with her from when I woke up in the morning until the specialist arrived around 11:00 p.m. in the evening.

I had one or two unexpected bursts of violent tears. Never in her presence, but maybe after I had been with her all day. The pressure cooker was on during those tense days, and the release of tears would just happen as I needed. It never happened around friends or family, but only when I was alone. I knew that bottled up emotions are bound to spew at some point.

Was there a moment of communication when you both acknowledge the seriousness of the complications to each other?

That is a very good question. Secretly, I knew she might die, but for fear of demoralizing her I never shared these thoughts with Alison. Also, I was holding onto the possibility that we might get a miracle from God for Alison's healing. In consequence, I think Alison thought I was in denial about her dying, so she never spoke about it for fear of upsetting me! The only real regret that I have—once the medics pronounced their final medical verdict on the situation—is that she and I did not have a solid discussion of closure with each other. I regret that we did not utilize the time to prepare ourselves to say "goodbye" to each other, and to thank one another for what our lives together meant to us both over the years.

This is quite possibly the reason why I found it so difficult to answer your previous questions about what we most appreciated about each other. A concerted effort to talk about those things needed to happen between us. Had that been an ongoing topic of conversation in the time that we were granted in September until she died, I think I might have been able to answer your questions with much more clarity.

So I lost out on that. I think Alison lost out, in the sense that she never really liked to ask where I was on things in regards to her parting, and I never liked to ask where she was. We had a chance to be open and honest with each other about our feelings, but we never broached the subject for fear of upsetting the other.

What kind of daily care did Alison need from you?

Initially, she was able to do most things for herself. She had good days and bad days. She had good times and bad times. But what she needed from me changed as the illness progressed. Once she came out of the hospital the first time, she needed care in just getting used to being home again. On bad days, she couldn't get herself out of bed. I was cooking, cleaning, and tending to whatever she needed. That's when I realized that we needed only to live one day at a time, and I really felt that the Lord was challenging me on that concept. I'm a great planner, and I love to plan! But I was wearing myself out planning for all the contingencies all the time. I'd spend ages thinking through 50 different scenarios, and most of the time miss the one that was actually going to happen. This was absolutely exhausting. Much more relaxing: don't plan, and fly by the seat of my pants! Planning was pure wasted energy. I had to settle back into the truth that each day was the day that I needed to focus on. That was it. Each day was an extra day of life. Good or bad, it was gift, and it was life. There were plenty of reasons to be grateful.

On a bad day, Alison would need everything done for her. She might not be able to get out of bed. There were days that I called the hospital because I thought she needed medical attention I couldn't give her. It required massive amounts of patience. Patience with the situation, patience with the medical system, patience with the doctors—it could be trying at times. Once I asked her oncologist if we were making progress against the cancer. He responded with, "We just don't know. We're doing the best we can, but sometimes there is no way to know. Have patience with us." So I rushed home to vent to God about it: "God, give me patience. NOW!" **[laughing]** Patience isn't my strong suit.

As time went on, Alison needed more and more care. Getting in and out of the bath was difficult for her. She was getting more and more emaciated by those later stages. People who knew her really well didn't recognize her when they saw her. The skin was just hanging off of those tiny arms and legs. It was just awful.

One of the most helpful things that people did for us was to cook their normal meals with a few extra portions. They'd bring us those extra portions. Then I'd put them in the freezer. That allowed me to offer Alison a variety of options from that freezer. Quick and ready meals in small portions! Often I'd warm up what she wanted, but once I served it to her, she couldn't eat it. This wasn't too bad with a frozen meal, but on the occasions when I had spent all afternoon preparing that meal, it was very disheartening to spend that much time and energy for something she couldn't enjoy.

Generally, what was Alison's response to your caretaking?

She was so infinitely grateful I think. Even through the whole process! I was so glad to have the time to devote to her.

How much of that overall burden did you shoulder by yourself?

A lot, but I did have friends who came to clean the house or whatever else needed attention. Other people did help shoulder the burden. Alison's sister came to stay, and my kids pitched in to help. In fact, the most help my kids offered was just to visit with Alison. Whether she was at home or in the hospital, their visits were pure refreshment for her. And our minister was amazing too. He often visited to pray with her and me and to give us communion.

When she had the surgery in August of 2001, the gynecologist told Alison to get her affairs in order and make some plans for how she wanted to conclude her life. The surgery had been successful in rectifying the bowel issue, but the cancer was still doing its damage. He assured her the cancer would return with vengeance. Upon that news, Alison stated clearly that her priority was to spend as much time as possible with her family.

One of my favorite pictures of her was taken three months after that debrief with the doctor. It's of Alison holding hands with her two-year-old grandson as they walked through a puddle of water. It's obvious that she was enjoying the puddle as much as he was. It's a very special image for me. She just wanted to be with her children and the grand-babes.

How well do you think you did under that stress?

Could I give myself 8 marks out of 10? Would that be about right? I'm not sure, but that's how I feel about it. I was doing the very best I could physically do and emotionally could manage. Nevertheless, there were a couple times that I upset her greatly.

First, in February 2002, as she was facing this decision about whether or not to continue with chemo, she was having a down day. I said, "Look, I hope you don't mind, but when you're down in a pit like this, I can't jump into that pit with you. One of us needs to stay on firm ground in order to help you out of the pit. If I jump into your emotional pit—if I let my emotions go the way that you've been forced to let yours go—then we're both in a pit together, and I'm not able to help to you." That really upset her. She felt that she wanted me as close to her at that time as possible. She didn't want me offering her a ladder or a rope so she could climb out. She was hurting and she wanted me. It was difficult for me as well, but I knew if I let myself go down into that pit, we'd both be in trouble. To that degree, I had to emotionally detach from her. I really hurt her, and I don't think we ever resolved that.

Then, just before she died, Alison said she regretted her decision in February to continue with the chemo; she'd only done it for the family. I said she shouldn't have considered the family, she should have thought only of herself. And I went on to say that if we'd asked the family they'd probably have opted to let her go in peace. I wasn't thinking of the impact of what I was saying—that really upset her.

Where did you find your strength and courage?

I found it with my walk with the Lord. He was very gracious to me. My sleep pattern was somewhat weird, and I read some very good books during that time. I had a lot of support from close friends, particularly my home group, and

I had friends all over the world. I knew I was being supported supernaturally. It couldn't have been handled in my own strength. God taught me some unique and valuable lessons during that time.

What were your big "priorities" before you found out Alison was sick? How were those things affected by the illness?

After my retirement in 1997, we had settled nicely into the empty nest and refocused ourselves in making ourselves useful in our local Christian community. We were beginning to build a new phase of our marriage. We were in a new place, and we were extremely excited at all of those new possibilities. I've already said this, but we were closer together as a couple than ever before. So we were ready for the new phase. Of course, we didn't realize that cancer was going to have such a massive role in that new phase, but we even put that in God's hands and moved forward as best as we could. We trusted that He was in it all.

Was there a point when you knew that your caretaking days were numbered?

Not KNEW, no... I was always hoping Alison might be healed by God. I never came to the point—openly to the point—where I was willing to admit that He probably wasn't going to heal Alison of cancer. I'm not sure I would have discussed probabilities with God anyway. I think internally, I had a serious theological quandary that I didn't fully face up to probably the way I should have. If I had to counsel anyone now, I would say that you must come to a point where you accept the fact that God may not do what you're asking him to do, and share that openly together and with others. His love for us is no less diminished in that truth, but it has to be faced.

Did you two ever talk about "your" future without Alison in the picture?

In one aspect, we did have a conversation the week before she died. She asked me if I had thought about whom I might actually want to marry if she died. I told her that I hadn't given that a lot of thought. We actually discussed some people whom we thought might be a possibility. But that was as far as the discussion went.

Looking back, how prepared were you to let her go?

By the last week, very prepared. Strangely enough, I wasn't destroyed when Alison died. In fact, I felt a release for myself, as well as for Alison. The last twenty months had been brutal. It was very intense, very focused, and very demanding for both her and me. She went through it all, but I was with her, and I had to watch someone I loved suffer that horrible disease.

It's like when you rest your foot on a soccer ball. The pressure changes the shape of the ball, but once you lift your foot, the ball goes back to its original form.

All that pressure had reshaped me over those 20 months. Once Alison died, the pressure lifted. To some extent, I bounced back. People were quite worried that I didn't seem to be grieving over Alison's departure. In one sense, I wasn't, because we had been grieving together once we realized the seriousness of her situation. So I didn't feel at all like I did when I lost my father. This was different. I felt an almost instantaneous relief. In this, my father's death prepared me for losing Alison, and I was glad I had so long with her before she died.

In the afternoon of the day she died, she said to me, "George, I have to do this alone. You've been with me so far, but there is only so far that you can go. I have to take these final steps alone. I can see a building, like a church building, that is full of people, and they're overjoyed at my coming. It's a city of people who are really ready to welcome me." At that point, there hadn't been a detailed discussion, but I realized that she needed to be alone. She didn't need me fussing around her being busy and all while she was having this vision of the heavenly city. I left her alone until the sons showed up later in the afternoon.

Alison was quite definitely ready to die. She even said to me, "George, I just want to ask you one thing. If anybody says that they would like to pray for me to be brought back from the dead, I'm willing for people to pray, but they must also pray that I'm totally restored back to full health. I don't want to come back to life and have to deal with this dreadful disease ever again, thank you very much." [laughing]

Back when she first got the diagnosis about the cancer, when doctors forecast her life to end within two weeks, she said to me, "George, I've had a quality life. I don't want to go on living just for the sake of living. There is no need for that. I've truly had a quality life, and I want to die knowing that!" So when it came to death, she was fine with it, but she wanted to be able to live while she was alive.

Was there an opportunity to say "goodbye" before her final sleep?

One of the saddest things was that, because of a medical emergency, neither I nor my sons were allowed to be with Alison when she actually died. We were denied that final chance to say goodbye and thank you.

So it's been 12 years since she passed. How are you doing?

I'm doing well. I can tell you a story here. Very soon after Alison died, maybe three days after her death, I was sitting to pray a bit, and I felt I heard the Lord say, "George, you do know that your marriage is over?" I thought, "Well, yes Lord, but what do you mean by that?" He said, "You don't have to be bound by what Alison might think any more. You don't have to wonder, 'What would Alison think of this?' You can make changes to the house, or whatever, without wondering how Alison would react. You must be released from Alison in this particular area of your life. As wonderful as your marriage was to Alison, it is over." That was a huge release for me. It allowed me to think about possibilities for new adventure in my life.

Now another thing happened around 3 – 6 weeks later. I said earlier that during the time that Alison was ill, I had been reading a lot of books. I began reading the works of John Galsworthy, who wrote the trilogy: *The Forsyte Saga*, set between 1880 and 1920. I then read the second trilogy, which was set between 1920 and 1930. In 1932, the author Galsworthy felt there was another trilogy in his head that needed to be written, but he didn't want to write into the future of another generation of the Forsyte family. So he sidestepped the issue and wrote the third trilogy about another family that married into the Forsyte family.

So after reading those first two trilogies, before I got into the third trilogy, I thought how much I'd enjoyed those two trilogies. But I was deeply interested in this fictional Forsyte family, and I didn't think I could hack making a jump into another family. After thinking about it, I decided to make a start regardless of my hesitation, and I ended up enjoying the third trilogy even more than the first two—much to my own amazement. I found the heroine in this third trilogy to be very selfless and absolutely charming. Anyway, it was just magic.

So about a month after Alison died, I was sitting with the Lord one day for prayer, and there appeared to me in my mind three large volumes. The first was entitled, *Before Alison*. It was on the left side of the table in front of me, turned face down, like it had already been read. Then there was a second volume entitled, *Alison*. It too was turned face down, on top of the first volume. Each of these volumes had masses of pages in them. Then there was a third volume, unopened and face-up, on the right side of the table, and it was called, *After Alison*. I felt God saying to me, "What about the *Forsyte Saga*? What did you do with that third volume?" I said, "Well, I didn't think I would enjoy it, but I thought I'd give it a try anyway." He responded, "Then what are you going to do with this *After Alison* volume?" I said, "I'll give it a try." **[chuckling]**

And it's been great! God has been so good to me. I've not been so good to him, but he has really been good to me this past 12 years. I had eight years of singleness, and then I met this lovely lady, remarried, and so now it's another story!

Each of those volumes was totally different, but each has been rewarding and totally satisfying! Before Alison, I had a wonderful childhood. With Alison, I had a wonderful marriage. And after Alison, I'm having a different life all over again. It's just great. **[laughing]** It's so good.

Do you ever sense that Alison is with you?

Only in dreams. I dream of Alison, every so often. But other than that, I never sense her presence, nor do I feel she is watching over me with a critical eye. As I've mentioned, I was released from our marriage just a few days after Alison died, and that release was total. It doesn't demean in any way what our marriage meant to me, and in a sense, still means to me. But I was no longer obliged to live my life contingent upon Alison's thoughts or directives.

I wouldn't say there was a theme or pattern in the dreams. We could be doing something very plain and ordinary, or we could be at Niagara Falls. I could be almost anywhere, and I'd realize that she was still around, or have the thought in the dream that she had come back to life. Shortly after her death, I'd have these dreams and they were so real. I could touch her, feel her, and even smell her. I'd wake up and just be gutted by the reality that she wasn't with me any longer. I'd be taken in by the dream only to realize it was only a dream. A little later, in a dream where Alison would show up, a loud voice would speak up, "George, you do know that you're about to wake up, and when you wake up, Alison will no longer be with you. I know you've enjoyed your dream-time with her, but that time is about to end, so prepare yourself." That allowed me to enjoy the dream, but prepare for her absence once I awoke. I didn't have to cry it out alone in my bed.

Most marriage vows contain the words: "For better or for worse... in sickness and in health... until death do us part." Describe what those words might have meant to George & Alison.

At the time that we took our vows, I genuinely believe that we were both sincere and committed. We had been well prepared, and we knew what those vows meant. We knew it might mean poverty. We understood it might mean ill health. We suspected that any kind of difficulty could arise, but we were ready to face that in God's strength. We were very aware that we were not alone in our marriage. God had a plan, and it was going to require us both to face it all together.

From the Newlyweds:

Were there times during the illness that you didn't think you could do it anymore?

There were times when I knew I couldn't do it. It forced me to absolutely rely on God's strength to move through me. There were many times like that, when I acknowledged that I couldn't go on. But never did God disappoint. Never did I break down to the point that Alison was actually concerned for me. There was always the grace to do what was needed to be done.

If my spouse were just diagnosed with a terminal illness, what advice would you give me?

Pray, and get friends to pray. Be absolutely open with your spouse about how you'll face the situation together. You can be open about it, or you can be closed. I respect people who want to keep everything they're facing private. We were not like that. We knew we needed the support of our friends. And we were communicating to each other about what we were going to do.

With cancer, the thing is to be aggressive. If the plan is to fight the cancer (and I respect anyone who decides not to), I wouldn't waste a single day. Attack, and attack hard with the prescribed treatment. Don't faff around. Get on with it if you're going to fight.

Again, I totally respect the decision if people choose not to fight. The circumstances are different in every case. To not fight could have well been our decision considering the condition that Alison was in. But we were given a fairly optimistic outlook for what might be accomplished with treatment. In our case, Alison opted for fighting, so we did that to the full extent. Right or wrong, that is what we decided.

How did your mate's condition affect your normal intimacy patterns as a couple?

On one level, we spent more time together while Alison was under threat during those first two months than ever before! I spent every waking hour with her. I didn't want to be away from her for a moment. Much the same after she went home. We had a lot of sweet times together.

On a physical level, the hospital stays removed all the possibilities for us. But once she was home, we were able to mostly maintain our normal patterns of intimacy. With that being said, because of the nature of her illness, the contact was much more difficult for Alison during the last several months of her life. There were days she just felt really bad and there were days when she felt fairly good. But there were no agendas or disappointments. We were blessed in those arenas.

How did you find joy together when so much time and emotion was filled with the illness and disease? How did you avoid not focusing on the bad all the time?

We had over 30 years of happy marriage. We had learned how to deal with difficulty and stay connected. Because of our love for each other, we both made the choice to not major on the bad. We knew how to speak encouragement to one another. We were not hiding our heads in the sand. The bad was there, huge, and it was real. It had to be faced, and it had to be dealt with. It took up a lot of our time and energy, but we worked hard to convert the flow of energy to the positive. We had always done this in our marriage.

Things might well have looked much different for us if we had faced this trial early on in our marriage. We might well have focused much more on the negatives and succumbed to fear, anxiety, and blame. But we had learned well that those things are destructive, and not helpful.

I only felt love, care, and sympathy for Alison. I didn't feel robbed of anything. After she was gone, I felt slighted and alone, but while we were in the fight, we focused on all the good around us. We didn't have the time to waste on negative impulses—nor the energy. There was no cover up. We were choosing joy, and joy isn't emotional froth. Joy comes from deep inside you.

What was the dominant emotion during your season of caretaking with your mate—as compared to your emotional state now?

I've seen pictures of guys in a war zone, particularly ancient pictures of a battlefield. That battle with Alison's cancer was much like that. There was a job to do, and you just get on and do it. You don't reflect a lot on that reality until after the battle is over. I didn't realize how many emotions I had buried in that conflict. I thought that I was being quite open with my emotions during that time, but it was some time afterwards that I realized that my emotions were in a deep freeze—they needed to thaw out again.

I find this question difficult for several reasons. One, I don't remember all the details of what I went through with Alison's sickness. Two, I'm not sure I'm totally aware of what those differences might be, even now.

Funny as it sounds, it was quite the adventure with a certain level of excitement. I'm not saying I'd ever want to relive it again, but nevertheless, it was a journey that Alison and I had never taken before. I have the same sensation now. I'm on a journey that I've never been on before.

What's the best thing a husband can do for his wife every day?

Cherish her. Nurture and encourage her. Make her laugh. Learn the joy of giving. The more you give, the more joy you'll have in yourself. Put her needs above your own, and you'll find the deep satisfaction of a God-given relationship. Put your needs first, and neither of you will find satisfaction. Figure out how to give her some space if she needs it. Trust that space for the good.

What's the best thing a wife can do for her husband every day?

I guess it's the same! [laughing] Don't make your life about you.

What one piece of advice would you give to a newly engaged couple?

Keep sex for marriage. Don't think that you'll know more about each other via sexuality. I know it's an antiquated response, but I truly believe it is the right answer. It's my advice, and I stand by it. You'll see the benefit from the other side.

What are your most important memories of your marriage?

Her ebullience. Alison bubbled over with excitement, joy, and an infectious posture of hope. It communicated to everyone who knew her. Her capacity for friendship was just awesome. It was one of the things that attracted me to her. Her gift of hospitality was amazing. My abiding memory of Alison was her ebullience. That's the only word I can think of. She could be like a little kid in that sense. She never grew up. **[laughing]** She was always a kid.

Do you still think that marriage is a great idea?

I think it must be the best idea that God ever had. Maybe the best thing he ever planned for mankind this side of heaven.

Any final words of advice for married couples of all ages?

Marriage is for life. The goal isn't for 3 years, or 5 years, or 10 years. It's for life. The real benefits of marriage are seen at the end. When you look back, you'll see the benefits. Not to say you can't see the benefits today, but it will be so obvious later. You may not appreciate all the benefits today, but you will later.

In Memory of
Alison Patricia Bewes Gilbart-Smith
August 24, 1947 – November 25, 2002

Ruthie

Introduction

Many times, only history affords us enough clarity to understand the significance of a moment. Sometimes life happens like a strong current beneath a sleepy sea. Sentience whispers, but you can't see it. January 1933 could be such a thing. Like bullets in a chamber, events took their place in the queue of time, waiting for the trigger to be pulled — and pulled it was. In cascading inevitability, shifts and transitions did their thing. A step here, a step there, and all of it was leading somewhere. Here is a sampling of what I mean:

In January 1933, Franklin D. Roosevelt completed his term as the forty-fourth governor of New York. Two month later, he would take office as the thirty-second President of the United States of America.

In January 1933, the leader of the Nazi Party, Adolf Hitler, was sworn in as Chancellor of Germany.

In January 1933, construction of the Golden Gate Bridge began. It all started with the anchorage for the tower at Marin on the north side of San Francisco Bay.

In January 1933, the infamous Clyde Barrow killed a Tarrant County Deputy Sheriff in Dallas, Texas. The story inflamed the American press to begin following the escapades of Bonnie and Clyde until they were both killed 16 months later.

In January 1933, the fourteen-year ban by the United States Navy, which prevented enlistments of African-Americans, was lifted because there were concerns that Filipino domestic help was dwindling. "Negros" were granted permission to join, but relegated to serve through the steward's department, i.e. food service and servants for officers. This move by the Navy set the table for the emerging heroics of Waco, Texas, native Doris Miller. Miller was awarded the Navy Cross for his bravery during the Japanese attack on Pearl Harbor in 1941, making him the first black to receive the award.

Also in January 1933, the world welcomed another baby girl into its arms. Without a lick of fanfare, Ruth "Ruthie" Mae Cooper Haynes was born at home with the help of a midwife, on a small family farm in Lee County, Texas. Sometimes the old sayings testify the greatest truths. The most precious things that we ever acquire arrive in the smallest of packages.

What you are about to read in this interview is special. What started out as an innocent friendship between two childhood neighbors ended up being a risky roll of the dice for love and companionship. For 33 years, to the very end of their time together, Harold and Ruthie Haynes lived and loved one another as real friends. That sounds so normal, but it's not. They made their choice and kept their word as opportunity, or fate, circled back around. It's not 1933 anymore and in this day and in this time that qualifies as something to be noticed and honored.

Getting to know Ruthie has been one of the highlights of this project. Her simple honesty rides on the most powerful horse in the arena: Wisdom. It has been pure joy working with this wonderfully dynamic lady. I hope you see her beautiful strength and amazing grace. She really is the loveliest gift.

With sincere joy and heartfelt respect, it is a happy pleasure to present to you Ruthie. Oh, do we love this woman! –MDP-

Tell us about how you two met and fell in love?

We met as children in 1943. I was about 10 years old, and Harold was almost 4 years younger than me. Our parents were friends, so we spent a lot of time together as kids. We didn't marry until 36 years later, and I'm not sure about that falling in love part—on my part **[laughing]**.

We met again in 1979. I was living in Waco, and Harold was living in McGregor with his mother at that time. He had been married three times. I was to be number four. I had been married 19 years, and my first husband was killed in a car wreck. So I had been single for seven years when I hooked up with Harold.

Harold told my son that he was coming to see me. They were working together at a body shop in McGregor. I told everyone, "He better not be coming over here to see me, because I'm not going to be bothered with him." At that time, Harold was doing some heavy drinking. I emphasized, "I am not putting up with a drunk!" Well sure enough, he made his way to my house, and that's how we got together. We met around Thanksgiving and married two days before Christmas.

When Harold was 8 years old, he told my daddy that he was going to marry me. I was 12 years old. I told him, "Nobody is going to marry you, because you are just a kid." Not really realizing that I was just a kid also! But after 36 years got tacked on to all that, who cares about the age [laughing]? Growing up when I did, girls didn't get to date boys who were younger than them. We always got along, even when we were children.

When I got courting age, if someone asked me out, Harold went along. He'd say, "Well, I guess I better walk between y'all," and then he'd grab my hand and hold it. The poor guy tagging along just had to watch [laughing].

Was it love at first sight?

Not really. Let me tell you how this marriage happened. He came over here and my younger children were just crazy about him. He'd bring chicken, and you know how young children are. The real truth is that our mothers were working behind the scenes. They were plotting to get us together. That's how that marriage came about.

Harold wanted us to get together, our mothers wanted us to get together, but I told them that all that could wait a couple of years. My mother said to me, "If he can pay his bills, and you can pay your bills, then you should marry and pay your bills together." We paid our bills separately for seven years, and then after that time we paid them together.

Were you in love when you married him?

I don't know. I really don't know. To me, Harold was just a sad person who needed someone to tend to him. That is basically why I married him. There was no deep affection. It was a matter of him needing someone to take care of him, and I needed someone to talk to [laughing]. He'd say, "Well, I can give you some money." And I'd say, "I don't need your money. I got enough money now to be a fool." So I had my bank account, and Harold had his, and that continued until he died.

When and where were you married?

We met in November 1979, and married December 22, 1979 in the First Baptist Church on Jefferson St., Waco, TX. We had a fine church wedding. We didn't have anyone in that wedding except my seven kids and my oldest daughter's husband.

How long were you and Harold married?

Thirty-two years.

What was the first year of your marriage like?

We got along beautifully. We always got along. We never had a fuss, nor did we ever have a fight. No one ever got mad really. If he was upset about something, I clammed up and went on about my business. We never had a fight. Not once.

Now, Harold was a weird creature. I say weird, but he was clinically diagnosed with paranoid schizophrenia. You know how they can just imagine things? Well, that is what he did. He was always seeing or imagining something strange. He just went on, and I didn't pay him any attention when all that was going on [**laughing**]. I accepted him and never tried to change him.

Harold was military. During his 18-½ years in, he spent most of his time in Germany, but he did two tours in Vietnam. The VA kept him on medication. I didn't know he had those things working when I met him. He wasn't paranoid with me, so how was I supposed to know he had all that other stuff going on? He always treated me real good. I didn't know how sick he was with that condition until after he died really.

He moved in with me at this very house. I've been here since 1967.

{The following is an excerpt from Harold's obituary: *In 1961, Harold Haynes joined the Army and served three tours of duty in Germany and two tours in Vietnam. During his military stay, he served his country with honor and distinction, receiving two Bronze Star Medals, the Purple Heart Medal, two Purple Heart Medals with Oak Leaf Cluster, the Air Medal, National Defense Service Medal, Vietnam Cross of Gallantry with Palm, Vietnam Service Medal with four Bronze Stars, Republic of Vietnam Campaign Medal, Combat Infantryman Badge, Good Conduct Medal Clasp Bronze Five Loops, and the Designation of Expert: Rifle. After the completion of his distinguished military career, he retired on February 1, 1980 from the First Calvary Division Army in Ft. Hood, Texas.*}

How differently were you both raised?

We were raised very similar, because our parents were friends. Both set of families were very spiritual people. My mom was fairly strict with the discipline. Harold's parents let those kids do what they wanted to. All of us did field work. We picked and chopped cotton. My mom worked all the time, but his mom didn't have to get out too much. My mom and stepfather raised me. Harold was raised by both of his natural parents.

Early on, what were some of your toughest challenges as a couple?

Honestly, it was dealing with a son who had a drinking problem. That was our toughest challenge. If I had married a gopher, he would have been mad about it. He was one of those kids who felt rejected by my marrying again. I spent a great deal of my time trying to convince my son that his acting out wasn't going to negatively affect my relationship with my husband. I could love them both. That was our toughest challenge.

Another challenge was in allowing Harold to have his say in our home. I was used to doing things my way, with my children, in my home. I had seven kids, and five of them were still at home. He moved into my home. My home had to become our home. I had things to do. I didn't have the time or the patience to wait around on him to make up his mind on the things he needed to do. But I learned to wait until he made up his mind.

My first husband was in the fleet Navy. He was gone most of the time, so I was used to having all the responsibilities to pay the bills, take care of the kids, or whatever—by myself. Then after he was killed, I had it all by myself. It took some adjustment. It was hard for me.

When Harold and I married, he was on temporary leave from the military. He retired from the military in 1980. So I was ready for him to find something else to do.

So as the marriage began to develop and mature, what did "normal" look like for Harold & Ruthie's relationship?

He worked at night, and I worked during the day. He had to be at work around 11:00 p.m. I had to be at work at 10:00 a.m. So we were on totally different schedules. We usually didn't get together until the weekends.

What part of your life with Harold was the most rewarding for you?

Once he retired from his work. Just being together.

Why was it rewarding?

Because he was at home and in my way [laughing]. I retired in 1998 from a business where I did alterations on clothes. I had worked that job for over 30 years. So when I came home, I opened my own business, doing alterations in my garage. Harold had his routines, but we spent a lot more time together.

Ruthie, did you love that man?

Oh yes! I did, and I still do. Do you know how some people are just lovable? He was that way. Harold was good and kind. He loved God. He loved his Bible. I think he might have loved his Bible more than he loved me, but that was okay with me [**laughing**]. If he wasn't out riding, he was sitting in that chair right there, reading his Bible. He could do that all day. I liked him like that. He was serious about God, and when a person is serious about God, you don't have a whole lot of trouble out of them. He wasn't out there running, ripping, snorting, drinking—acting a fool. He didn't do any of that. He did plenty of that before I got him, but he didn't do any of that after I got him.

When we met again, he kept a red cooler in the car that was full of beer! Up until we married, Harold was drinking all the time. He smoked 3 packs a day. He quit all of that when we got married.

I just gave away his clothes last week. It's not that easy to let go of the things that you associate with someone you love.

What have you learned the most in your life that Harold taught you?

First, he taught me to love God. Second, he taught me how to live, and how to die. He did live. Harold did plenty of riding and looking. He had his routine, and you didn't interfere with his routine. After he retired, he went out in the morning, he went out at 12:00 p.m., and he went out in the evening. He'd ride and look. To me, that was the biggest waste of time, but it was his routine. He'd go over to the Dairy Queen and just sit and look.

Another thing he taught me was what we think is important is usually not that important. Most people are materialistic. Harold didn't care about things. He'd keep a car for a couple years and then give it away. That was a strange part of living with a paranoid schizophrenic. I'd wonder about his car, only to find out that he'd given it away. I'd ask, "Where is the car?" He'd say, "I gave that car to so-and-so. They chasing me in that car!" [laughing] That man thought someone was chasing him in that car [laughing]. I'd tell him all the time, "People don't even know you're living. Don't nobody care about you or your car." [laughing] He had three or four cars that he just gave away because he thought someone was watching him. If he went somewhere, he'd never come back the same way. Very seldom did he come home the same way. He might drive five or six miles out of the way to come back home. I'd say, "Where are you going now?" [laughing] He was going home, but he wasn't going home the same way he went out.

Do you think some of that was inflicted due to his military experience?

He was paranoid. Shit, he was crazy when he went into the service. He was crazy when he got out [laughing].

Harold had gotten real sick. He was never down in the bed sick, but he just felt real bad and had gotten weak. Up until the last six months, he handled all of his own doctor appointments. One day I knew he had an appointment. When I asked about what the doctor said, he informed me that he didn't go. He went to his brother's house and spent the day. From that point on, I quit sending him to the doctor, and I started taking him to the doctor. So we made another appointment with the VA cancer doctor. Harold asked about going to Florida because my son was retiring from the Air Force. That doctor said, "In no way, under any circumstance, are you allowed to go to Florida!" When my son retired, Harold was in Florida for his retirement! There were 7 of us that went to Florida for the ceremony. When Harold made up his mind to do something—that was it, regardless.

What do you think you taught him the most?

To understand that it doesn't really matter what other people think or say. You know right from wrong. Do right, and you'll stay out of trouble. That was my message with him from day one.

When did Harold's medical complications begin to surface?

I think Harold knew he was in trouble for a long time. In fact, he had been preaching and doing ministry, and when he retired from that in 2006, I think he knew how sick he was. The family didn't know it, but I think he knew. He had lung cancer. My suspicion was confirmed months before he died, when the VA doctor in Waco said to Harold (in my presence), "So you finally decided to go to the VA in Temple for treatment?" His doctors had been trying to get him to address the cancer for a long time. He knew he was dying and wasn't telling anyone about his condition.

The reason I say he knew he was dying was because he was exposed to Agent Orange in Vietnam. When he told me of that exposure, I started researching what the effects of that might be to Harold. He was a paratrooper, so he spent time in the bush. There were a lot of side effects to Agent Orange, but Harold's cancer came from that.

He knew he was sick, and he knew he was dying. He didn't call me Ruthie. Harold either called me "Babygirl," "Punkin," or "my wife." Once we finally had a cancer diagnosis, he'd say, "Babygirl, I'm dying." But he'd been dying ever since I met him. He'd say that ever so often, but I just thought he was being paranoid. I'd say, "Well, everyone is dying." But I think he knew, and he wasn't telling anyone.

Sometimes he'd come in and say, "Babygirl, let's go ride." I'd say, "Ok, where we going?" "Let's find out. I got something I need to tell you." So we'd go and be gone a couple hours, but he'd never tell me anything. I think he was trying to work up the courage to tell me he was sick and dying, but he just couldn't do it.

So was there an official diagnosis of cancer?

We got an official diagnosis of lung cancer on February 15, 2012, while at the doctor's office at the VA hospital in Temple. He died March 9, 2012.

In November of 2011, they started giving him breathing treatments, and inhalers. I would tell him, "Harold Edward, you're not supposed to have pneumonia every year!" He had it in 2010, 2011, and 2012. The doctor told us at that time that he had a tiny spot (about the size of a dime) on his lungs. He suspected it was cancer, but they were going to send his report to Maryland to make sure. The man told me that treatment of any kind was impossible. He said, "If we give him chemo, he might last 2 hours, or he might live 2 months."

By the time we went back in on February 15th, they said the cancer had covered his lungs entirely. But there wasn't an official diagnosis until February 15th. The reports from Bethesda, Maryland, showed that he had a rare type of lung cancer.

While he was at the doctor's office that same day, he fell ill, and they checked him in thru the emergency room at the VA hospital in Temple. They didn't expect him to live through the night. He went down that fast.

What was amazing to me was that Harold expected to die that first night in the hospital. When he woke up that next morning, he said to me, "I'm still here? Where is Jesus? What's taking him so long to get here?" I'd say, "He'll come get you when he's ready. He's not quite ready for you right now." I'd always tell him, "Jesus is busy building on your house. It ain't got no top on it." He'd say, "Girl, it's taking him so long." Well, he wore out one room, and they moved him to another room. He wore that room out, and they moved him again to another room for a whole week. Every morning, "I ain't dead yet? When is Jesus coming?" I'd say, "He'll be here soon enough."

On the 29th of February, we left the Temple VA, checked him into the Waco VA Hospital, called hospice in, and he was dead in 9 days.

I was always very truthful and straight with Harold. He asked me when they checked him into the Waco VA, "Did they bring me here to die?" I said, "Yes." He thought a moment and said, "Babygirl." I said, "What you want?" He replied, "I'm ready to go home." I pointed, "My house, or your house up there?" He said, "It doesn't make me any difference. I'm tired. I'm ready to go home." He died early that next morning.

[laughing] I guess I'm naïve, but that old boy still looked pretty good to me when he said that. I was surprised when he did die. My daughter and I left the hospital that night at 9:00 p.m. It was misting rain and the weather was nasty. I prayed, "Lord, you're gonna have to take over here. Somebody is gonna have a problem out in this nasty weather." We had family trying to come in to see him from Ft. Worth, and I was concerned. I said, "Lord, it's time for him to go home. He's asking, so do what you will." My nephew woke me at 3:00 a.m. to tell me that Harold had died.

It was obvious that God had moved on everyone's behalf. There was nothing to do for Harold, but the family was falling apart all around us. I trusted His timing.

How did he handle his complications emotionally?

Harold never complained, never said, "I don't feel good." He never said anything negative. From February 15th until he died, Harold was hungry the whole time, he laughed and talked, and he knew everybody that came to see him for a visit. We got him interested in the Baylor girls basketball team, so he wouldn't miss a game on the TV. He was alert and engaged with everything and everyone.

Was there a moment of communication when you both acknowledge the seriousness of the complications to each other?

There really wasn't a conversation, but he didn't want me leaving his bedside for any reason. When he was in Temple, I stayed with him every day, and I slept there every night. If I needed to go home he'd say, "They can go, but you have to stay." I stayed right by his bedside in a chair. That told me right there that he was aware of his condition, and he didn't want to die alone. If he knew I was right there with him, then he could die in peace. He didn't really want me out of his sight. He didn't mind me going, but I had to get back in a hurry.

When we moved to Waco, they had a separate room for me, but he didn't want me there. He wanted me either in his room, or at my home. I went to see him in the morning, and again at night.

What kind of daily care did Harold need from you?

From about September 2011 until he went into the hospital in February 2012, I helped him sort his meds and made sure he took them. He was on oxygen and he had to be reminded to keep it on, and I took care of all his meals. Much earlier, I had started researching his diet, and I started growing a garden and fed him things out of our garden. I'd tell him, "If I grow it, you have to eat it."

Generally, what was Harold's response to your caretaking?

He enjoyed it.

Really, that was his response?

Oh yeah. He loved the fact that I was waiting on him. I had raised seven kids, so waiting on him was no problem to me. I liked serving my husband. Cooking, ironing, washing... all of it. Someone asked me one time, "Do you miss your husband?" I said, "For what? He didn't do anything **[laughing]**." I miss his laughing and talking, but he didn't do anything around here. He paid my nephews to mow the yard. He didn't wash or scrub anything. He sat in his chair and read his Bible.

Harold was a thankful and grateful person. He really was. The man was sick, and he was just happy to have someone to help take care of him. He didn't have to die alone.

How much of that overall burden did you shoulder by yourself?

All of it. He was my husband, so I was the one that did all that stuff. Everyone else in the family had jobs elsewhere. I told them all, "Go do your job, and I'll tend to Harold." So I did what he needed. I even drove him around on his rides. The man enjoyed living, and he enjoyed dying. That's the only way I can put it. He knew where he was going, and he had a beautiful funeral.

How well do you think you did under that stress?

I think I did real good! I didn't toss him out on his head [laughing].

Where did you find your strength and courage?

Well, I tried to teach my kids that you don't need someone around you all the time. You don't need nobody, because you are always four. It's you, God, Jesus, and the Holy Spirit—that makes four. You always got four people. So I didn't need anyone to help me tend to him.

What were your big "priorities" before you found out that Harold was sick? How were those things affected by the illness?

My work. My sister and I work together to alter clothes. I'd tend to Harold's needs, but he never demanded things be done on his timing. He'd wait until I could get to him. Working at home made tending to him a lot easier.

He'd say, "Girl, you working today? You go on to work." He always wanted me to be busy. So I'd go out to the shop and do my work. Then I'd come in and check on him, and he'd be sitting right there in that chair, reading his Bible. He didn't demand, he didn't interfere, he wasn't hard to get along with, and he was easy to please. Not that much changed.

Was there a point when you knew that your caretaking days were numbered?

I knew he wasn't going to last forever, but I didn't really think about it. My idea was always, you do what you have to do, when you have to do it. I took care of everything he needed, including buying his clothes. I did all the washing and the scrubbing—all the cleaning and the cooking. When Harold left this earth, I said, "Hallelujah," and started on the next thing.

How was Harold processing his decline?

A lot of people who are sick will complain about their condition and their circumstances. Not Harold. He never complained, not one time. He never said, "I don't want to be sick." He was never mad at the government, he wasn't mad at anyone. He was what everybody ought to be. He lived thankful for what he had.

Did you two ever talk about "your" future without Harold in the picture?

No. Because, I didn't think he was going to go anywhere [laughing]. I really didn't. My son and I were laughing just the other day. My son said, "You know, I thought Harold was getting better. Even until the last day, I wanted to say to him, 'Old man, get up out of that bed, and let's go home!'"

They lowered his bed almost to the floor at the Waco VA, because they were concerned he might fall out of the bed. The night he died, I sat down on the floor by his bed and we ate a 3 Musketeers bar together. See? He didn't act like a sick person. So we were just being normal together. I knew he was dying, but he didn't act like he was dying. I didn't realize that was the night he was going to die. Never had the thought, this is it.

Looking back, how prepared were you to let him go?

When he was ready, I was ready. Harold had been sick a long time. He was exposed to Agent Orange way back in the 60's. It was eating him up on the inside for many years. He'd have scars and rashes on his neck because of it. I'd ask him about it, and he'd say, "Its just psoriasis." I told him one day, "That isn't psoriasis. Psoriasis will heal up, and this never goes away." Strange enough, when we changed his diet, only eating stuff out of the garden, it healed up. He also had a bald spot on the top of his head which filled back in with hair—all because of what he was eating. When Harold died, he had a full head of hair.

Was there an opportunity to say "goodbye" before his final sleep?

I told him "goodbye" the night he died, at 9:00 p.m. I said, "Goodbye, Harold." He said, "I love you." I said, "I'm going on home." He said, "Ok." So I left. I went home, and he went home [laughing]. So we both went home. I went to my house, and he went on to his heavenly reward.

When I'd leave at night from the Waco VA, Harold would always say, "I'll see you in the morning." He didn't say anything that night. Not that night.

So it's been two and a half years since he passed. How are you doing?

I am fine—busy as a bird dog. Harold died in March 2012, and one of my daughters had a stroke the next month. So I brought her to my house take care of her. About the time she got well, my other daughter's husband had surgery, so I kept him at my house until he got well, and that took about six weeks. After that, my granddaughter and great-grandson came through the door needing some help. They've been staying with me. So I've been busy. I like it that way. For as long as I can remember, I've been busy. All of my life I've been that way.

Do you ever sense that Harold is with you?

Yeah, everywhere I go I can sense his presence. I figure if he's doing fine, I'm doing fine. I can come into this room and look at the chair you're sitting in and see his glasses setting there, and I can feel him.

Most marriage vows contain the words: "For better or for worse... in sickness and in health... until death do us part." Describe what those words might have meant to Harold & Ruthie.

I took it literally. That means that you stick together through thick and thin.

Regardless of what happens or what comes. I'm certain that they meant the same thing to Harold.

I've been looking for the tears you're supposed to have when someone you love dies. I haven't found them yet, but I'm still looking.

From the Newlyweds:

Were there times during the illness that you didn't think you could do it anymore?

No. My only concern was if he got to where he was bedridden. But, he never got that way. There was only so much oxygen they could give him at home. So as long as that was good, I knew we could manage everything at home.

If my spouse were just diagnosed with a terminal illness, what advice would you give me?

To keep them at home as long as possible. The end is coming somewhere down the line. Most people are afraid of dying alone. I believe that is why Harold Edward wouldn't talk about his sickness. I think he was afraid of being alone, or I wouldn't keep him here at home. If the vow says, "Until death do you part," then stay to the end.

How did your mate's condition affect your normal intimacy patterns as a couple?

We hadn't had physical intimacy for many years, but that didn't bother me. We hadn't really been together in that way since 1995. We were able to cope with that part because we both understood that there is more to a marriage than sexual intimacy.

The way we got along, you'd have thought we was getting' it on [laughing]. We truly just enjoyed each other.

How did you handle those changes?

He had the desire, but the medicine he was on had shut him down. I didn't want to make things worse by insisting on something he couldn't do. I coped just fine. Even when he was dying, he was still in that "want to" stage. He was just too sick.

Were you two still able to play together during your mate's decline?

Most of our play was in our own communication. There was a lot of laughing when we were together. He'd always want to be hugging and all that stuff. There was a lot of affection and fun in our communication.

I'd be in my shop sewing, and he'd be in here sitting in his chair. So I'd go check on him. He'd say, "Girl, come here," and I'd say [attitude], "What do you want?" And all he wanted me to do was to sit right here on this coffee table, like I'm sitting right now. He'd say, "Just sit right there. I'm gonna look at you!" [laughing] So I'd sit here while he'd just stare at me, and then I'd go on about my business.

I enjoyed all of that. Knowing he was in here. Seeing him step into the shop. I just enjoyed him being around. We'd get into the car and drive to church in McGregor. We might go over there and never say a word to each other. We didn't have to. He might reach over and pat me on the leg. It just felt good to be together.

How did you find joy together when so much time and emotion was filled with the illness?

My idea is this: We are supposed to have illnesses. Jesus suffered, and we're probably supposed to suffer also. Sickness is a normal part of life. So I didn't dwell on him being sick. There is always something to be thankful for.

What's the one piece of advice you'd give someone just starting out in marriage?

Develop the relationship beyond sexual love. If that's all you got, it's shallow. Because when the thrill is gone, the marriage is gone. Learn how to be a friend, get along, and make up your mind that you are staying in the relationship through thick and thin. Be flexible. You can't get everything the way you want it all the time. Let God have his say in your marriage. I tell people, "God put us together. I don't have the right to not make it work."

What's the best thing a husband can do for his wife every day?

Respect her and treat her like you want to be treated. Talk to her kindly. When God was passing out brains, he didn't give you all the brains. Your wife has brains too. God threw a few brains my way too [laughing]. Everybody has a portion of common sense. It would seem that highly educated people are lacking common sense, but look for it. It's in there somewhere. Ok, so you have a degree, that doesn't mean that you know everything. I used to tell Harold Edward, "God could make a whole new world out of the things you don't know." [laughing]

What's the best thing a wife can do for her husband every day?

Let him be a man. Most marriages fall apart because women want their men to be like boys or children—someone they can direct, control, and tell what to do. They want him to be under their thumb, so he can be told exactly what all they want done.

There was no sense in my asking Harold to do anything that he had to do with his hands or fingers, because he was going to tear it up. But that man had a brain, and he could do just about anything I asked that required a lot of thought. Let that man do what he can do, and you do what you can do. It solves a lot of problems together.

What one piece of advice you would give to a newly engaged couple?

Pay attention to that person's habits and attitudes. If they think they know it all before you get them, they'll think they know it all after you have them. Don't get that person. Leave them alone. Don't try to change anyone, because you can't. You can change yourself, but forget changing someone else. If you're skippin' over here, and they are skippin' over there, then let them keep on skippin' [laughing]. You'll never come together like that.

Beliefs matter. Being unequal in major beliefs can be a problem for you. Don't think you can make a silk purse out of a sow's ear. You are not going to change that person to your way of thinking.

Knowing all that you know now, what would you have done differently in your marriage?

I would have married Harold earlier than I did. I would have cut out one of those wives that he had [laughing]. Other than that, there wouldn't have been anything I'd done differently. I have no regrets. None whatsoever.

What did you learn about your spouse that caused you to love him even more?

His humility. Harold was a very humble person. He treated everyone with kindness and respect. I used to say, "If one of us has to die, I want Harold to die first." I said that because I didn't want anyone to misuse him. He was too good and humble, and I didn't want anyone to mistreat him. That's why I said that—because you'd have a hard time misusing me, honey [laughing].

He was so easy to get along with. Ever since I knew him, even as children, we got along beautifully. He'd been a good companion a long time.

Do you still think that marriage is a great idea?

I think it's the best idea there has ever been. It really is. But whoever said it was a 50/50 arrangement was a liar. Everyone has to treat it like it is 90/10, and you got the 90. If everyone will do that, there won't be any more divorce. I think marriage is wonderful. I don't know where people get all these ideas of stackin' and shackin'. I don't like that.

Any final words of advice for married couples of all ages?

First, know God. Second, love the person He gave you, and understand that God made that person unique. They're not supposed to be like you. Let them be an individual. Appreciate the differences. That's my final word.

In Memory of
Harold Edward Haynes
October 17, 1937 – March 9, 2012

Mike

Introduction

"Cancer, we now know, is a disease caused by uncontrolled growth of a single cell. This growth is unleashed by mutations—changes in DNA that specifically affect genes that incite unlimited cell growth. In a normal cell, powerful genetic circuits regulate cell division and cell death. In a cancer cell, these circuits have been broken, unleashing a cell that cannot stop growing."

—Siddhartha Mukherjee, M.D.

"Cancer is no friend. It's a cruel bastard—a hateful bitch."

—Anonymous

If you've never been to Archer City, Texas, well, you ain't missed much. It's the home of Larry McMurtry, who wrote *The Last Picture Show*, *Lonesome Dove* and *Terms of Endearment* among others. *The Last Picture Show* movie was also filmed in the small town. Outside of that flash of notoriety, it's pretty much just a small West Texas town, located about 25 miles south of Wichita Falls.

Patti and I moved there in August 1985. I had started seminary in Fort Worth just three months earlier. When we made our first official visit to Archer City to interview for the youth minister position at the First Baptist Church, it was our first real introduction to West Texas. We had lived in Northwest Arkansas, East Texas, and Central Texas, but we never considered living in West Texas. In fact, when we were driving the stretch of road between Windthorst and Archer City, Patti said, "This is the ugliest place I have ever been in my entire life." I quickly agreed and we planned that our strategy was to be nice and cordial that weekend, but no way were we going to seriously consider living in such a place. We would just inform God "No, thank you." Those were famous last words. Without a doubt, it was some of the best days that she and I have ever known in ministry. We fell in love with the people, and they fell in love with us. God knew exactly what he was doing.

It was there that I preached my first real sermon. I also officiated my first funeral. I remember there were about 25 people sitting in the pews at the Aulds Funeral Home to pay their respects. Twenty of those people looked like they belonged in the nursing home. I was 29 years old at the time, green as a gourd and full of myself. After the service, all those little senior adults came to thank me for my words. I was the man — the new preacher man.

After the room cleared, a short, fat kid, dressed in a nice suit (he looked 19-years old) came up to me and said, "Not too bad for someone who doesn't know what the hell they're doing." Before I could expel a nervous laugh, he whispered, "Don't worry about it Paschall. The person in this casket is dead and the rest of them in this room are almost dead, so you can't tear up too much by what you said." That fat kid was the owner of the funeral home. That was J. Michael Aulds. He became one of my best friends in that town. There was never a dull moment when he was on the scene.

I was commuting back and forth to Fort Worth for school. There were a lot of days and nights that Patti, Nicole and Paige were home alone. Mike loved my family and provided a lot of comfort to them while I was out and about. My kids didn't call him Mike. To them he was "Mikeaulds." Like it was one word. That's how they addressed him. He'd walk into our house and within seconds they'd be draped all over him like little spider monkeys. We made a lot of trips to Wichita Falls and Mike was always buying our dinner or putting gas in our car. We had hundreds of church friends, but not many did the stuff for us that Mike did. If I had a kid in my youth group who needed money to go skiing or some other pressing need surfaced, Mike dished out cash. Preachers need friends like that. I had Mike Aulds. He was always there for my family and me.

We left Archer City in 1987. Since then, my contact with Mike has been sporadic, but whenever we've connected, it's like we've never been apart. I was around Pebbles Aulds only a couple times. I must confess that I too had that common thought most men have about another man's beautiful wife: "How did he get her?" Talk about beauty and the beast! Unbelievable.

Pebbles was instant sunshine on anyone's cloud. She possessed a beautiful smile and that slow southern drawl sucked at your heart. A mint julep couldn't have been any smoother than this woman. One thing is true: once Pebbles showed up, it wrecked my friend Mike Aulds for good. What they had together was truly magic and it is an honor to recognize them both in this interview. Mike Aulds is one heck of a storyteller. Just know that you are about to encounter is a real love story. It's rarified air. Slow down and breathe it in deep. Let it help improve what you now have with your own mate.

Mike, you did good my friend. You did real good! It is my distinct honor to present to you my dear pal Mike Aulds. -MDP

Tell us about how you two met and fell in love?

I had been set up by some friends for the first blind date of my life. It was Valentines Day 1992. The date was not with Pebbles, but with another girl. I had a horrible time. I felt like a piece of meat. This chick was pawing all over me. I'm not kidding you—it was horrible! So the next day, I told my friend Laura, I'm going back to the La Cima Club in Las Colinas (Irving, Texas) tonight and I'll get my own date! She said, "Well, make reservations for us also, and I'll see if I can get Roger to come and get me in Wichita Falls." So I made reservations and invited another buddy of mine, John DeLoach, to go with me as a fifth wheel. Roger was out, so Laura was finding it difficult to catch a ride to Dallas, so she called the clothing store where Pebbles used to model and asked if anyone was going to Dallas. It sounds strange, but people in Wichita Falls go into Dallas all the time. The person who Laura was talking to said, "Pebbles was just in here, and she said that she was going tomorrow." Laura and Pebbles had modeled clothes together, so she called Pebbles. "I know you're going into Dallas tomorrow, but would you be willing to go today? We're going to have dinner at the La Cima Club tonight, and you could join me and my friends!" Pebbles said, "Sure. I don't have anything else to do." Her employer, Du Pont Pharmaceuticals, had just transferred her to Wichita Falls.

Pebbles had asked Laura about what she should wear, so Laura offered to pick out her outfit. Pebbles had been in beauty pageants, and when she was representing Burleson in the Miss Texas Pageant, a leather shop had given her a red snakeskin miniskirt and matching jacket. That is what Laura picked out of Pebbles' closet to wear to the club that night. Pebbles had never worn that outfit before, but they gave it to her for a photo-shoot, and she got to keep it. So that is what she had on when she showed up at La Cima Club. Of course, the girls show up an hour and a half after our reservations. When they stepped off the elevator, I saw Pebbles at a distance and thought: Holy mackerel—who is this? She was absolutely beautiful. Drop-dead gorgeous. Both of them looked like a million bucks.

I did have a date that night with a friend that I ran around with, but Pebbles landed at our table and instantly took over the party. About halfway through the night I thought, *I could marry this girl, and I could teach her how to dress,* [laughing] because she had on that crazy outfit. That wasn't typical attire for a funeral director's wife [laughing].

My date leaned over towards me at the end of the night and said, "This girl has Mike Aulds written all over her!" Naturally my friend John, the fifth wheel, was falling madly in love also. As we're sitting there, Pebbles started making plans for all of us go to church together the next morning. So John got up Sunday morning and picked up Pebbles, and they were the only two that went to church. That was the beginning of them dating some. She lived in Wichita Falls, and John lived in Dallas. Therefore, John was at a disadvantage. She and I would spend every free moment we had together. I would drive to Wichita Falls to meet her for lunch, and then she would come to Archer after work or I would drive back to Wichita for dinner.

The next weekend, Pebbles was giving up her crown as Miss Burleson. She invited John and I to come to the pageant. Of course I was willing to do whatever to be around her. While driving to the pageant, I called and ordered flowers. I'm in the funeral business—I know how to order flowers. I know flowers. I sent her a massive bouquet of beautiful flowers and put both John's name and mine on the card. While still in route, I got a call; someone had died, and I had to turn around and go back to Archer City. I called John and left him a voicemail that I had a body, I wouldn't make the pageant, but I forgot to mention the flowers. Pebbles and John were also playing phone tag about their travel arrangements to Burleson, but she left him a message to thank him for the flower arrangement. When he got the message, he didn't know that I had sent them, so he thought that Pebbles might be dropping a hint that flowers were expected. There were more missed calls and the details were worked out, but she once again said, "Thank you so much for the flower arrangement. It is absolutely beautiful, and please tell Mike 'Thank You' too." So John calls me, "Mike, is there something you forgot to tell me?" I replied, "What? I'm busy here. I'm embalming. I don't have time to figure out what you're talking about. What do you want?" "Do you know anything about some flowers?" "Oh crap, I forgot. Yeah, we sent flowers to Pebbles." [laughing] When John picked Pebbles up, he saw the flowers and said the flowers were indeed incredible. He was thinking he was going to get brownie points for that spread of flowers.

They go to the pageant in Burleson, and the next morning she flies out to DuPont's headquarters in Wilmington Delaware for a week of training. John started feeling bad about taking credit for the flowers. I had ordered and paid for them without his involvement. Evidently, Pebbles went on and on about how beautiful they were. So he decides to send flowers to her in Wilmington. He thought that would even it up. She calls him that night and says, "John, I don't really know how to say this...but I'm doing it so you can call and complain if you want or need to. These flowers are nothing like what you sent before! This is a pick-me-up bouquet in a coffee cup. I just want to make sure you didn't get taken advantage of [laughing]. He confirmed that was what he ordered, and she immediately went into her "Thank You" mode.

After she thought about it a little bit, she called me from Wilmington and asked me if I was the one who had sent the original flowers. I told her I had. "How did you know what to send?" I replied, "I know flowers. I told them exactly what I wanted and I wasn't going to pay for them if they didn't meet those standards." When she got back, she called me and we started meeting for dinner. We weren't "dating" because John still had an interest in her. I knew I had to just back off and wait for things to develop.

About a month later, John invited Pebbles to go to Florida with him to meet his family. She agreed to go because it was a trip to Florida. I knew John was going to ask her to go, so I told her she'd have a good time. She happened to mention to me that she didn't know what to wear for the trip. She said she had gone to Banana Republic in Dallas and tried on a bunch of clothes, but she just wasn't sure about the attire, so she didn't buy anything. So on Monday morning I called Banana Republic. I said, "Hey, does anyone remember this beautiful woman that was in the store last Saturday that tried on a bunch of clothes? She's unforgettable, she's gorgeous, bubbly, and she looks like she's got money!" The girl on the phone said, "Was her name Pebbles?" I said, "That's her! Do you remember what all she tried on?" "Yes I do! She was a blast!" I said, "Wrap it all up." She replied, "Excuse me?" "Whatever she tried on, wrap it up, and I'll come get it. Here's my credit card number." So the girl got it ready, I drove to Dallas to pick it up and brought it back home with me. That night, I met Pebbles for dinner and told her I had a little gift for her. She totally freaked out because she couldn't figure out how I knew what to pick out. It was a lot of fun to watch her open up those bags of clothes.

I was at her house the night before their trip while she was packing up the clothes I had purchased for her. She said she felt kinda weird going on a trip with him after all the time we had been spending together, and especially packing all the clothes I had bought for her. I told her, "Just go, have a good time, and compare him to me. That's all I ask. Just pay attention." She wanted me to ask her to start dating, but I told her, "Not until this John deal runs its course." She said, "Well, what if I fall in love with him or something?" I said, "You won't. You're not his type, and he's not your type. Go have a good time, but all I ask is that you pay attention and compare him to me."

So she goes to Florida, but she's calling me constantly. "Oh my gosh. He doesn't open the car door for me like you do! He didn't order for me like you do!" She was there with John, but she was thinking about me the entire time. When they flew back to Texas, he mentioned something about getting together the next weekend. She told him that she didn't want to hurt his feelings, but she believed she was interested in pursuing a relationship with me. He said, "Mike? Mike who?" She said, "Mike Aulds." John said, "Mike Aulds from Archer City?" She said, "Yeah." "You want to go out with Mike Aulds?" She replied, "Yes. He's funny and I kind of like him." John was the perfect image of what her parents wanted for Pebbles. He was tall, thin, good looking, and athletic. He said, "Let me get this straight, you'd rather go out with Mike than me?" Pebbles said, "I'm not putting it that way. I'm just saying I want to explore a relationship with Mike and see where that goes." That was it for John and Pebbles.

We had our first official date on my birthday. We flew to Vegas and then chartered a helicopter that took us to the bottom of the Grand Canyon. There we had a picnic. That was our first date. It was all love from that point forward.

So, it was love at first sight?

Oh yeah. She stepped off that elevator, and it was on. Even my date on the night I met Pebbles recognized the inevitable.

When and where were you married?

We wanted a small intimate wedding, but Pebbles' mom was insisting on the wedding she never had. We were married April 15, 1995 in Natchez, Mississippi. That was six hours from where she grew up and ten hours from Archer City. We purposefully got married on the Saturday before Easter Sunday to try to keep it as small as possible. Her mother insisted on inviting over 700 of their nearest and dearest friends to the wedding. So we decided to have it on a conflicted weekend (Easter), in the middle of nowhere (sorry Natchez), and we still had over a hundred people show up.

How long were you and Pebbles married?

Twelve years.

What was the first year of your marriage like?

A honeymoon. On our 1-year anniversary, Pebbles said to me, "If this was supposed to be the toughest year of our marriage, we are going to have a blast!" I know it sounds like a crock of bull, but it was perfect. It was a yearlong honeymoon. There were some adjustments, but we were older. I was 35 years old. She was 30 years old. Actually, she was 29 and eleven months. I think she just lowered her standards to get in under the 30-wire. I just happened to be in the right place at the right time [laughing]. We were mature and ready!

Did you move her into the funeral home in Archer City?

Yes, at first we lived in the funeral home. I hadn't really thought anything about it. I'd lived there my entire life. That is where my dad and mom raised me. Pebbles was freaked out. She'd never been around the funeral business until she started dating me. We got married, I moved her in, and there were dead people lying in caskets on the other side of our bedroom wall. It took an adjustment on her part [smiling]. She thought that sharing a home with dead people was a bit strange.

A couple months after we had gotten married, she went back to Wilmington for more training. While Pebbles was gone, unbeknown to her, I moved us into one of my rent houses in Wichita Falls. When I picked her up at the airport in Dallas, it was obvious that she was really tired and just wanted to crawl into her bed. I drove straight to Wichita Falls, pulled in the driveway and said, "We're home." She saw the disarray inside the house and said, "What have you done?" "I moved us!" She cried, "I just want to get into my bed." I said, "Your bed is set up." She fired, "No! I want all this stuff organized and set up [laughing]. We lived there about a year. Finally, she began to question why we were giving up rent income by living in the rent house. She had gotten used to the funeral business. Once I was trying to do the makeup on a 35-year-old woman who had died. When Pebbles saw what I was doing, she said, "No Mike! That's not going to work." So Pebbles ended up doing the makeup on that body. This was the same woman who had been freaked out about living in the funeral home, but the mascara was clumped on the woman's eyelashes, and she wanted her right for the family. Eventually, at her suggestion, we moved back into the funeral home.

How differently were you both raised?

When it came to values and character, we were raised the same. She was Baptist. I was Methodist, but she got me fixed right off the bat [smiling]. Pebbles came from money. I didn't, but you would have thought I did the way I courted her [laughing]. Her parents did not want her to marry me and pretty much did everything they could to keep it from happening. They had some really good excuses for why they didn't approve of the marriage.

By all means—tell us the story.

Now that I have a daughter, I understand. When DuPont hired her and wanted to move her to Wichita Falls, her dad did not want her to take the job. He said, "You'll get to Texas and meet some hairy legged boy, fall in love, and never come back home." Pebbles assured him she wouldn't, but her dad knew better. Sure enough, that is exactly what happened. Her parent's expectation was that Pebbles would marry a U.S. Senator, a doctor (or preferably a surgeon), or an attorney. Not some short, fat funeral director from Archer City, Texas. **[laughing]**

We were on our first date in Vegas and we walked past a small wedding chapel. Pebbles said, "Come on, let's get married!" I said, "It ain't happening!" I don't know how serious she was about it. She swore until the day she died that she was serious. I wasn't worried about repercussions, but it wasn't my first rodeo either. I knew that impulse weddings aren't always a good idea.

We dated almost three years before we got married. After two years of dating, Pebbles decided it was time for us to start dating other people. I knew that this was probably the break up before the make up. She was trying to just get me off high center. So I said, "Ok, that's fine." It took me about an hour to figure out, who could I date to really get under her skin? Once it was decided, I called a good friend of Pebbles who had worked in Young Life with her. I took her out for about a week or so. She was getting interested in me, and I had to tell some of our friends to communicate with her that this wasn't going anywhere. It was Pebbles attending the J.M. Aulds attitude adjustment seminar. **[laughing]** Pebbles and I were still communicating that week, but eventually she came to me and said, "This is not working." She had gone out with a guy I called the "Ab Man." She told me she had gone to a pool party with the "Ab Man," and he made sure she had seen the six-pack abs. I told her, "You don't like those kind of guys! You don't like tall and muscular. You like short, fat guys like me." After a couple dates with him, she called and said, "You misunderstood what I meant. What I meant was that I was going to date other people, but you were going to stay home and pine over me." I said, "What does that mean? I've never heard of that word 'pine'." I knew what was going on, but I played it up pretty good. "Why didn't you just say that?" She said, "It's time for our relationship to move forward." I said, "I agree, but that isn't what you told me. You said you wanted to date other people." It got pretty serious after that.

We decided we were going to get married. She wanted me to go ask her dad for her hand. My attitude was, "Why? I'm a grown man. I don't need him to pay for the wedding. I don't need his permission." She said, "You don't understand. This is how we do it in the south." Lord, I knew all that, but I was just trying to aggravate her. So I said, "Okay, I'll do it."

Her dad was going fly-fishing in Northwest Arkansas. That was when Pebbles wanted me to ask her dad because he was away from her mom and isolated from the family. It was quite an ordeal to pull that off! My bags were packed, and Pebbles was about to take me to Dallas to fly to Little Rock. The phone rings, someone had died, so I called Pebbles and told her that I couldn't make the trip. Well, once I picked up the body, I found out that it was a pre-arranged funeral for a Fort Worth funeral home. All I had to do was pick up the body, embalm, and deliver the body to Fort Worth! I called Pebbles to tell her, "It's back on," and all she could say was, "Hurry Mike! Make it happen!" It was probably the fastest embalming ever recorded. **[laughing]**

That was only the beginning of the drama! On the way, I realized that there wasn't enough time to drop off the body and make the flight at Love Field. So we drove straight to the airport, but we had a friend meet us at the airport to drive the body on to the funeral home. When she got in to drive, she drove so fast in order to drop us at the terminal, she hit speed bumps and the body is flopping all over the place. We started yelling to tell her to slow down. She slams on the breaks, and again the body is sliding off the stretcher. **[laughing]** Pebbles' brother was going with me, so the girls drop us at the terminal, and we are literally running through the airport to catch the flight.

We made the flight, and her dad had left a car at the airport in Little Rock. It was a 1978 Plymouth Fury that her dad had inherited from an aunt. When we got into the car, the car wouldn't start. With jumper cables that were left in the car, we jump the car off, yet it died several more times. I'm in a suit, I'm sweating like a fat man, it's hot and humid, and every time you made a left turn with that car, it died. So we pull into a service station and change out the battery cables. Eventually, we made it to within 5 miles of the fishing camp. By now, it's almost 10:00 p.m. Pebbles' brother was driving, and we needed to make a left turn, and I said, "Alan, don't do it! Move left, and then make a right hand turn, and come in from that direction!" The battery was getting weaker and weaker. He assured me it was going to be ok. He turned left, and the car died.

We were in the middle of hillbilly nowhere, with a dead car. Alan said, "We're close, so let's start walking." Again, I'm in a suit, it's late, pitch black, and we walked uphill for at least a mile. As we inched near the top of the hill, a pickup truck pulls up. "Hey! Y'all need a ride?" These people were missing a lot of teeth, and I could hear the Deliverance tune playing in the back of my head. I said, "Oh no. We're fine." They insisted, "Come on. We'll give yer a ride—hop in!" Alan jumped into the back of their pickup, so I followed. They took us straight to the fishing camp! But the whole time I was telling Alan, "Alan, we're done for. These are not civilized people. They're going to kill us, mug us, and then rape us out here! We're going to squeal like a pig!" **[laughing]** When I saw the railroad tracks I thought, "This is it. There is where they rape and kill me. It always happens at the railroad tracks." [laughing]. Thirty seconds later, I could see the lights to the fishing camp and smell the water.

By now, it's about midnight. I didn't sleep a wink, because I was trying to figure out how I was going to get an opportunity to talk to Pebbles' dad. By early morning, the guys were all getting their gear together, and I approached her dad and said, "Can I talk to you for a moment?" He said, "Sure!" So I indicated that my reason for showing up had nothing to do with fly-fishing. "Well, why not?" He didn't have a clue. "I came to ask for your daughter's hand in marriage." He said, "You want to do what?" I said again, "I came to ask for your permission to marry Pebbles." He asked, "Does she know about this?" I affirmed she did. "Y'all want to get married?" Again, I confirmed. "I just thought y'all were friends!" I said, "Well, we are. We're pretty good friends." [laughing] He went there again, "Seriously, you want to marry my daughter?" I gave him the same answer. What I'm about to tell you are the exact words: "Well, I don't know. Let me see if I can talk her out of it first." That was the answer I left the fishing camp with. For about six weeks, her parents did just about everything they could to talk her out of marrying me. I was not what they wanted for her, nor was I what they had envisioned. Her marrying a funeral director in Archer City wasn't the plan.

On their first trip to Archer City after our engagement, we showed them a rent house in Archer City that I had owned for several years that we were going to remodel and move into. Her dad called it a shack. He told Pebbles, "When I was his age, I was moving your mother into a mansion." Pebbles reply was pretty good: "Well Daddy, he's got 16 different shacks that we could move into. That is the one I want to fix up, and we'll make it very nice!"

Pebbles dad also told her, "I've always heard that if you marry a divorced man, you should always talk to the other spouse." I had been married before. Pebbles replied, "I've already done that. Not only did she recommend that I should marry Mike, she'd love to have him back!" After an extended barrage of that kind of stuff, the best friend of Pebbles' mom told her, "If you don't stop with all this, you're going to lose a daughter. I've been around Pebbles all her life. She's never looked at another man the way she looks at Mike. She's been telling you that she's in love for two years. You're in denial! This is who Pebbles is going to marry." They just thought we were hanging buddies. I finally got permission to marry her, but it wasn't easy.

The day after Pebbles' funeral, when her parents got ready to go back home, her dad approached me and said, "I want to thank you for taking care of my daughter the way you did." **[crying]** "I can't imagine anyone who would have taken better care of her. You gave her a wonderful life. You're the only one that could have pulled that off." **[crying]** "I want to thank you for that." That was it. That was when I finally knew that I had met his approval.

Pebbles' dad asked her one time, "Where do you get the doctors and the people who take care of you?" She said, "Mike finds them. I don't know how he does it, but I've had world-class medical attention." It came late, but I eventually got the blessing that I was in the family. Now, he had always pointed to a specific meal before the wedding that was prepared in their home (leg of lamb) that supposedly sent the signal that I was in, but I missed the memo that the "preparing of the fatted lamb" meal was their sign-off. All they had to say was that they were on board and approved! **[laughing]**

Early on, what were some of your toughest challenges as a couple?

My relationship with her family was about the only challenge. Keep in mind, I antagonize a lot, and when I found out that I wasn't good enough, I went there. The very first time I met her parents, her dad made me a martini. I'd never had a martini—ever. So I'm at their house the first time, and I pounded these martinis until I was hammered. Their family watches pageants like we watch the Super Bowl. The talent portion for one of the girls was clogging. So they called me into the room to watch this girl do her clogging routine. My loud commentary during the dance was something like, "Work it... come on girl... work it for daddy." It was totally obnoxious and inappropriate. Pebbles' mother asked her, "Does he always drink like this?" Pebbles responded, "No, mother! I've never seen him do this!" I said to her mother, "Dot, I'm sitting right here. You could ask me the question." That was my first impression with her family. [laughing]

Soon thereafter, her brother called to appeal to Pebbles that the family didn't think that I was a good enough Christian for them. Pebbles became very irritated and said, "Excuse me?" He went on, "The first impression was ugly, and we're pretty sure he is all wrong for you." After the conversation, Pebbles told me that she felt that they knew I had made my choice, but it rocked them that I had stood up to all of them—especially her mom. No one in that family had ever done that. That was part of why Pebbles fell in love with me—I stood up to her parents.

I remember the discussion about holidays. Her mom declared, "Oh no. My children will be at my house every holiday." I couldn't leave something like that alone. [chuckling] "You better hope she doesn't marry me, because we won't be here every holiday." You just didn't cross momma, and I couldn't help myself. I'd pop off, and her mother supposedly had this evil eye that was supposed to get you back in line with her thought. If she shot it my way, I'd say, "Dot, is that supposed to intimidate me? If it is, it's not working." Pebbles was a grown woman and hadn't really stood up to her parents, but that quickly changed once she started dating me. It was very difficult for her parents to lose that kind of control.

Pebbles grew up with luxury. She was never really required to work. She did it because she wanted to. After we were married, I saw a signed blank check in Pebbles' purse one day. "What is this?" She told me that her mom had given it to her in case of an emergency. I made her send it back to her mom. Pebbles' parents were always concerned about my ability to take care of her needs.

What were your shared goals and ambitions?

Mostly, having babies. Our clocks were ticking. We never used birth control. We were married in April 1995, and we had Alexandra in November 1996. The first year of our marriage was a honeymoon, and the second year was filled with excitement about our kid. I quit drinking because of it. I didn't have a drinking problem, but I didn't want anything to impede my judgment in case one of our kids got hurt and I needed to respond. Pebbles loved it. She always had a designated driver. She could have a glass of wine, but not me. My brother asked me one time about why I stopped. I told him it was because I had kids. He said, "And that's the exact reason you'll start drinking again someday!" [laughing]

Pebbles stayed pregnant. She wanted five kids, but we managed three (Alexandra, John Michael, and Abigail). We were financially very blessed. The plan was for Pebbles to stay home with the kids. She had Alex, was on maternity leave, and then she was going to resign from her work. While she was on maternity leave, our pastor's wife offered to keep Alex for us. This wasn't a babysitter. This was another mother who was vested in our lives and loved our baby! Pebbles worked locally as a pharmaceutical rep, so she could work a couple hours, see her doctors, and then pop in and feed the baby. It worked beautifully! She had amazing favor with her company because her sales and retention rates were some of the best in the country. Awards and bonuses were very common. She just had a way that influenced everyone that she sold products to. Everyone loved her.

Once Michael came along, that was it. She stayed home after that. She was in full-on mommy mode by now.

While she was still nursing Michael, while at the very end of her maternity leave, Pebbles discovered that she had a benign neurofibroma that appeared on a cranial nerve in her neck that went to her vocal cords. Since having Hodgkin's disease as a teenager, the radiation treatments she had received back then were now producing multiple benign tumors. She had a history with benign tumors in her body. The day before the surgery was to happen to remove this tumor in her neck, they wanted to inject dye into her bloodstream. That meant she couldn't breastfeed for 24-hours. Pebbles was a human pacifier. Michael had never taken a pacifier, nor had he ever had formula. She was the meal plan. So this created a small crisis for feeding Michael. On top of that, her boss called to tell her that he was taking her off of maternity leave that day, and she was to report to work the next day. She said, "I can't do that. I'm going to Dallas for a surgery that is scheduled for tomorrow!" He said, "Fine. Take a sick day, but you're off maternity leave... now!" That brilliant move right there by her boss made Pebbles eligible for short-term disability. That gave her a year off from work, with full pay. She kept her company car, with the gas card, with full pay, for a year! After a year, they took the car and moved her to long-term disability and reduced her pay by 40 percent.

So as the marriage began to develop and mature, what did "normal" look like for Mike & Pebbles' relationship?

When the kids were little, we were on the move with parenting. We dated a lot. We had a high school girl who loved our kids who was always calling us for work. Her parents were wealthy, but they were trying to help her understand the value of money, so she had to work and buy her own clothes. So we kept her busy with baby-sitting.

The relationship was just blessed. I wouldn't know how else to say it. We weren't wealthy, and we didn't live outside of our means, but we did what we wanted to do. Honestly, I only remember one fight. We were still living in the funeral home, and I can't remember what the fight was about. She got mad and stormed out of the house. She didn't grab a coat, car keys, her purse—nothing. She walked out the back door in her pajamas. [laughing] I saw the direction she went because a night-light flicked on around the corner. I was without attire of any kind, but I followed her out to see what was up. I'm hiding to see what she was going to do. As I'm watching her, I could tell that she was waiting for me to come and get her. So I just kept watching. After pacing and huffing a bit, she turned to go back in, and when she passed by me I said, "I was wondering how long you were going to wait out here." She exploded with, "You jerk! How long have you been standing there?" [laughing] I whispered, "The whole time." She kept on, "Why didn't you come get me?" I'm laughing now, "You weren't going anywhere. You didn't have car keys, you didn't take anything, and you're barefooted." She elbowed me when she walked by, and that was it [laughing]. We just didn't fight.

We had decided never to go to bed mad. I was in the funeral business. I had heard horror stories about couples that fought, someone would say, "kiss my ass," and then later one of them had a heart attack and died—that being the last conversation between the two. We didn't want that. We prayed together at night before bed. There were plenty of nights I prayed out loud, "Dear Jesus. Would you please make Pebbles quit acting like an ass?" [laughing] She had her own prayers for me too.

We had an absolutely wonderful physical relationship—up until the day she died. I remember that Paula, who is my manager at the funeral home, used to call and gripe all the time to Pebbles that I would never come into work once the kids were off to school. We had names for the days. Pebbles would tell her, "Paula, he can't come in for another couple hours. It's Moaning Monday!" There was also "Touchy Tuesday." Wednesday of course was "Hump Day." "Thrilling Thursday" was also popular. But, the best was "Freaky Friday." [laughing] It really was like that. We had a blast! Pebbles would take the kids to school and then come back and bring me a cup of coffee. People who knew me would say, "You don't drink coffee." I'd say, "I do when Pebbles brings it to me, but I'm not getting out of bed to make coffee."

Pebbles took care of me as much as I took care of her. She even ironed my boxers. Who does that?

What part of your life with Pebbles was the most rewarding for you?

Every bit of it. I know you want specifics, but I'm telling you the truth. When I sent her flowers, the card always read: Thank You for marrying me. I told her that all the time. The last thing I said to her was, "Thank you for marrying me." [crying] How do I parcel that out—the most rewarding part? Where we had been, what we had done together, having the kids—it was all perfection for me. Watching Pebbles be a mother was beautiful and amazing. When she got sick, we got closer. I know that's hard to believe, but it's the truth. Now, I'd get frustrated with things because Pebbles sickness would rattle my nerves and put me on edge. I was mad that my girl had to go through all she endured. I remember Fern Starnes telling me one day, "Mike, you don't need to be bickering over stupid things." She was absolutely right and straightened me out.

It's hard to convey how good it was being with Pebbles. It was like a dream. It was the best twelve years of my life. We crammed a lot of living into those twelve years. Probably more in that time period than most people ever do in a lifetime. I was fortunate to be able to be with her non-stop when she got sick. Paula ran the funeral home, Luke Lunn and other friends in the funeral business covered a lot of bases for me, and I took care of business. My sister Karen moved to Archer City to help take care of the kids. There were a lot of trips to doctors and hospitals, but we didn't want the kid's lives to be put off schedule. All of that allowed for Pebbles and I to have the quality time we wanted and needed.

It was all good. No lie. It was all good. I can't pick a part that was better. I worshipped Pebbles. She warned me all the time that I couldn't make her my god. I'd say, "You're the most important thing to me." She'd say, "You can't do that." I'd come back with, "I'm sorry. He gave you to me. So, you're my priority. It's His fault—not mine."

What have you learned the most in your life that Pebbles taught you?

Be nice. She was the sweetest and kindest person in the world. A friend's sister told me one time that I was an arrogant, obnoxious asshole. She said, "Aulds, you got just enough asshole in you to keep you interesting." [laughing] And I really was. Still am to this day. [smiling] I probably have a little bitterness packed in there now—a little bitter, angry, short fat man. But that wasn't Pebbles! She would talk to anyone. She loved everyone, and everyone loved her. For her, a quick trip to the grocery store for milk might last an hour. She'd see someone and then come home with some long story that she'd gotten wrapped up in while at the store. She gathered a lot of information with everyone she met. I'd pop off, "Where do you hear that crap? I go to the store, buy milk, and come home!" "Well Mike, I talk to people. I ask questions." I'd say, "No one tells me all their crap!" She'd smile, "That's because you're an arrogant, obnoxious asshole." [laughing]

Pebbles worked hard to help me be nice to people, but I didn't have the time or interest to be nice to people. I'm strongly opinionated. I'm also redneck, and I have a low tolerance for liberal lifestyles. Pebbles worked in the modeling profession, so she was much more tolerant of less traditional lifestyles. She coached me constantly to be more considerate. She reminded me often that

God loves everyone. Pebbles was unmoved by all of my barking. There is nothing politically correct about me. Well, actually, I am politically correct. It's the rest of the dumb-asses that have it wrong. **[laughing]** I like confrontation. I'll square off with anyone. Pebbles reeled me in. I'd get revved up on something, and she'd put her hand on my arm and squeeze gently. That was the signal. Or, she'd grab the inside of my thigh and pinch the crap out of me. **[laughing]** I knew she'd had enough.

What do you think you taught her the most?

Probably tolerance **[laughing]**—that she deserved to be taken care of, loved, and worshipped. She never could figure out why I treated her the way I did. I would tell her, "When I say thank you for marrying me, I mean it! It is an honor to be your husband!" I hit the jackpot. She was so humble that she never really saw why I thought like that. I think I helped her realize that she really was that good of a person. She deserved to be treated like a queen. I've never met anyone like her. Not even close.

Everyone loved Pebbles. She had a zest for life that was infectious. It was one of those personalities that sucked you in. She had a history with Hodgkin's disease at 15 years old. Obviously I didn't know her then, but she found a knot on her neck, was diagnosed with Hodgkin's Lymphoma, had surgery to remove the knot, and was given radiation treatments. Losing her hair didn't faze her in the least. All those nurses who treated her back then at St. Jude's Hospital fell in love with Pebbles. They all became friends into her adulthood. When she'd drop in to visit after we were married, she was like a celebrity or something. I had never seen anything like it. The rapport she had with people was astonishing!

I have to tell you this story. Pebbles had a friend in high school that was the school nerd. Picture the classic nerd, and it was this guy: pocket protector, books in a briefcase—classic. Pebbles was always very kind to the kid. In fact, she was the only person in the school that would be nice to him. He didn't have friends, so she basically befriended him. That kid was brilliant. He graduated a couple years ahead of his class. Eventually, he became an oncologist. He credits Pebbles with being the motivation for his career path. When she got sick with Hodgkin's, he decided that he wanted to find a cure for cancer. He didn't want anyone like Pebbles to suffer with cancer [crying]. That is how she affected people.

So that was the beginning of Pebbles' medical complications?

Yes. She was 15 years old and they removed her spleen and treated the Hodgkin's with high doses of radiation. I'm not sure of all of the details, but that was the background of Pebbles' personality. She was lucky to be alive and lived with a lot of gratitude and grace.

In 1980 people died regularly of Hodgkin's. But in Pebbles' case, I think she got her treatments and was cleared of cancer within two years. Up until we met, she'd probably had a dozen desmoids tumors removed. She had scars everywhere. You did radiation treatments to kill the cancer cells in the lymph system for Hodgkin's. So she had radiation under her arms, neck, and shoulders. The doctors were now discovering that the radiation was causing tumors 20-25 years later. Pebbles had her share. She had so much radiation, Pebbles didn't have to shave under her arms. There was no hair growing there anymore.

Pebbles was told that she'd probably never get pregnant. Bullcrap! We'd go on conception vacations just to make it challenging. [laughing] We didn't plan Abigail, but the other two were planned. Pebbles had told me that southern girls only ovulate in very expensive places. She explained, "If we're going to get pregnant, you need to take me to Maui." Stuff like that. I still thought it was bullcrap, but she got her way, and it seemed to work! [laughing]

In summer 2005, we found a lump in Pebbles' breast. She had just had a lump removed not long before then that was benign. She basically ignored it and agreed to have it checked out after the kids went back to school after the summer break.

Soon thereafter, a friend discovered she had breast cancer, so Pebbles decided to go have a mammogram. They saw something that didn't look right and had the thing biopsied. Remember, Pebbles knew all these doctors professionally. We actually dropped by the pathologist to pick up her report ourselves. We were in the car and read the report before we went to see her doctor. We were floored! I could not believe what I was reading. We were shocked.

The same oncological surgeon that had done the surgery on her cranial nerve that led to her vocal cords was who Pebbles wanted to do the lumpectomy. He also removed her lymph nodes. It was a big deal, because this guy only did head and neck oncological surgeries. His staff was amazed that he had agreed to do the surgery, but he loved Pebbles, so he did it for her. He normally only did surgery in what he called 'high priced real estate.' On the morning of the surgery, Dr. Preskitt came in and said they were ready to go. Pebbles wanted to breastfeed Michael one last time before surgery. Her mom had the kids and was running late to the hospital, so she told the doctor he'd have to wait. The doctor said, "Good. That will give me more time to sober up." It's 6:30 a.m., and he's talking trash, but he got the message. "Just tell the nurses when you're ready, and they'll come get me." When she was done nursing about an hour later, they called Dr. Preskitt.

After surgery, we're all in the waiting room. He was shooting for clean margins. So we asked immediately, "Did you get clean margins?" He said, "No, I did not." Next we asked, "Was it cancerous?" He said, "We'll have to wait until Monday until we can get the pathology report." **[crying]** Everyone was at peace with his answer, but I wasn't. When Preskitt did the previous surgery on Pebbles, he told me that he could tell if that particular tumor was cancer or not. He said, "I can do anything the pathologist can do. I can put it under a microscope and look at it. I'll know when I come out of surgery." I remembered him saying that to me. Internally I was thinking, "You lying SOB." **[crying]** He talked to everyone but me. He wouldn't look me in the eye. I knew. Everyone else was encouraged and hopeful—not me. He delivered the news and moved on quickly. I told them that he wasn't being forthright. My sister-in-law had been around this doctor also, and she concurred, "No, Mike is right, he not telling us what he knows." Pebbles asked me what he said as soon as she woke up. I told her. She grimaced and said, "That's not good is it?" She knew too. In actuality, the cancer was out of the breast and lymph nodes. Cancer cells were floating throughout her body.

Later we met with Preskitt and he referred us to an amazing breast oncologist—Dr. John Pippen. He immediately began rounds of chemo, did a bilateral mastectomy, and radiation. The chemo was rough. That almost killed her. The details are now a blur, so I can't be too sure on the dates, but I believe by September 2006, the scans indicated that she was cancer free. It had been a hard season, but life was good, and we were flying high.

At Thanksgiving 2006, we were at my brother's house to celebrate the holiday. Every time that Pebbles laughed (and that happens a lot with my family), she grabbed her shoulder in pain. She finally told us all to stop making her laugh because it was bothering her so much. It stays that way through the holidays, and she decided to go get her shoulder checked out, because she figured that she might have torn a ligament or something. She already had an appointment scheduled with Dr. Pippen for a 3-month checkup, so she also scheduled an appointment with a shoulder specialist. That was our first appointment for that day. He checked her out, but didn't think there was a joint issue that might be causing all the pain. He didn't really offer too much information. So we go over to Dr. Pippen's office for her check up, and he enters the room with, "What are y'all doing here? I told you I didn't ever want to see you in here again." This guy was a major cut-up. He knew all about Archer City. He hunted quail about ten miles from there. So we had a connection with this doctor. Pebbles loved him.

Dr. Pippen asked her how she was feeling, and she told him that we had just visited with the joint specialist about her shoulder. "What did he say?" Pebbles said, "He said I have a slight tear in my rotator cuff, but that's probably not my problem." So he mentioned that he wanted to do some scans to see if he could figure out what was going on. They do the scans, and we go have a nice lunch and then go back to the office for the results. We suspected nothing. Not worried at all! Once we get back to the office, Dr. Pippen came in to the office where we were, and he had tears in his eyes. I was standing behind Pebbles, so I couldn't see her face, but I knew those tears were not good news. His voice is cracking and he says, "Pebbles, your cancer is back." We were in shock. She asked him, "What do you mean?" He said, "Your cancer has metastasized. It's in your liver and your lungs." I don't remember exactly what Pebbles asked him, but it was basically, "Is that real bad? It's not like it's going to kill me." Dr. Pippen said, "Pebbles, this will probably take your life." [crying] I was totally floored, and so was she. It never entered our minds that she couldn't beat this cancer. Ever. Not once did we consider the possibility of her dying of cancer. Never even remotely had a thought like that.

What was the progression from that point?

Dr. Pippen wasn't worried about the lungs. He felt we needed to do something about the liver. Because the cancer was loose in her body, she was never really a liver transplant candidate. The liver filters the blood. Whatever is in the blood—gets into the liver. So that was out. I had been in the funeral business a long time. I knew that anything to do with liver or pancreas was a serious problem. They started with radiation and chemo. It was brutal and so hard on her. They were giving her the stuff they call 'red devil'—which was a badass chemo. She was very sick, dehydrated, and constantly in and out of the hospital because of it. They were pushing anti-nausea meds simultaneously with the chemo. It was tough.

There were giving her shots in the abdomen after her chemo treatment to fight the nausea. Those shots were $4,000 to $6,000 a piece. Fortunately we had the means to give her the best care. My family constantly offered to do what was necessary to help with expenses. One day a wealthy gentleman from Archer City called and asked me to lunch. He offered to pay for all of Pebbles' care. His wife had colon cancer when they were younger. He explained that he knew how financially devastating cancer could be to a young married couple. Because they loved Pebbles, and also because of their experience, they wanted to cover all cost. I said, "I didn't know you liked me that much." He shot back, "We don't, but we love Pebbles." **[laughing]** I've already said this, but we were really blessed. I thanked him, but graciously declined the offer. I felt it was my responsibility. I had many options to consider before I took that one. Some people are simply amazing!

Dr. Pippen made sure she stayed on the pediatric floor in the hospital. We thought it was so strange. I asked him one day, "Why do we have her on this floor?" He shot back, "The nurses on this floor are the best in the entire hospital. I want Pebbles to have the best." Being with Pebbles was like being with royalty. The best always showed up to take care of her. She smiled at everyone. Greeted everyone. We'd walk into a restaurant and heads would turn. She had that effect on everyone. People looked my way, and I'm checking my zipper, because it feels weird to have all those eyes on me. All that ignited her. It was crazy.

The chemo made her sick, but it also was wrecking her immune system and her blood wouldn't clot. She lost a lot of weight and became very weak though it all. Her lips cracked and bled constantly. Still, I never thought she'd die. **[crying]** Pebbles had no plans of giving up. Those babies needed her.

About a month before she died, Pebbles is in the hospital in Wichita Falls because her normal doctor (Dr. Pippen) was out of the country to give a lecture. Another doctor came in and started giving Pebbles the quality of life speech. The implication was for her to consider that it might be time to stop with the treatments. Her suggestions were probably right for some, if not most people, but not for Pebbles. When that doctor left the room, Pebbles got out of bed and started putting her clothes on. I inquired. "We're going home. If they've given up on me, we need another doctor." And that is exactly what happened. That doctor called Dr. Pippen to tell him that she had given Pebbles that speech. Dr. Pippen said, "Doctor, that was the wrong person to give that speech to." She said, "This treatment is doing a number on her." Dr. Pippen replied, "You don't know this girl. She's a fighter, and she's not done." As were driving back to Archer City, the phone rings. It's Dr. Pippen, "Pebbles, what the hell were you doing in that hospital anyway?" She told him that she didn't want to bother him while he was out of town. He said, "You have my cell phone number. I told you to call me if you needed anything!" She was really sick, and we had excuses, but I took her back to Baylor in Dallas the following Monday. She could get these nausea shots, and she'd bounce back. Once she stopped throwing up and got some liquids in her, she'd start to feel better. But overall, the chemo was really beating her up. She drove herself to get radiation treatments. She could drop the kids at school, drive to Dallas, get her radiation, and be back in Archer City in time to pick them up from school.

We stayed in that rhythm until the summer. The kids were going off to Camp Kanukuk in the Ozarks. She wanted to go, but she did not feel good enough to make the trip. She insisted she was going, but I squelched that idea and told her I would take them. Pebbles complied, but informed me that she would be going on the back end to pick up the kids. They have all these ceremonies, and she wanted to be there for the award presentations. So I drove the kids to Branson for camp and then immediately turned and drove back to Archer City. Fern would drop by to check on Pebbles a couple times a day. If I was working a funeral and Pebbles wasn't doing too well, Fern would call, "You might want to cut it short and get back here to Pebbles." If she felt bad in the mornings, I wouldn't leave her. But feeling good in the morning didn't always mean good in the afternoon. It could turn on a dime. After a week, it was time to go back and get the kids. I could tell that Pebbles was too weak to be in the car for ten hours. So I hired a couple college kids to drive my Suburban to Branson. I then chartered an airplane to fly us both to an airport just outside Branson. My plan was for Pebbles to go to the ceremony and then fly right back home to Archer City. That wasn't Pebbles plan, "No, I want to ride home with the kids in the car so I can hear all about camp. I don't want to miss that!" That trip killed her. Looking back, it was too much on her. [crying] The kids wouldn't ever go back to that camp because they associated the camp with that drive home with her. It took two days because we had to keep stopping for Pebbles. She was so uncomfortable. As soon as we got home and got the kids settled, I took her on to Baylor Hospital. She didn't come home after that. She lasted a week there.

Did you call in Hospice?

We did not. Pebbles was not in that kind of mindset. She was still fighting. One of her family members called in Hospice a couple months before she died. The Director of Hospice came to see us to enquire, and he took one look at Pebbles and knew that call was premature. Pebbles didn't have plans to die. She was going to hang on no matter what.

She kept declining, her lips were bleeding, but she was still fighting. I called her dad and asked him to alert the family that I didn't think she was going to go home this time. I wasn't sure that I totally believed that, but that was the message I gave the families. God had told me that she was going to be ok. The same God that had told me that Alexandra was going to be a boy. I guess God forgot to give her the boy parts. [smiling]

About three days before she died, they were giving her morphine, she's lying there, and I'm trying to keep all the visitors out of the room. You could tell that she was hurting. I leaned over to her to put some medicine on her lips. [crying] She hadn't opened her eyes for almost 24-hours, and while I leaned over her I said, "Pebbles, we're going to be okay. You can give up and stop fighting." I wasn't even sure if she could still hear me or not. She hadn't moved or talked in a while. She said through gritted teeth, "I'm not ready." [crying] She wasn't giving up. She wasn't ready to die. Next question.

[crying] I've been mad at God ever since. Pissed as hell. Why would he take the mother of my children? I would have been the perfect candidate to go. [crying] I had so much life insurance in place. She and the kids would have been set up for life! I thought I had all the bases covered. I did everything I could do to protect my wife and kids if something ever happened to me. Uhhh... I don't get it.

Becky and I were there with her. It was about 9:00 p.m., and her heart rate had really slowed—her breathing became very shallow. She gasped, and I realized she quit breathing. That's when the monitor went off. Becky jumped up, shook her, and said, "Pebbles!" [crying] I said, "Don't. Let her go." And, that was it.

We had already lined it out. We didn't think she'd make it through the night, so a couple of my funeral home friends were already on their way to Dallas to pick her up. I called Luke as soon as she died, and they came and got her body and took her to Henrietta where a couple more of my friends were waiting at the funeral home. My four friends embalmed her and prepared her body.

I left the hospital and went to a friend's house to get the kids and told them that their mother had died. It was the hardest thing I've ever had to do in my life. [crying] (Alexandra was 10 years old, Michael was 8 years old, and Abigail was 7 years old.) I know it happens. I just don't know why it had to happen to her. I know I am a survivor, and I don't want to be selfish for me, but that was the mother of my children. I lost my dad when I was 15 years old, but I just can't understand this loss—the mother of my kids. I begged God to take me and leave her. Her kids needed her. [crying] It's bad, because the two youngest are starting to turn out like me. [smiling] They've got attitudes.

How did Pebbles handle her complications emotionally?

She was one of the most optimistic people you'd ever meet. She wasn't going to let cancer beat her. When Dr. Pippen told her that he had done everything he knew to do, her response was, "Well then, I need you to help me find another doctor. I need to find someone who is smarter than you. I'm not going to die and leave my husband and children." She wasn't beating him up, but it was just her thought process. He said, "Pebbles, if I knew someone to hand you off to, I'd do it." She wasn't going to let it get her down. She died, but it wasn't for the lack of fighting. She fought her ass off, and it was for those kids. She told me one time, "If something ever happens to me, I know you'll be okay. It's the kids that I think about." Those little kids needed their mother. I tried my best, but they needed their mother.

I used to be the spiritual leader in our home. Now I'm just pissed.

How did you handle Pebbles' complications emotionally?

Honestly, I was probably in denial. Because she was so determined to beat it, I bought in also. I just didn't believe that cancer would win. When we got the diagnosis about it being in her liver, I started bargaining with God: "Give me ten years! Let me get these kids grown!" We met a woman that had beat liver cancer. She took small doses of chemo for 10 years. Dr. John Pippen was her doctor. I thought if he could keep Dorothy alive for that long, he could certainly do the same thing for Pebbles.

What kind of daily care did Pebbles need from you?

Primarily just being emotionally there for her. My life was to serve her.

Generally, what was Pebbles' response to your caretaking?

She wasn't a complainer and she was very independent. She apologized all the time. She didn't want to be a burden on anyone. Pebbles wasn't a burden. It was an honor to serve her.

Usually, I worked when I had a body. That could be at any time of day or night. People asked her if she was okay with that. She'd say, "As long as he kisses me before I go to bed, and he's there to kiss me when I wake up, I don't care what he does all night—as long as he's making money!" [laughing] That's exactly how she was. I haven't worked a lot since she died. I don't really work in the funeral home much anymore. I can't wait on the families properly. It's too emotional for me. I'm a full-time mother and daddy now. That's my job.

How well do you think you did under those conditions?

Damn good. But, you have to remember, if she felt like doing stuff, Pebbles was taking care of the kids. She didn't miss a whole lot of parenting. She made most of their school functions. Even when she was deathly sick, she'd power through to do what she could when it came to those kids. It just wasn't a burden. I loved serving her.

Where did you find your strength?

I loved my wife [crying]... more than anything. I didn't need strength to love her. She made my life. Her medical challenges forged us closer together. I didn't want her sick, but I liked being around her. We stayed on the move. It was awesome serving her.

Was there a point when you knew that your caretaking days were numbered?

Not really. I could see the severity of what we were facing, but I didn't think it would kill her. Three days before she died, when I told her she could go on, was the first time I had really thought I might lose her.

Did you two ever talk about "your" future without Pebbles in the picture?

Once she mentioned that if something went wrong and she couldn't get past the cancer, she wanted me to promise that the kids would maintain a relationship with her parents. I said, "Excuse me?" "Mike. Promise me." I said, "Okay." "No! I don't want okay. I want to hear you say the words that you promise." Again, I said, "Pebbles, that isn't fair." She smiled and said, "Why do you think I'm making you promise that you'll do this?" So I promised. People ask me all the time, "Why are you dragging the kids all the way to Mississippi? It's because of Pebbles. I promised. I knew they weren't crazy about me. It got a little better after the grandbabies started popping out. But I wasn't their choice. Not even close.

Pebbles went to the mall and picked up three Build-A-Bears for the kids. They had these little voice recorders that you could put inside of the bears. Pebbles recorded a message for each one of the kids, and then they stuffed them into the bears. It was like: "Abby, I love you. I wish I were there to tuck you in. Goodnight. Your mommy loves you." [crying] All three of them had their own message from Pebbles. When the kids hugged their bear, the message played from the recorder. I'd tuck them in at night, and then when I was closing the door, I could hear Pebbles voice talking to those kids. [crying] For anyone that is facing a similar situation with their kids, they need to be sure to record something so their kids have something to hold on to. My kids wore those bears out! She had recorded those messages when she was sick and going in and out of the hospital. My kids didn't go anywhere without those bears. Abby had just turned 7-years old when her mommy died. She has great memories, but those bears helped.

What was going on in your head and heart during the few final days with Pebbles?

I was waiting on God to do something. It was time. She was going down and getting weaker by the moment. I knew she could die, but I thought something was going to happen to turn it around. My God wouldn't let her die. Why would he let her do that? Those were my thoughts then. Those are my thoughts now. I don't buy that "God needed another angel in heaven" bullshit.

Looking back, how prepared were you to let her go?

I did not want her hurting anymore. That was the only reason I released her to go. That was for her. I knew we'd be ok, and I knew that kids are resilient and would move on. Living without her—how could I ever be prepared for that?

Was there an opportunity to say "goodbye" before her final sleep?

Ah yeah. [crying] The last thing I said to her was, "Thank you for marrying me." She heard that everyday for 12 years. She didn't say anything, but she squeezed my hand. It was her, "I hear ya buddy." She was so tired. It had been a brutal fight.

So it's been 7 years since she passed. How are you doing?

I'm surviving. I'm still mad at God. But life goes on. You just have to suck it up and go on. That's the only choice. It really hasn't gotten any easier—you just get numb. The first Christmas came along, we made it through that, and then the second Christmas shows up, and you think: Hell, we made it through the last one—we can make it through this one too. I'm just used to doing it by myself now.

My kids are happy and well adjusted. They're spoiled rotten [chuckle]. They've got a lot of their mother in them. Alex is a clone of her mother—talks to perfect strangers, smiles at everyone, and will give you the shirt off of her back. Michael is more like me: on task and not a lot of time for people's drama. Abby looks exactly like her mother but got stuck with her Daddy's aggressiveness.

Most marriage vows contain the words: "For better or for worse... in sickness and in health... until death do us part." Describe what those words might have meant to Mike & Pebbles.

We made a vow before God. We believed that God had put us together, and we were determined to let nothing interfere with that union. We never spoke the word "divorce." Ever. I heard Tim McGraw make a statement about his wife yesterday on the radio. Evidently he used to have a drinking problem. He said, "My wife would have walked through hell soaked in gasoline for me." I would have done the same thing for Pebbles. I would have gladly given my life for hers.

I had a suicide yesterday, and I had to go get the body. I've seen lots of women that I'd kill for, but Pebbles was the only one that I would have died for. If that trade could have been made, I would have done it in a heartbeat. I would have walked through hell soaked in gasoline for Pebbles, and I'd never bat an eye about doing it.

I took those vows seriously and certainly Pebbles did too, but I had been divorced before. It wasn't my idea, and I did everything I could to stop it, but it does happen. It takes two to stay married, but she wanted out, and I don't blame her. I was an arrogant, obnoxious asshole... well, sorta. [laughing]

It's been 7 years. I don't date. I have no desire to date. I tell people all the time: if I meet someone in Pebbles league, I might consider dating. But I tell my kids all the time, "Aulds don't settle—for nothing." So I won't settle for second best.

From the Newlyweds:

If my spouse were just diagnosed with a terminal illness, what advice would you give me?

Cherish every single moment that you have with them. You never know where or when it ends.

How did your mate's condition affect your normal intimacy patterns as a couple?

It didn't, because it drew us closer. We probably had more intimacy because of our situation.

On the night before our rehearsal dinner, we had our premarital counseling session with our pastor. We were close friends, so it was relaxed and an easy connection for us. Six weeks of sessions was the norm, but we were older, mature, and they knew us very well, so we didn't have to jump through all the hoops. That night he quoted 1 Corinthians 7:5 "Abstaining from sex is permissible for a period of time if you both agree to it, and if it's for the purposes of prayer and fasting—but only for such times. Then come back together again." Pebbles, trying to be cute, popped off something that was an exception to the rule. The Pastor basically implied that he was in charge and she needed to listen to what he was saying [laughing]. So he went on to say to me, "Mike, when you crawl into bed at night, tell her that you're starving and ask, 'did we not have dinner tonight?' She'll blow up in attitude and carry on wildly about how hard she worked to prepare that meal, and you didn't notice! That is when you reminder her: #1 We aren't fasting; and #2 the way she is acting sure enough isn't prayer—so, pony up momma!" [laughing] Of course the girls went straight into: "How about honoring your wife, you big jerks!"

I couldn't have asked for more. We had an amazing relationship. The intimacy was awesome. Pebbles took care of all my needs. I took care of hers. It was amazing. I was very blessed.

Were you two still able to play together during your mate's decline?

Oh yeah. We stayed on the move. We slowed it down when she didn't feel good, but overall we just lived like we always had.

The way my job worked allowed me the luxury of flexibility with her. I know it's not a fair comparison for everyone. Not everyone can drop everything and tend to their ultimate priorities. I would never say, "This is how you're supposed to do it." It's just how we did it.

What was the dominant emotion during your season of caretaking with your mate—as compared to your emotional state now?

Now, I'm just mad—probably bitter. Back then I just loved every minute with her. I was never fearful because I knew she was going to beat it. I could not believe that I'd lose the mother of my children. I knew I was sorry enough that I might actually deserve to lose Pebbles for myself, but not my children. My kids were her life. No doubt about it. [chuckle] I mean God was in her mix also. She had it all figured out. I think that stemmed from her living though Hodgkin's as a teenager. She felt she was spared for a reason. Then she realized it was all about being a mother to our children. I was just a means to an end to get those kids. [laughing] I was at the right place at the right time.

What's the one piece of advice you'd give someone just starting out in marriage?

Put God first, pray together every night, and don't go to bed mad. Smile and laugh together. Enjoy your life together every single day.

What's the best thing a husband can do for his wife every day?

Thank her for marrying him. He's lucky he got her too.

What's the best thing a wife can do for her husband every day?

Forgive him. We're idiots. We're a screw up waiting to happen. [laughing] I'm serious.

What did you learn about your spouse that caused you to love her even more?

She never gave up. She wasn't a quitter. All of her values stayed true under intense fire.

Do you still think that marriage is a great idea?

Without a doubt. It was the best thing that ever happened to me! Pebbles filled a part of me that I didn't know was empty. I had the best. No doubt in my mind. People asked me constantly, "How in the world did you get her to marry you?" We had been married about 3 years, and I asked Pebbles if people constantly inquired about how she got me to marry her. She said, "No. Why do you ask?" I'd change the subject. I don't know how I pulled that off. I caught her at a weak moment. I tell single women all the time, "Stop whining about not having a man. Just do what my wife did—lower your standards." **[laughing]**

Any final words of advice for married couples of all ages?

Love God, you can't out-give the Lord, cherish each other, and work to make each other happy.

If I was around, Pebbles didn't get into a hot car in the summer, or a cold car in the winter. She didn't open doors—that was my job. Even with what I did for her, it didn't touch what she did for me. She made my life.

In Memory of
Pebbles East Aulds
May 15, 1965 - August 17, 2007

Tommy

Introduction

"If I give everything I own to the poor and even go to the stake to be burned as a martyr, but I don't love, I've gotten nowhere. So, no matter what I say, what I believe, and what I do, I'm bankrupt without love."
—The Apostle Paul, 1 Corinthians 13:3, MSG

Before Patti and I conducted our first interview, we speculated about how hard it would be to find people who would talk to us. IF they were indeed willing to talk to us, would there be stories worth hearing and passing on to you? We were still in a *planning, praying* and *thinking about it* mode. The very first call I made once we felt ready to test the waters was to an administrator of the nursing home in my hometown of McGregor. After we swapped pleasantries, I told her what we were thinking of doing and I asked, "In your long history of working with that nursing home, is there a person that we need to interview? Is there a story out there that we need to know about?" She shot back in an instant, "Tommy Leutwyler. Definitely. You need to talk to Tommy." Then she proceeded to tell my why. Once you have read Tommy's interview, you too will understand why there was zero hesitation in her voice.

Gentle souls who are humble, soft spoken and careful with information about themselves seem to be almost non-existent these days. Even though Tommy was very forthright about his love affair with a childhood friend, you can tell when you're with him that there is an undercurrent of loving passion that existed exclusively for he and his "one and only" — his true sweetheart. It's much like the young woman who hides the box of Valentine's candy that she's received from her beloved. In secret, she nibbles for months to savor and relish every small piece. Why would she do that? Partaking in the hidden place is gloriously satisfying.

A friend once told me that you can usually spot the people who have been loved well in their lifetime. "They always look younger than they really are." I can't verify if that is a scientific fact or not, but it's true enough in this case. Tommy is close to his mid-seventies, but he looks as if he is in his mid-sixties. He'd make a fuss about me saying that and guffaw it off, but it's true. No, Tommy didn't find the fountain of youth. He eventually married the woman of his dreams, his forever friend, the one who had always made his world bright. She infused him with love and understanding and that would be a game-changer for anyone.

Tommy will convince you in his interview that Nancy Marie Leutwyler made his life very rich. And when Alzheimer's did it's worst on his gal, Tommy responded the way we would all hope we would. He's a man of few words but big on action. No fanfare or gushing self-praise is to be found anywhere near the man. There isn't a presumptuous bone in his body. Tommy did what he did because, "I loved her." He made a promise. It really was that simple.

I have enjoyed getting to know this quality man. Even though Alzheimer's robbed him way too early of his wife's attentive faculties, it could not touch their love. Alzheimer's was in the script, but love was always the stronger prevailing theme. This is a story of second chances, love and service. It just doesn't get any better than that.

Meet Tommy: a real, gentle man. –MDP-

Tell us about how you two met and fell in love.

Well, we actually met when we were children. We knew each other through most of our childhood. We actually started dating while we were in High School. Once I graduated, I enlisted in the service, and before I shipped out with the Navy, I bought a ring and asked her to marry me. I gave her the ring, but I hadn't asked her dad for her hand. On the day I gave Nancy the ring, her dad went into the hospital. It was late at night, and I was told by her mom, "You'll have to ask that man up on the second floor." But it was too late to talk to him because visiting hours were over, so it would have to wait until the next day. Nancy's dad died that evening. Eventually, I got the blessing from her mom, but I had to ship out before we could get married.

We were trying to make a long distance relationship work while I was in the service, but I made a terrible mistake. Basically, I lied to her in an attempt to make her fall in love with me more. The plan backfired, she didn't take it very well, and out the door I went. **[laughing]** I'm laughing, but it wasn't funny at the time. While I was in the Navy, Nancy got married to another man and they had two children.

Once I was discharged from the military, I came back to Waco and went to work at the glass plant. It was there that I met my first wife. After some time of being with her, I began to realize that she hadn't told me the truth about much of anything. I was twenty-two years old, and she was about ten years older than myself. I was told she had two children, but the truth was that she had seven children from a previous marriage. It was a wild goose chase! We were married for about five years, but I finally broke it off. She just couldn't be trusted to tell me the truth at any level.

After my divorce, my job sent me to Vietnam to repair damaged helicopters. I had been trained as an engine and structural mechanic while in the Navy. I was there one year. After I got back to Waco, I was walking down an aisle in the grocery store, and I ran into Nancy. I came to find out that she had two sons, but she had divorced the man that she had married. We got together fairly soon after that and started going out as a couple. We were pretty much inseparable after that.

Was it love at first sight?

Well, she was about ten years old, and I was eleven the first time I saw her. I immediately fell in love with her. We were at the First Baptist Church in Hewitt when her folks came into the church. That is where I first saw her. She really got into my heart. After some time, her family left our church and went to help start another church that was meeting in their home. As I've said, it feels like I've known Nancy all my life. The reconnection was an instant connection. Instant.

When and where were you married?

We married on December 28, 1973 at her mother's house in Waco.

How long were you and Nancy married?

Forty years.

What was the first year of your marriage like?

It was wonderful. We understood each other. It was like a dream. We were back together, and it was as natural as it could be. We knew how to get along, because we always had gotten along. I think we were very accepting of each other. If she needed to ask me about something that she didn't like, it didn't push my buttons. I could ask, "Hey, explain it to me." And then she'd explain it to me. We could talk about anything! There was a lot of love in the relationship. As I said, it was wonderful.

How differently were you both raised?

I don't think we were raised too differently. Before farming, my dad was military police. He knew a lot of guys who were at Pearl Harbor on the day it was bombed. Around our home, you did what you were told. On a farm there were lots of chores to do! I made the mistake only once in asking, "Why?" I was told, "Because I told you to do it." That was the end of that discussion. **[laughing]** Our house was run with strict authority. My mom could get after me too. I was the baby of the family.

The only time I remember my father telling me that he loved me was when I was home on leave while in the Navy. I was on the way to the Philippines. My father said, "I may not be here when you come home. I love you, and take care of your mother." That was the only time I heard those words. I was raised in church, and it was there that I learned that the Lord loved me.

Nancy was more of a city girl. She had eight siblings, and she was the third youngest. Church was very important to her family.

Early on, what were some of your toughest challenges as a couple?

Well, she came into the marriage with a couple kids. It was fine with me, but there were some adjustments to be made. We both had jobs, but it was soon apparent that she needed to just stay home to take care of her kids. A couple years later, our first child showed, and a second soon thereafter. Nancy decided to help her sister with a childcare center and eventually took that business over herself. She loved it, but it was a lot of work.

What were your shared goals and ambitions?

We didn't really have a big plan. We just did the things that needed to be done. We wanted to get the kids raised. There wasn't a lot of focus on us. It had more to do with getting them what they needed.

We bought ten acres and moved out of town. My work had me on the road quite a bit, and Nancy and the boys would go with me. So we wanted to establish a strong home base for kids. We were raising four boys, so there was never a dull moment. We eventually moved back to the family farm.

What part of your life with Nancy was the most rewarding for you?

Being loved by her. She made it very obvious that I was important to her. That changes a person, and I loved her for it. We had two kids together. They're both now serving the Lord in the ministry.

If it weren't for Nancy—if I wasn't given a second chance to have her in my life—I imagine my life would have been filled with sorrow. When I was in the wrong, she set me straight. She was my joy and balance. Nancy was always on top of things. Always loving.

When did Nancy's challenge with memory health begin to surface?

We were living in Houston in 1990. I was working for a Pipe company at the time, and I began to notice how forgetful Nancy was getting. I didn't pay a lot of attention to it at first, but I did notice that her memory was slipping.

Were there big things happening that alerted you of that the disease was progressing?

Yes. We'd be going somewhere, and she'd ask several times about where we were headed. Her routines were off. As I said, there was an overall battle with forgetfulness. She had a hard time remembering much of anything.

One day I was about to leave for work, and Nancy was outside talking very loud. She was saying to no one in particular, "Come on. Hurry up. Let's go." I walked up to her and said, "Honey, what's going on?" Nancy said that she and the kids were going over to a friend's to visit. I think she thought that she was at the kindergarten rounding up kids. I told her, "Honey, just take them on in the house. The lady will be by here in a little bit." So I left and went on to work. About an hour after I got to work, the police called me. Evidently, the neighbors saw Nancy out in the yard carrying on, and it must have scared them because they didn't know she had Alzheimer's. So I had to go home to sort it out.

After that deal, I decided it was time to have her checked out by a doctor. He diagnosed her with Alzheimer's. Nancy didn't say a whole lot about it, but she did not agree with the diagnosis. She was only 50 years old at the time.

After that meeting, the doctor sent some medicine and a book entitled, *The 36-Hour Day: A Family Guide to Caring for People Who Have Alzheimer's Disease, Related Dementias, and Memory Loss.* That book opened my eyes to what I was dealing with regarding Nancy. It all finally made sense. It also taught me a lot about how to deal with various situations that were happening frequently. I'll give you one example. One day I came home from work and came in the front door to our home. That was the way I entered the house every day. When I opened the door, Nancy was sitting in a recliner next to the door, and she started screaming at me, "What are you doing in my house? Get out of here! This is my house!" I had read in that book to just back away and try a different approach. So I backed out of the house, waited a couple minutes, and walked around to the other side of the house and entered through the kitchen door. When I opened the door I said, "Honey, I'm home." She said, "Where have you been? I've been waiting on you." It was as if nothing had ever happened. [laughing] Stuff like that was going on all the time, and it was progressively getting worse.

I noticed another time, when we were driving back to Houston from Waco, that she couldn't figure out how to make the proper change for a 75 cent toll. She had a handful of coins, and couldn't figure out to make 75 cents.

It finally got to where I was afraid to leave her at the house by herself. My oldest son was without a job at the time, so I paid him to come and stay with her during the days while I was at work. She was still continent at the time.

Nancy was a diabetic, so there were battles about her diet. Alzheimer's really hampered with her filter of how to take care of herself. She could have good days, and she could have bad days. If I was with her, she usually was at peace, but if I wasn't with her, she could get agitated, lost, and confused.

She used to like to ride in the car and go places, but it got to where riding in the car made her sick. So I had to stop taking her places unless it was absolutely necessary.

So your son had her in the days. What did Nancy need from you once you got home in the evenings?

There were only a few wild episodes at night. Nancy had a nightmare one night that woke her and me both up. It scared the daylights out of me. But she usually slept well and responded ok to what we needed to do.

Was there a moment of communication when you both acknowledged the seriousness of the disease to each other?

You couldn't really talk to her about it. She was suffering the effects, but she was in denial. So I just left it alone and coped as best as I could. She could get upset if she got too confused.

What were the determining circumstances that forced your decision to put her in a nursing facility?

From 1996 to 1997 I knew I'd eventually have to have more help with her. One day my son and I were at the house, and Nancy walked through the room where we were after she had taken a bath. She was only covered slightly with a towel. That had never happened before! NEVER, and that was what woke me up. I knew it was time to get her in some place. Things had advanced beyond what my son needed to handle, and I couldn't quit work at that time to take care of her.

The year and a half prior to that event, Nancy had really declined. My son had stayed with her about eight months, but now she needed more attention than what we were capable of giving her. I had to put her in Depends, and it was just too much for my son to have to deal with every day.

My family suggested the nursing home in McGregor. It had a new Alzheimer's wing, and so I moved her in there. Soon thereafter, I quit my job in Houston and moved back to Waco for another job. I needed to work for another eight years before I could retire in 2005.

She was 54 years old when I put her in the nursing home in 1997. She could still walk (she did a lot of walking) and communicate fairly well. She could tell me if she needed to go to the restroom and such, but she didn't always communicate what she needed.

How difficult was that decision for you to make?

It was tough in a way. It was best for her, but that was my wife. Life the way we had known it was now over. That was the hard part.

How much of that overall burden did you shoulder by yourself?

Until she went into the nursing home, it was my son and I taking care of her. Once I put her in the nursing home, I saw her on weekends until I moved back to Waco. Once I was back, I saw her every day after work, and on the weekends. On the weekends, I might take her out for a ride to go see the family. But it got to where she didn't know anyone, so we stopped doing that. Especially when she started having bouts with carsickness. I'd stay with her until I could tell she was bored, and then I'd leave and go take care of my business.

I made the mistake one day of telling her that I was going home. She pleaded, "Take me with you." I learned real quickly to tell her I was leaving to go to work, or anywhere else, but never home. After I retired, I saw her three times a day.

You saw her every day?

Yes, three times a day. Nancy had gotten to where she couldn't feed herself. When I realized that she wouldn't really eat for anyone other than me, I took over the feeding duties. She had lost her teeth, she ate slowly, and she ate for me real good, so I just handled it. It was just a better routine for her if I'd feed her. There might have been a time or two that I didn't get over to feed her and someone else took care of that, but I did that until she died.

Also, by then she was done talking. She could answer me with a "yes" or "no," but most of what she communicated happened by her nodding her head. I could ask her a question, but if she couldn't nod her answer with a "yes" or "no," she wouldn't answer at all. I'm pretty sure she knew me until the day she died.

Was there anything else other than Alzheimer's that ended her life?

Not really. She died late afternoon. I noticed the day before that she hadn't really eaten anything. You could put food in her mouth, but she just mouthed it. She would not respond in any way on the day she died. I was with her when she died. I wasn't really too surprised that it happened like it did.

Generally, what was Nancy's response to your caretaking?

By that time, feeding her was about the only time you got any kind of reaction from her. A few years earlier, she might grab my arm and try to mumble words, but I never knew what she was trying to say. She ate for me, so that was something she wasn't really doing for anyone else. I think that was a positive response. I'm convinced she wanted me there, and I was glad to do it.

How well do you think you did in those circumstances?

Well, I think I was more than ok with it because that's what needed to be done. She benefitted from my help, and that meant something to me. I miss it—if that tells you anything. I miss the interaction with her. She was important to me. It was the only way I got to be with her. She meant everything to me. That's why I did it.

Where did you find your strength and courage?

The good Lord.

What were your big "priorities" before you found out Nancy's Alzheimer's, and how were those things affected by the illness?

I'd say making money. I traveled a lot with my job, because I was trying to meet the needs of the family. Nancy would go with me, but that had to stop once Alzheimer's took over. I still had to work, but she became the greater concern.

Did you two ever talk about "your" future without Nancy in the picture?

No. We were busy holding on to the moment.

What was going on in your head and heart during the few final days with Nancy?

I could see what was happening, and knew she wouldn't be here for much longer. I had been thinking about her death for quite some time because of the misery she had been through. Of course, it was a great loss to me. I was in pain, but it was nothing compared to what she had endured.

Looking back, how prepared were you to let her go?

The journey had pretty much prepared me. The first symptoms had shown up 23 years ago. We're all going to die some day. I sure didn't want to lose her, but I knew the day was coming.

Was there an opportunity to say "goodbye" before her final sleep?

I won't say that I told her "goodbye," but I did tell her that I loved her. I didn't tell her that I was going to miss her or anything like that. I didn't want to discourage her or make her feel bad. I had gotten so used to talking to her, trying to make her feel good, and I didn't want to get in the way of what was happening. It was my loss—she was my loss, but I didn't want her to worry about it. I believe she knew what was going on as well as I did. There were times that she'd reach up and grab my hand. She didn't do that for anyone else. I was blessed to have her for my wife.

So it's been almost two years since Nancy passed. How are you doing?

Well, I miss her. I've had a few medical complications, but overall I'm good.

Do you ever sense that Nancy is with you?

There will be times at the house that I find something that she wrote, or a picture that I've never seen, and the memories flood me.

Most marriage vows contain the words: "For better or for worse... in sickness and in health... until death do us part." Describe what those words might have meant to Tommy & Nancy.

That is exactly what we went through... to the very end.

From the Newlyweds:

Were there times during the illness that you didn't think you could do it anymore?

Not really, but the issue for me was having the time to attend to her. I had to work, and she needed more from me than I could give her. That's why I made the decision to put her in the care facility. I was willing, but the situation forced a different response. Once I retired, it was more like I wanted it and probably more of what she needed.

If my spouse were just diagnosed with a terrible illness, what advice would you give me?

Hang on to them as best you can. Do what you can for them. If you love them, that is what you'll do. You'll do anything you can.

How did your mate's condition affect your normal intimacy patterns as a couple?

Until she went into the nursing home we were still able to be together in that way. It had started tapering off, but that part of our life together was still active. Maybe a year after she was in the nursing home, I'd bring her back to the house for a visit. That happened two or three times, but after that we were done.

How did you find joy together when so much time and emotion was filled with that disease?

I still was able to enjoy my wife's company! There were times that Nancy was an angel. Just like the old Nancy I'd always known. It might only last for 15 minutes, but it was wonderful. [laughing] We could laugh together. I was thankful I still had her.

What's the one piece of advice you'd give someone just starting out in marriage?

Love and trust your mate. Work hard to get on the same page together. Love and trust makes the world right.

What's the best thing a husband can do for his wife every day?

Love her. Help her in anyway he can. She is a part of your very foundation. Take care of her.

What advice would you would give to a newly engaged couple?

Work hard to understand each other during that engagement. Don't go so fast that you skip the friendship. Make sure that you want the same things out of life.

What are your most important memories of your marriage?

Knowing how much my wife loved me. No one ever loved me like she did. There are times when I'll have a moment of memory of something we were doing together, where she made me feel loved and special. I might dig a hole, and she'd plant the flower. Little things no one can ever take from you. Nancy instigated a lot of activities only because she knew I'd enjoy it. I enjoyed serving her in what little ways I could.

Knowing all that you know now, what would you have done differently in your marriage?

I wouldn't have done anything different our marriage. But back when I was an idiot, when we were engaged the first time, I wouldn't have lied to her. It cost me a lot of years! I was very fortunate I got a second chance.

What did you learn about your spouse that caused you to love her even more?

I knew that Nancy loved me. It wasn't just words. But the worse she got, the tighter she held on to me. It seemed that she loved me even more while in her decline.

Do you still think that marriage is a great idea?

Now? I'm a little old for that! [laughing] Yeah, I think it's great when two people care more for each other than for themselves. That's when it's great!

Any final words of advice for married couples of all ages?

If you can love today, then love today. You don't have any idea of what tomorrow will bring.

In Memory of
Nancy Marie Bledsoe Leutwyler
August 11, 1942 – February 5, 2013

Jackie

Introduction

From June 1982 until May 1985, the Reverend D. Michael Toby was my pastor. Deep in the Bible Belt of America that has certain connotations. Most apply here, but the personal relationship between Mike Toby and myself was something that moved way beyond church and religious duty. Mike was a brother, a real friend and a guy who I loved very much. He also was a proactive mentor, an example—someone who inspired me to "want to be like Mike." He taught me the skills of preaching, showed me that a man's man could be extremely focused and committed to spirituality while serving mankind. The man had "a call" and he lived it every day of his life.

Fridays were our days to hang out. For many years, he and I were either in a bass boat stalking our prey, walking behind his hunting dogs or engaged in intense combat on the racquetball court. Competition was the norm and both of us loved the edge of clashing swords. Mike was 10 years my senior, but I had no advantage in strength or stamina. The man was a machine. Once his mind and heart was set on a task, he was a powerful and driven force to be reckoned with. Just ask the staff and leaders who served in the churches where he pastored.

Mike Toby lived to grow people, grow a church and to point them both to God. Grounded discipline was his mantra. And around those gifts and passions, a 4,000-member congregation grew to also love and trust their leader's passion and vision for the things of God.

Mike was a good and solid man. He loved his beautiful wife. He loved his sons. He loved his daughters-in-law and grandchildren. He was a man of mission... a man on a mission. He made his mark. I am positive he's received his "well done, good and faithful servant."

A man of Mike's intense qualities needed spectacular diversity. Enter Mrs. Jackie Toby. She's a force to be reckoned with too, but in a totally different way. The air around Jackie is freeing, liberating, artistic, beauty-filled, colorful and downright easy. Patti says she has the best laugh ever, and she's right. There is no pretense with Jackie. What you see is what you get and it's a beautiful thing really. That takes courage and an elegant self-confidence to pull that off the way this strong woman does.

Jackie doesn't necessarily see herself as a businesswoman, yet she has run her own business for many years. Her skills as an interior decorator are marvelous and obvious. Go into her home and you're instantly engulfed in beauty and cozy love. It's a unique gift that beautifully blends that easy smile and genuine flow of alluring peace. Jackie is feisty and she's free—like a fresh cool breeze when you need it the most.

We adore this classy woman and, as you read her story, you'll understand why. What a joy for us to present to you a very special lady: Our longtime friend, Jackie. We love her so much. -MDP-

Tell us about how you two met and fell in love?

We met in college. When we both started school, it was called Houston Baptist College. By the time Mike graduated, they had changed the name to Houston Baptist University. I was a freshman, and Mike was a sophomore. At that school, part of the orientation was to make the freshmen (boys and girls) wear beanies. So the upperclassmen would get the beanies off the heads of the freshmen girls' head in the women's dorm, line them up, and toss them as a game. It was a way to get to know each other. That's how we met. Mike was trying to throw a beanie on my head. Later that night, he and his roommate asked my roommate and me to go out for a Coke. All soda drinks in Texas are called "Coke." I already had my eye on Mike's roommate, because I thought he was funny and I liked humor in a guy. Mike was tall and very serious, so I didn't pay him a whole lot of attention. So when we were about to get into the roommate's VW Beetle, Mike opened the passenger side door and funneled me into the backseat. I was asking myself, how in the heck did this happen?

We ended up dating a little bit, and I don't know if I was awe-struck with his seriousness or he just wasn't into chatter, but we didn't really talk when we were together. I kept thinking, well this just isn't working out very well. I was looking for connection, and it wasn't happening. I guess he felt the same way and didn't call for a long time. I was kind of glad about that and started dating other guys. Well, one day he called the dorm, I answered the phone, and he basically asked me if every woman in that dorm was available to go out on a date with him. **[laughing]** So get this, he's on the phone with me, asking me who might be and might not be available to go out on a date. For every girl he asked about, the madder I got. Finally I said, "Well, who do you think I am to take this message from you and give you any information? Who do you think I am... a second hand?" Then I got very dramatic, "A second hand... a second hand..." I couldn't think of anything to end that tirade with, so I inserted with great indignation: "dog?" He knew he was in big trouble. He didn't laugh then, but later he told me that he thought that was the funniest thing he had ever heard. He teased me all the time about my being a second hand dog. But he knew I was not happy with him.

Later, we saw each other as we were both making a visit to a mutual friend in the hospital. I walked into the room and thought, "Oh darn. There he is." He's looking at me like, "Please don't kill me here in front of these people." I visited for a minute and then left to go, and I realized that Mike was following me down the hall. He said, "Would you want to go get some ice cream?" I was thinking that this was crazy! **[laughing]** But I did go with him, and we got a chance to talk some more and get on a better footing.

So it wasn't love at first sight?

Oh no. It had to grow! We dated some more, and things were progressing, but I do remember when I fell in love with him. We were sitting in some little fast food place one night, and he started telling me about the purpose for his life and the ministry that he was going to have. It had never entered my mind to marry a pastor. He was a youth minister at the time, and not a pastor, but he had a huge vision to reach kids. I also knew I had a calling and had felt that as a sophomore in high school, but I never really had a lot of understanding about what to do with it.

I sort of felt I might be the first woman music director in an SBC church. There were none at the time, so I figured it might as well be me, since I was seeking a degree in music. Mike was so excited about his mission and purpose that I was absolutely excited about all of that. I definitely fell in love with him, but I also fell in love with his purpose and direction. It answered a lot of questions for myself. I fell in love with the man and his purpose at the same time.

Our courtship went really fast. We were two strong personalities, so we were either oil and water, or everything was flowing. We had some clashes, and we were strong together, but things moved very fast.

When were you married? Where?

We were married in Odessa, Texas on August 19, 1967. I was 19 years old, and he was 20. His dad had to sign for him to get married. You had to be 21 to get married back then. Isn't that cute? **[laughing]**

We got married right before school started his junior year. So we had a very short honeymoon because classes were starting. We also switched schools to Sam Houston State University in Huntsville, because he had gotten a job as the Youth Minister at First Baptist Church in Huntsville.

How long were you and Mike married?

45 years.

What was the first year of your marriage like?

For me, it was a major transition. We all have expectations about marriage. Our families were different, we hadn't really dated very long, and the expectations were probably very different. Mike came from a family that talked plainly and bluntly. If you had a problem with someone, you said what the problem was. I came from a very sensitive family. We tiptoed around each other's feelings, and you didn't blurt out what the issues were. Honestly, I cried all the time. Mike would say, "What did I say now?" I thought I had ruined my life with all this open honesty, plus I got thrown into the ministry with Mike. People at church had expectations for me to produce and perform. I could sing, because I had done that for years, but I had never spoken publically. I was 19 years old, carrying a double major, and piling on the hours so I could graduate at the same time he did. Mike talked me into changing my major from music to teaching, because he figured we'd be traveling around a lot and those jobs were more plentiful. I had never even considered being a teacher. I cried about that. I cried about the stress I was under with all the extra curricular work. I felt he was disappointed in me because the floor wasn't clean or dinner wasn't on the table, so it was extremely stressful.

How differently were you both raised?

Some things were similar, and others were very different. Mike came more out of a middle class background. I came more out of poverty. My dad was an artist and musician, and he struggled with finding his place. We didn't have much in terms of financial stability, but Daddy always worked hard to meet all of our needs. My mom was a stay-at-home mom who took good care of us and showed us love in many ways.

Mike's dad kept a steady job, and it was more of a traditional household. Mike's mom was very loving and kind. He got a lot of support from his mother. Mike's dad was the authority around the house and could be hard at times.

My mom was the authority; my dad was the one who showed more approval and unconditional love. I didn't hear my dad talk a whole lot, my mom was the talker. There were some major differences in how we were raised. We had to learn how to deal with the effects of those things in our marriage.

Early on, what were some of your toughest challenges as a couple?

As mentioned earlier, making those transitions into a new identity. We went from only thinking about our own individual thoughts about our future, to a shared future. I had no plans to fall in love with a guy and make such a drastic change of direction that early in my life. I didn't fully realize I was marrying into the ministry. The expectations on us were huge. Mike thrived on that because of his calling. I had a calling too, but I didn't really know what that was. I had to settle in my heart— part of my calling was to be his wife... a pastor's wife. None of that was defined early on. At the time, I didn't see how being married to a minister would be any different than being married to any other man. Some things are best-left unknown, I guess. It might have changed everything if we had all that understanding up front.

Most people had freedom on the weekend. We worked all weekend. Mike was a strong individual. Adjusting to a driven, committed, disciplined individual was a major challenge for me. It wasn't all ambition on his part—some, but the man wanted to get on down the road and accomplish what his heart was set on. He was highly structured. I'm a free spirit.

Looking back, it usually makes sense, and it looked like it worked well for us, but early on I had my doubts about how any of it was going to work. Many times we looked at each other in amazement and wondered, "How in the world did we get stuck together?" **[laughing]** We could see it in each other's eyes. Love was never the issue. I used to say, "Mike, we don't have a lot in common," and we didn't. But he'd always remind me, "Jackie, we have common values. That's what counts." I'd be thinking, "Well, not at the moment it doesn't." **[laughing]** But I'd soon settle that he was right. That was what was important.

What were your shared goals and ambitions?

Honestly, I'm not too sure what all his goals for the marriage were, but for me, I'm not, and I wasn't, a high maintenance woman. I just want to be happy and make others happy around me. If I can make that happen, I can usually be happy. He was pretty much a perfectionist. I can be that way about myself, but not on others. I usually make no demands on others about much of anything. I usually felt under pressure because of the way he was. I'm very sensitive and struggled with feeling that I didn't live up to his expectations. I felt many times I was disappointing him in some way. That was a hard thing for me. Honestly, it had more to do with my own insecurities than anything Mike was projecting on me. He seemed to be basically happy with our relationship.

We were married seven years before we had kids. It wasn't in my plans. I was the oldest of three kids, and I was like the second mother to my siblings. I had always been taking care of kids, and I didn't really want to do that anymore. My sights were on being a career woman. I had my own ambitions. Mike approached me one day about having kids and I said, "I thought we talked about that? I thought we were not going to bring children into this evil world?" He had a response. He always had a response and he was usually right. [laughing] "Jackie, there's another way to look at this. If we bring good children into the world, it can help make this world a better place." I thought it was indeed a good thought, but I wasn't sure I was buying it. [laughing] He could sell you his ideas. "You know Jackie, we're with all these young families, they all have children, and we need to be role models to them." Of course I said, "Oh, that's why we're having children? To be role models? I don't think so!"

This is how he was... highly structured, and it made sense to the overall plan. As much as I didn't like that conversation then, I'm praising God now that I listened to him! My children have been my whole life! And now my grandchildren are such a blessing to me! I'm very glad he was right in that situation, as he was in many others!

When it came to money, and most of the normal shared decision making basics, we were pretty much always on the same page. We worked hard to be a team. We both made sacrifices that were for the benefit of the marriage and our family. We both had a strong work ethic, and we both came from families that had a strong work ethic. You do what you have to do to make things work for the family.

So as the marriage began to develop and mature, what did "normal" look like for Mike & Jackie's relationship?

We both had extremely busy lives, so we operated a lot independently. We were both secure in our relationship with each other. That allowed us both to grant the freedom to do our own thing. He was giving himself to the church, I had my own ministries inside the church, I was raising two precious boys, managing a household, and later, as the guys entered junior high, I was operating a business. We'd always come back together at night, watch TV, eat dinner together, and do all the normal stuff that everyone does.

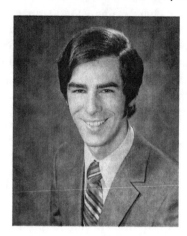

What part of your life with Mike was the most rewarding for you?

I always saw him as my earthly protector. I knew God was my protector, but I saw Mike as my rock... my protector. That was who he was... how he was. That was his essence for everyone.

Scott, our younger son, is a lot like Mike. People call him a gentle giant. Mike was more of a dynamo giant. Josh, our older son, is like Mike in strength also, with Mike's strong energy and decisiveness. Mike was strength for anyone around him. He was the strength for a huge church. People just about fell apart when he got sick and died. They are recovering and doing well now, but it was tough. That was his essence... what I depended on in him.

What have you learned the most in your life that Mike taught you?

He taught me a lot of things. We grew up together. Discipline is one thing he lived in front of me. Not that I am disciplined at his levels, but he showed me the value of his way. I used to ask God, "Why in the world did you put me with someone that is this structured? I can never measure up to that kind of discipline!" But he was a great role model for the kids and myself. He lived the value of discipline. I saw him do many things that I'm pretty sure he did not want to do. But he did it out of duty. People were counting on him. He learned that from his mom. She was very duty bound. Mike only missed one day of school his first 12 years of education. And that was because he was very ill that day. He was amazingly disciplined. Imagine living with that! It was hard for this free bird. **[laughing]**

Mike wasn't one to explain the methodology. It was more: "Hop on board... this train is leaving!" He and I would be somewhere, and he'd say, "This train is pulling out. You better get on in here." He taught by action. He was extremely punctual. You had to be there early. On time was late. This trait has led to one of my tips for a happy marriage: Two cars!

What do you think you taught him the most?

Frustration... [laughing] Irritation and frustration. He had to be thinking: "Is this woman trying to drive me insane?" [laughing] Everyone in our family knows that my job was to soften his edges. I think I taught him softness and beauty. One person in every couple has this job I think. I really do think that is a traditional perspective of how God brings together the different strengths and weaknesses of a couple. My prayer was to bring him comfort, softening, and nurture when he needed it. I hope that is what he got from me.

Did you ever see him cry?

Not really. I saw him extremely upset and on the verge of tears early on at one of the churches where the pastor told him that he was disappointed with him. Mike was such a high achiever, a perfectionist, and probably a people pleaser also. He was so hurt. He wasn't good with letting anyone down. He eventually got it worked out with that pastor, but he was really wounded in that situation. I also saw him cry when Josh and Scott were born. He was so happy! That guy was tough. He didn't show those kinds of emotions easily.

When his parents died, he was a rock. He loved his mom so much, and even preached his mother's funeral. He was so strong, and full of faith throughout her illness and death. I had to tape my vocals for the funeral because I knew I wouldn't be able to emotionally handle it. Mike conducted the service beautifully. Amazing strength. I was having such a hard time when his mom died. I couldn't turn off the tears. Mike gently reproached me, "Where is your faith? You know where she is right now." A couple of minutes later, Scott came into the room—he was about 8 years old. I was lying on the bed crying, and he said, "Mom, I know you loved Grandma, but you've got to pull yourself together." [laughing] I got a double-whammy from two of my guys that day. One was old, and the other one young! All that just shows how solid Mike was in his convictions and how it affected those of us around him. That lesson on faith really helped prepare me for what I was going to face when Mike got sick. He had amazing faith and sharp discernment. He could figure out someone in a heartbeat.

When did Mike's medical complications begin to surface?

Sometime around July or August 2012. It could have even been earlier than that. Mike kept complaining that he couldn't get his contacts on. Mike wasn't a complainer when he was ill, but he was getting very frustrated with that issue. After his death, a staff member who manages the church's workout facilities (Charlie Dodd), mentioned that he noticed that his workout routines were changing. The church staff had also noticed some changes. Looking back, little things were subtly changing on a regular basis.

We had gone to Colorado for our summer vacation, and I noticed a lot of things were different with him. He was much more introspective. He talked to me more on the trip out there. That was unusual for us. I'd usually dive into a book, and he'd just drive. He asked me right before we got into Pagosa Springs if I thought it would be okay to ask the Personnel Committee for a 3 month sabbatical. I told him that 35 years as one church's pastor surely warranted that kind of time off. I thought it was a marvelous idea. Mike had been looking tired to me. He said, "I think I need to do that." That kind of put my antenna up.

On our past visits to Pagosa Springs, he was constantly on the go to fish and golf. It was vacation... that is what he did. When he'd go fishing, he'd be out all day. That was normal. On this trip, he returned from fishing almost immediately. I said, "You're already back?" He replied, "Oh, they weren't biting." The next day he went to the golf course. He was gone less than an hour. "You're already back?" He said, "Yeah, it's too windy," or some excuse like that. That was not normal for Mike. It was like something was heavy on his mind. It was just strange.

On the way home, he pulled out in front of a car. He had always had great vision; he never took risks like that, and I couldn't believe he didn't see that car. He never even noticed what had happened. The same thing happened again after we got back to Texas. He pulled out in front of another car. I thought, "My goodness, do we need to have his eyes checked?" Once we found out about the brain tumor, it was clear that he was losing his sight on the left side. All those little things were accumulating quickly.

The week before events in his illness really escalated, we were at the church together on a Wednesday night to have our picture made for the new directory. When he met me for the sitting, I noticed that his tie was tied in a very tight knot and it hung kind of weird. It looked strange, and he didn't look put-together. He was meticulous about how he dressed. I asked him if he wanted to re-tie the tie. He said he didn't have time for that. I suggested he had plenty of time to re-do it. He got frustrated. "I don't have time for that. We've got to get this done." I said that was fine, but asked him if I could at least loosen the knot a bit. He was agreeable, and I did that, and we got our pictures made. Well now days those directory services have digital images, so you can see the proofs immediately. He said, "I've got to go." I said, "Don't leave me with this. You know I'll spend too much money on pictures. You'd better stick around here." **[laughing]** He snapped, "Jackie, handle it. I've got to go." I thought, something is very wrong here. I couldn't figure it out. That picture turned out to be our last formal portrait. His eyes displayed his illness.

When a big, strong man is losing control of his body, it has to be enormously frustrating. He never was mean or irritable, but it was obvious that the loss of dexterity was extremely frustrating. I think he handled all that with amazing composure.

When did he get the diagnosis that he had a brain tumor?

All of this was happening gradually. He was trying to get ready for a trip to Israel. He decided to check with a sports medicine therapist and ask a few questions about his hand. He was having all those issues controlling his hand. The therapist actually recommended for him to go see a specialist, but the thought was that there was a problem with the nerves in his hand.

October 14, 2012, he preached his last sermon, and it was obvious to everyone that something was badly wrong. Mike seemed shaken, he had to use his glasses (since he could no longer get his contact on), and he told the church that he almost didn't come that morning.

Something like an electrical sensation passed through me upon seeing him and noticing the difference in him. I'm sure many in the congregation felt the same way.

I put the incident in the back of my mind as just a temporary setback. Mike always bounced back. He was never one to let anything hold him down. Perhaps I was in denial. How could I consciously accept that the vital and energetic man I had lived with on a daily basis for forty-five years could be that ill?

Our last church function in which he spoke and seemed perfectly normal was the annual Deacon's Banquet on October 18, 2012.

I'm not an early riser, but I woke suddenly (5:22 a.m.) with a sense of panic. I also sensed that he was still at home (Mike usually left home at 6:00 a.m.). I asked him, "Honey, are you ok?" He said, "No. My hand is totally numb and unresponsive." I thought he might be having a heart attack and told him we needed to get him to a doctor immediately, but he said that he already had a scheduled doctor's appointment that morning.

By the next Sunday, October 21st, which was to be a big celebration honoring Mike's 35th anniversary at First Baptist Woodway, he was too ill to attend, and it was cancelled. It was apparent to everyone at that point that something was dreadfully wrong.

Monday, October 22, our younger son, Scott talked with the staff of the church after Mike was diagnosed with brain lesions. His left side was drastically affected. His balance was immediately off.

Friday, October 26, a series of tests, scans, MRI's began. People's care, concern, inquiries were constant. Mike was wearing down. Everything was surrealistic. I had just begun organizing my store after moving it in July, thinking things were finally slowing down and stabilizing so that I could plan and normalize my life again. It's amazing that while you are busy planning a life, life has other plans!

Mike and I used the same woman (Sharon Calloway) to cut our hair for about 30 years, and she told me (after Mike's death) that she had cut his hair and he was having trouble sitting straight in the chair. His hand and arm were dangling to the side. She said she had to ask him if it was okay to pick up his hand for him and put it in his lap.

My son, Josh (anesthesiologist) told me that Mike had described some of his symptoms and he thought it might be nerve damage in his arm or shoulder. But Josh didn't think that his dad saw it as anything more than that. Josh suspected something much worse.

Once he had the MRI, it was obvious that there was a bigger problem. There was a brain tumor in the right side of his head, along with multiple lesions. They found the tumor towards the end of October, 2012.

When he went in for the MRI, he was leaning to one side, really having trouble walking. The nurse helping him started crying. Dr. David Myers came to our house to give us the results of the MRI on November 6th. David seemed concerned. I knew immediately it wasn't good. We went to the dining room. Scott sat to my right and Mike to my left. Mike wasn't saying anything. Not normal. David said that they had found some lesions in Mike's head and that they didn't look good. I took the lead and asked, "Does that mean cancer?" He said that he didn't like to use the word cancer. I responded, "Well, let's use it anyway. Is that what it is?" He said, "Yes." I said, "By looking at you, I can tell that this isn't good news." He said it wasn't. So I asked, "What does this mean? How much time are we looking at?" David responded with 3 to 6 months. In reality it was 2 and a half months.

Was there a progression to the illness?

Yes, I've already explained most of that, but it was primarily that he was losing his abilities on his left side. He started leaning more in that direction. His whole left side was deteriorating because the brain tumor was on the right side of his brain. I didn't realize it at first, but he was also losing his vision. When I look back, even to the car incidents, it was obvious that his vision was a problem for him. Very quickly he couldn't walk anymore and his voice weakened at the end.

Scott had to take off from work to help me because the neurosurgeon didn't want him to go home after an evaluation. They wanted to take him straight to a care facility. When Mike heard that, he started trying to get up out of the bed. He said, "I'm not doing that. I'm going home." The doctor adamantly insisted that he not go home. I could tell Mike wasn't having it. So as he was putting his clothes on, the nurse and doctor were trying to get him to get back into bed. I said, "No. He's going home." Because I knew that is what he wanted. The doctor got angry with me and said, "You do not need to take him home because I can tell by looking at you that you're going to try to move him, and I'm telling you that you can't move him. He's too tall and too big and you're going to hurt him and hurt yourself too. Do you understand me?" I said, "I do understand you, but he's going home." Later, one of our associate pastors told me, "Jackie, you've never been in one of those places... Mike has. That's why he wanted to go home." So we went home.

When we rounded the corner to the house, Mike seemed uncharacteristically emotional and said, "I thought I'd never see our home again." I was so glad that I brought him home. The way that the people needed access to him, it just wouldn't have been the same if he'd been somewhere else. It needed to be in our home.

He was still walking at the time, and equipment was sent out at first for physical therapy. That was before we got the final diagnosis. He had a couple more MRI's and other tests before we knew what we were finally facing. The physical therapist came out, took one look, and said, "This isn't going to work. He doesn't need physical therapy." She saw it immediately. So we moved that equipment out to the garage, and Scott started helping me move him around. Things were moving so fast he went straight to a bed. He used a wheelchair one time at Thanksgiving to take him to see where he was going to be buried. He wanted to see that. That was his last time out of the home and the only time he used a wheelchair.

How did he handle his complications emotionally?

He was amazing. You'd think he would have been very frustrated and resent his condition—he never did. The hardest thing for him was that he needed to see a clock at all times. I asked about that and a nurse told me, "He's a very powerful man, he's use to structure, schedules, and being in control. Those types normally have to be able to see a clock." So we tried to keep a clock where he could see it, and after a while we realized he was going blind in his left eye, and would have to move it to the right place and angle for him to see it. Small things like operating a tape player got to be a frustration because the man was self-sufficient, and was losing dexterity and vision.

Mike was in control through most of this process. He made the decision about not having surgery, not having treatment, and he wasn't going to be talked out of it. He was still managing the affairs around him as well as he could. One day the staff was coming for a visit. They had planned to pray for him and share communion. I said, "Honey, we can cancel this if you're not up to it. If you feel bad, let's reschedule." He said, "No, no. It's scheduled." See the structure? So I met them outside and suggested that we keep it brief, he wasn't feeling well, and everyone was in agreement. Typical Mike Toby, they come into the room, and he comes alive! He's asking questions and making recommendations, totally in his element. Those guys are all looking at me like: "We thought he felt bad?" [laughing] That was so typical of who he was. Totally in control and doing what he did with his staff. There was still some expectation for him to lead them. They were like sheep without a shepherd. It was painful to watch. He'd tell them to just keep doing what they had always done.

None of us were really talking through all of this. We're all talkers, but it felt like we could just look at each other and knew what the others were thinking. When

Dr. Myers came to the house to give us the final diagnosis, I noticed that none of us were crying. It might have been shock, but I honestly felt that we were dealing with the facts: This is what it is... and it's going to be ok. It was a very weird feeling.

The day Dr. Myers brought the final report; God spoke very clearly to me. "We do not grieve as those who have no hope." (1 Thessalonians 4:13) I also remembered the lyrics of an old hymn: "Grant us wisdom, grant us courage, for the facing of this hour, for the facing of this hour." As I was walking back to my bedroom after Scott and Dr. Myers had left, God spoke clearly again, "Focus on me—not on yourself." All of those things were perfect for what I needed. Those three things took me through everything.

How did you handle Mike's complications emotionally?

I went into action mode. When you've got those kinds of difficulties facing you, you man-up and get strong in the Lord. I had to focus on Mike and his needs, because he had serious needs. And then we had a large number of people who had needs. Everybody was upset. This was their pastor who was very sick. Lots of people were upset. Josh (older son) lived away, so the burden fell primarily to Scott (younger son) and me. People were calling and texting, and I couldn't handle it all. I said, "Scott, I'm going to disappoint everybody. There is no way I can get back to all these people." So he set up a Facebook page, which was genius for us. It gave us a way to give factual updates because there were all kinds of weird rumors flying around about what kind of sickness Mike had. People were talking about it without the facts. Some just made up their own stories, I guess. Scott kept that page up to keep people informed. It was very helpful.

Scott was a major help and then friends started showing up to assist me. I had nurses and quality help, but the biggest stressor was that we had people everywhere who were hurting. I felt loved to death. People were genuinely concerned and offering, "What can we do?" But there were 20-30 people in the house almost every day from the time Mike went into the hospice bed until a week before he died. We shut down the visitors that last week. We were glad to do what we did, but it was hard. I like my alone time, but I also knew my calling and my role as a pastor's wife. I do love the people. I knew we had a responsibility to the people who loved Mike. I wanted to facilitate the people's access within reason and not totally exhaust him.

We had to get the church staff in, we had to get the attorneys in to get the legal affairs in order—it all came in layers. Then we had our best friends begin to show up, you guys came in, and family. I tried to let anyone come who asked to come, if Mike was up to it and if he wanted guests. We only turned away one couple that whole time, and that was only because Mike was spent and done. That prompted me to pray and ask the Lord for all the visitation to stop. After I prayed that day, not one person called to ask for a visit. Isn't that amazing?

After a visit with Mike, people would come out of his room crying. They'd go in with the intentions to help and bless him, and almost every time, people came out helped and blessed. It was awesome! He just had this gentle grace during all that. He got softer in those days. He was always sweet and kind, but he definitely got softer.

Was there a moment of communication when you both acknowledged the seriousness of the complications to each other?

We already knew it was serious. We didn't have to talk about that. The most special times were when we were alone, and we didn't get very many moments alone because we were both so committed to meeting the needs of our people. I knew my time would come later. At night, I would read to Mike all the cards and letters that were being sent to him. That was a special time, and it was important to me that Mike heard everybody's words. If those words were important enough to be written down, they were important enough for him to hear them.

He got some of the most amazing cards from people who wanted to share how he had influenced their lives. So that was our time together. I would sit in this big chair with my legs crossed over the arm and read all those notes to him. He loved to listen to those words.

One time I did ask him, "Are we ok here? You and me, are we ok?" He said, "Yeah, we are." And I started crying. He said puzzled, "You're crying." I said, "I know, Honey." And he said, "Jackie, you've got to stop being so sensitive." [laughing] All through my life with him he'd say, "You've got to stop being so sensitive." I said, "But you're dying!" [laughing] He said sternly, "Even so, Jackie, you've got to stop being so sensitive!" [laughing] I thought that was so funny. He didn't want me crying. I walked out of the room laughing and wiping away my tears, and I said to the Lord, "Ok God, you've got to help me control this." And that was the first time I had cried in front of him during this whole ordeal. I thought I had done really well, and I got scolded for that! [laughing] I realized I didn't get any points for that.

We had great communication through all of this. I've written most of it in my journal, but I remember that Mike asked me a few times to sing to him. He didn't really seem to care for music that much. I never felt that he enjoyed hearing me sing, so I stopped years ago. I haven't sung publicly in 18 to 20 years. It's not that he criticized me, but I just didn't feel I appreciated my singing... that it made him nervous when I got up to sing at church. I had kind of gotten burned out on it too, so I just stopped. He had asked me twice to sing to him. And I just blew it off and said, "Ok, maybe later," and just walked out of the room just because I didn't want to. When I came back in to the room, we had some music playing on TV, and he said to me again, "Are you going to sing to me?" And sort of confused, I said, "Ok." Mike said from his hospice bed, "Well, something is missing here." He was pointing to a space on the side of the bed. I said, "What's missing, Honey?" I thought he'd misplaced his tape player. He said, "You." I said, "You want me to lie down there?" He said, "Yeah." It was amazing. That song that was playing on the TV, I knew exactly every word. *Can't Help Falling In Love With You.* I lay down beside him and sang every word to him. **[crying]** I think more than wanting to hear me sing, he wanted closeness to me at that moment, and probably knew my insecurities about my musical abilities and wanted to heal past hurts.

[Excerpt from Jackie's personal journal: *December 14, 2012 - Mike can't sleep even after several meds. I'm standing beside his bed THINKING about how he had asked me to get into bed beside him the other night. As I was THINKING that he said, "We could try it." "Try what?" I asked. "You lying beside me," he answered. I read later, after Mike had left this home for his final home in heaven, about a little girl who had gone to Heaven and had come back to earth. Her mother was asking her questions about her experience. "Do they talk to each other like we do?" The little girl answered, "They can, but it's easier to talk with your mind."] I was thinking, "I will never have this moment again - even in eternity since there is no marriage in heaven. As I was thinking that he asked, "Is the camera there?" "Take a few pictures of us." So sweet! A moment I will treasure forever!]*

What kind of daily care did Mike need from you?

Just various needs like giving him meds. At first, he'd yell if he needed something, but his voice got weaker, and I gave him a little bell. I truly began to realize why the Lord wanted us in this new house, because the accommodations were perfect for me to be close to him at night. I prayed a lot that I'd be aware and able to hear him when he needed something. I felt many times that the Lord woke me up in the middle of the night because Mike was awake and he needed something. Towards the end, all he could eat was popsicles and ice cream. I'd feed him those things to help his meds go down easier.

There were some basic bodily needs that I handled for him. We had a huge blessing when Aziz, a male nurse who was also Muslim, started helping us. What a wonderful man! He'd come to the door and say, "I need to see my pastor."

He'd go into Mike's room, and Mike would pray with him every morning. I've had coffee with Aziz several times since then. He and Mike really connected. They loved each other. So Aziz was there most nights since I got so tired after a couple of months of caretaking with all the people in the house.

Generally, what was Mike's response to your caretaking?

Oh, he was wonderful—so sweet and appreciative for everything going on around him! He didn't hesitate to ask for anything, because he knew I was there for him, as he had always been there for me too. He'd call when he needed me. His voice was strong, and he knew I'd come. I tried to keep him comfortable. His response to all that was pretty much as it had always been. Always courteous and kind... very thankful!

How much of that overall burden did you shoulder by yourself? For how long?

I'm not sure I saw it as a burden. I saw it more as me having limited time with him. I was getting to be with him. It wasn't a burden to me. I had two days off during that 2 and ½ months. People were in and out, taking care of him, and I just needed to get away for a little while. I would drive through and get a Blizzard ice cream, find a cul-de-sac, park the car, and just look over that open field. My friends (Doralyn Dyson and Ginger Burlison) insisted I get out of the house, and it was good for me. When you've got limited time, you don't really want to waste time. You want to be around.

Scott was also there a lot at night. I remember one evening staying up all night in the den with Scott because Mike was constantly calling us. We were taking turns checking on him. Nights could get intense, but usually either Scott or Aziz was there to help. It was much harder on the front side, because Mike was trying to maintain control of his body, control his life, and he was calling all the time for something. That was his way... his personality. But the end was much easier than the beginning.

How well do you think you did under that stress?

I think I was doing amazingly well, because I knew that God was giving me the strength. I knew it was superhuman from the very beginning. From the minute I heard the diagnosis until the end, I don't remember crying privately about any of it. I watched other people cry, and I still haven't really cried a whole lot about it. Something might hit me, and I may shed tears. I miss him at night, but for the most part God has given me amazing strength and peace.

Early on there were so many questions, and the little questions would really get to me... especially about food. "What do you guys want to eat?" Nobody was eating around here. Mike wasn't eating, I wasn't eating, and inside I was thinking: Just throw a loaf of bread on the porch and leave us alone. Of course, that's how people minister and want to help, and I knew that, but I was also done with all the questions about food. I was spending all day answering questions about so many different things. It would get so intense that I moved a bench into my closet, and would put my head in my hands and just pray. Then I'd get up and go back out and deal with all the people. That's how I saw my role. As long as Mike was being taken care of, I was free to minister to the people coming in. Everyone was hurting so much.

The way you get past your own grief is by ministering to others. It's trite and very classic, but it's also very true. It's hard to feel for yourself when you feel for someone else. It's amazing.

Sounds like you had a massive extended family to tend to. You couldn't just focus on your family?

No! We could have, but that would have been selfish. I guess that's a value of our family in that we've never wanted to be selfish. That's a decision that everyone has to make. Sometimes you have to set boundaries for self-preservation. But if you can just be open and let God direct, things will work out.

Where did you find your strength and courage?

In the Lord! Yes. Absolutely. I don't see how people can make it through these kinds of difficult times without the Lord. He is our strength, our peace, our joy, and everything else to us. You really can have all of those things in the midst of the most severe situations.

I've been in those hard situations. A business loss, I also lost a husband, and I've had a lot of losses this past decade in a lot of different ways. There are plenty of people who have had much worse losses than myself. I've read some history books, mostly to search for answers when I was battling my own depression. I would read about the people who went through the Holocaust, wondering how those people coped with depression and adversity. I went to the worse case scenarios looking for clues on how they did it. I was always amazed at how people found their strength. As Christians, we absolutely find our strength in the Lord, and it grows with each new adversity. It's confirmed over and over that He is taking care of us.

What were your big "priorities" before you found out your spouse was sick? How were those things affected by the illness?

We had gone through several business losses during the recession, and I have moved a retail business now four times in ten years. Then I've moved houses three times during that span, and once we moved into this last house, I was immediately called to go to Tyler to take care of my grandbabies. My daughter-in-law's father had passed away in Russia. I came back from Tyler and was trying to unpack and straighten up the house at the same time. I was lying in bed one morning, and I was telling the Lord that this was not my home... I didn't like this new home. It was painted all in beige; it was new construction, and I thought: "Poor me... just get over it!" So I picked up my iPad and was looking at some news and saw where

Phillip Phillips had just recorded a new song called *Home*. I listened to the video and thought, how amazing is that? That was exactly what I needed in that moment.

One part of that song says, "Don't give no mind to the demons. They'll fill you with fear. Just know you're not alone, I'm gonna make this place your home." Is that not perfect? The whole song was perfect. What I came to realize was that it wasn't about this home I had moved into, but it was about my entire life situation, because my life had been in chaos for the last decade.

God then said to me, "You see what that says? Get up and get going." I accessorized this home faster than any home I've ever done. I hung every picture and every flower was in place in like... four hours. Mirrors, pictures—everything hung in a very short period of time. I was amazed at how fast it was finished. The reason that God allowed all that to get done so quickly was because He knew what was coming. I've seen how God goes before us in so many amazing ways. He knew we had a whole bunch of people coming into our house... and that our house needed to feel like a home. It needed to be comfortable for everyone coming in. Also, God knew that once Mike was gone, it needed to look like a home. God loves me so much, [crying] he knows that is important to me. He knows I need a home to be pretty. Some people may not care. It's vitally important to me. I came from a life of poverty. Growing up, we moved from rent home to rent home, and they were never pretty. So Mom would sew the draperies, and I would paint. God knows us so intimately. [crying]

I was still trying to put a store back together, because I had a chance to sell one of the locations. It didn't work out, so I had to move the store again. I moved it back and forth across Main St. in July. July in Texas is brutally hot. We spent a lot of blood, sweat, and tears, not to mention all the money. I do not understand all this turmoil that we've had with the business. All I know is that it's made me stronger; it hasn't killed me; we lost a lot of money in all that—yet God is providing beautifully for me. All that to say, God is right there, no matter what you're going through. That's what was going on. I was trying to put a home together, a business together, a daughter-in-law together after she lost her dad. There was a lot going on. Mike's illness and death capped it all.

Was there a point when you knew that your caretaking days were numbered?

Oh yes, very much. It was like when I knew that the kids were going to be leaving home. I knew empty-nest syndrome was coming. We could feel a transition coming. You can usually feel that before it happens. If it's hard stuff, we usually fight it. I kept saying, it's coming, and I can't stop it. It was the same way with Mike. It's coming, and I can't stop it. I didn't have quite as much time to be as dramatic as I was with empty nest. It's amazing how one thing prepares you for the next step. Yes, I could see it marching toward me and I couldn't stop it.

How was Mike processing his decline?

Mike didn't make time for self-pity... ever... his entire life. The nurses told me early on that a person of his caliber and personality would have everyone in the house jumping as he was trying to manage the problem through his decline. They were right! One of my friends told me one day, "He can issue orders to every corner of the house!" [laughing] And he was, but we just laughed about it. He knew what was going on, but he was trying to keep control of his life by controlling everybody else. We didn't see it as a bad thing. It was what it was. This was the strength of who he was. Those strengths were paramount to all he accomplished. Early on in my marriage, I wanted a leader, but I had no idea of how strong of a leader I was getting. He had to soften some, and I had to toughen up some. Stop being so sensitive. [laughing]

Did you two ever talk about "your" future without Mike in the picture?

Not really. We were so focused on what he had going on... not so much about my future. I remember saying to him that time I was being sensitive, "Honey, I'll never marry again. I'll never love anybody like I love you." He said, "Never say never." I thought, "Well, okay." That was it. That was the only discussion we had about going forward. We didn't talk about finances; we didn't talk about any of that, to the point that it was kind of bad. I didn't really know if I had any finances or not. It was all handled with his retirement, but I didn't know about it until the bookkeeper contacted me. With these kinds of things, there wasn't a lot of talk. It was more feelings and doing. Not a lot of talking.

When did it finally sink in that your remaining time with Mike was near?

Immediately. When we got the diagnosis from Dr. Myers and I saw the tears in his eyes, I knew. That's when God told me, "We are not to grieve as those who have no hope." "Grant us courage for the facing of this hour." The hour was there! I knew it was imminent. Mike was totally good with it because he knew where he was going. We're Christians, so we believe what we believe. I tell people all the time, for his sake, I wouldn't want him back. He's already where we're all headed. So he's happy. I miss him, but I choose purposefully to not allow myself to be dragged down in self-pity. That would not help anyone in any way. And I know that neither Mike, nor God would want me to be sad. Mike had worked hard and fulfilled the mission God had for him to accomplish.

What was going on in your head and heart during the few final days with Mike?

There were many things going on all around us, but ultimately I felt covered by God's peace. Josh and Olya were struggling because they couldn't get here. His work schedule didn't allow him much freedom. I kept telling them, "Don't feel guilty. It's ok." They were able to come in the weekend that Mike died. Olya had said to me, "Mom, please go to bed. You look so tired. You have to be exhausted." I said I felt like I needed to stay with him, but, she insisted that I go to bed. "You're right there next door. I'll call you if something happens. I'll stay right here with him." His breathing was getting shallow and erratic. I had just gone to bed and she came in and said, "Mom, come quick. It's happening. Come quick." So I had to throw on my pants because Josh was coming in. By the time I got in there, he was gone.

It's interesting to me that there was a gap over behind the headboard of his hospice bed and the wall. Josh and Olya were kneeling beside him at the front side of the bed. So I had to go around behind the headboard, and I remember thinking, "Lord, this is so strange. I wasn't the one holding his hand when he died." The Lord spoke to me so clearly, "Olya needed to be the one to hold his hand. It is closure for her since she has now lost her two dads." I thought, "How beautiful is that?"

The hospice nurse had told me that sometimes your loved ones will only die when you leave the room because they don't want to hurt you by dying in front of you. And remember that Mike knew me to be super sensitive. Isn't that awesome? Josh felt so much better by getting to be there, so we all had the closure we needed. Scott and Monica, Marlena and Gisele all had their time. I had gotten mine. It was time for Josh, Olya, Evan, and Conrad to get their closure. I am so thankful that Mike got to say goodbye to all of his children and grandchildren. It meant so much to each of them that he told them he was proud of them. What a beautiful blessing on them. Priceless!

When they came to get Mike's body, Olya and I sat in my bedroom and shared some of the most beautiful thoughts together. She shared with me exactly what had happened. She said, "Mom, it was like he stayed with me for another minute or so after he stopped breathing. I could still sense that he was still here. It was like he went over to that corner over there and watched the whole thing." There were numerous comments about that corner in the room as people visited with Mike. Mike would ask if someone was standing in that corner behind the headboard. I wondered if it was an angel just watching over us. Some would think that's too strange to be real, but that's what we felt.

Looking back, how prepared were you to let him go?

I was totally prepared somehow. It wasn't that I did anything, but I do feel that God prepared me. I had two and a half months to be prepared. I was very blessed to get to have closure with Mike. Honestly, most of what I feel as grief is my own self-pity, and I don't want that, nor will I accept it.

When you see a person of Mike's strength and vitality decline and push into the point of no return, it would just be mean to keep them around to suffer.

Was there an opportunity to say "goodbye" before his final sleep?

I told him goodbye every day. I told him I loved him every day. I try to do that with my friends and family. Tomorrow is not guaranteed for any of us. We need to live giving closure.

So it's been 15 months since he passed. How are you doing?

I'm doing well. Truly, I'm doing great. I know he is happy, and he lived a very fulfilled life. He was pleased about the way he lived his life, and I too was pleased with it. Anyone who watched his life would have to say that Mike was a quality person. He did the best he knew to do. We all have our faults, but I'm good with how things turned out with Mike.

I have goals and ambitions. I'm goal oriented. I want to use my spiritual gifts of service and mercy, and I love helping people. There is still a lot for me to do.

Do you ever sense that Mike is with you?

I don't. But with some of the blessings that I've been receiving lately, I feel he's up there pulling strings for me somehow. I sense he knows what I'm going through, what we're going through—our sons and their families have faced various challenges as well—and he's trying to help. I've gone through and faced some very hard circumstances with my business. There was so much to accomplish in very little time—I've been blessed, and the challenges were overcome in superhuman time. Of course God is definitely helping me, but I can't help but wonder if Mike is assisting Him in blessing me, our family, and church family.

So do I sense him near? No, I don't. Mike and I used to go through a ritual we had at night. We'd get up in the middle of the night to go to the restroom. We called it "intermission." We'd always crawl back into bed and search for each other's hand. I'd get nestled in, and he'd cover up my hand with his big hand. I'd say, "How are you doing?" and he'd reply, "You go nite-nite." That was just the ritual. That was Mike. So for a while I had to put my hand under a heavy stack of pillows so I could sense his heavy hand on mine. I don't do it too much anymore, but for about 6-months it was necessary for me to get back to sleep. I found that I needed to remind myself repeatedly during the first days of losing him that he would never be back—I would see him again but not in this life. I knew facing this reality was a major key to my healing.

It also dawned on me one day that Mike has now met two of our children that I've never met. I had a tubal pregnancy between both of our boys. I almost died. And then I had a miscarriage after we had our youngest son. So the two children I've never seen are already with Mike. How beautiful is that? He can't be with his children and grandchildren here, but he can be with our kids there. That is a beautiful thought to me. He will one day be introducing them to me!

Most marriage vows contain the words: "For better or for worse... in sickness and in health... until death do us part." Describe what those words might have meant to Mike & Jackie.

Ah, they mean everything. It's a commitment. There are times in marriage that you want to toss that commitment. There were times I wanted to say to God, "I didn't know what I was doing. I was nineteen. I didn't know." He'd always say, "Yes, you did. You knew exactly what you were doing." **[laughing]** Of course you have your ups and downs in marriage, and there are some really bad marriages out there, but ours was not that kind of marriage. We were both very committed to the Lord, we both knew that God led us together, and that got clearer as we grew together, even though there were times I thought God had sent me to the wrong guy. But ultimately, we knew that God put us together. We made a commitment and we made it work.

From the Newlyweds:

If my spouse were just diagnosed with a terminal illness, what advice would you give me?

Focus on God, and not on yourself. Those were the instructions straight from the Lord. And it was perfect advice, because if you go introspective and analytical on yourself, you'll wring your hands and wonder how you'll ever live without that person—and you won't make it. You can't make it, because you're so steeped in yourself. Anytime your eyes are on yourself, you make it difficult for God to actually get through to you.

How did your mate's condition affect your normal intimacy patterns as a couple?

Those things stayed normal as they always were until they couldn't function anymore. Our lives stayed pretty normal. We still communicated. We still touched. Normal.

How did you handle those changes?

I just let those things progress normally and I saw them for what they were. I have a saying that cycles often in my life, "It is what it is." If it is what it is, then you deal with what it is. You don't conjecture or lament what it could be, or what it ought to be, or should be, but it is what it is. It's like Nike, "just fix it... just do it." I'm highly analytical, and that's good to a point. But after a certain point, you're just harming yourself and everyone else around you. So if you're in a triage situation, and that is what I had, you deal with what is bleeding. You don't worry about what color the bandage is that you're using. That's my practical way of looking at things and it seems to work for me.

Were you two still able to play together during your mate's decline?

You know, we had gone to Pagosa Springs together, and that was something that we loved to do twice a year. I don't know that we ever played together because our interests were so different. He golfed and fished, and I'm pretty much sedentary. We ate out and went to movies together.

I loved his dry wit. The neighbors had a Springer Spaniel that would play in the yard outside of the window where Mike's hospice bed was located. He called me into his room one day and asked me if maybe the neighbor would bring the dog in his room so he could scratch the dog behind his ears. Mike had a Springer when he was a child. I said, "Probably so, but Honey, you know the neighbor is a bit strange." Mike said, "Yeah, don't do that. That guy would probably bring that dog over here everyday." **[laughing]**

Mike had a very playful humor. He loved to scare people. He loved to scare the grandkids. One of the little boys told me one day, "Poppy really scares me." And I said, "I know. Is it really bad?" Conrad said, "No. I like it." [laughing] He was all the time jumping out at the staff... scaring them. So he had a great sense of humor.

It was one of the things that so attracted me to Mike. Later, I saw he did have that side I hadn't seen at first. It was a part of why I fell in love with him. He was real, accessible, and genuine. What most men tell me about Mike is that he was a man's man, yet authentic and non-judgmental. He wasn't put off by people's vices or weaknesses—whether it was drinking or swearing. He just loved people where they were. I'm very much that way myself, so that was an easy connection.

What was the dominant emotion during your season of caretaking with your mate—as compared to your emotional state now?

Probably just alertness. I had to stay alert to his needs. Alert to people's needs around me. I was on call. Standing to serve.

What's the one piece of advice you'd give someone just starting out in marriage?

You know, that's a big subject. When I was having all my bridal showers, the ladies would tell me that I had to let him know who the boss was right off the bat. Just starting off, how was I supposed to know how to handle all of that? How do you let a Mike Toby know that you are going to be the boss? [laughing] You might try to be the boss, but that isn't happening. Pray a whole bunch. Pray, pray, and pray some more. It's a cop out answer right? [laughing] But it's true.

What's the best thing a husband and wife can do for each other every day?

Don't tell each other what to do! That's in general, not just marriage, but marriage too. If you feel that you've married a capable person, then there is no need to be a controller. It's an insult to those who are not controllers to have to deal with those kinds of attitudes and actions. It's really more in the "how you said it," the tone, that a thought is expressed. You can make suggestions with tact.

Be courteous and respectful. That's it. It goes so far and "love covers a multitude of sins." In that love is kindness, consideration, and courtesy. Courtesy is a big "C." The other big C's: Communication & Compromise.

What one piece of advice would you give to a newly engaged couple?

Look at the family that you're considering marrying into, because you don't realize what's coming your way. I've seen this happen several times. Thankfully

I had a beautiful family that was coming my way. I had a mother-in-law that I loved dearly, and my father-in-law was a character, but he was so sweet to me. Ask, "What are the real family dynamics here?" That person you are going to marry came out of those dynamics. It plays a massive role in who your mate has really become. Get to know that family. Family complications can spill into your marriage. It's not just their parents either. It can also be a sister a brother... whoever. It can be a really big deal.

What are your most important memories of your marriage?

I think of how important it was for Mike and me to have similar values and love for the Lord. We had a desire to please each other and please the Lord. Our reputations were important to us. We both wanted to be the best we could be... so yes, values in those terms. We both had a strong work ethic and goals we wanted to accomplish. We took vacations. Mike and I travelled extensively to do mission work. We were usually so involved with everyone else, we were hardly together, but we went and did those things as a couple. But the sweetest are just simple times—quiet and alone together.

Knowing all that you know now, what would you have done differently in your marriage?

I wouldn't have been as sensitive. [laughing] I wouldn't have gotten my feelings hurt as easily. I was extremely sensitive, but I was also 19 years old and a baby. I would have communicated my needs more maturely, instead of doing what most young women do—we use our emotions wrong in trying to communicate with our husbands. I think you have to be more factual inwardly and confident about your needs. I would have said, "Honey, I don't really want to do that... and here is why." I'd be straight and more to the point—more factual. I think men would have much more understanding with all that because they don't know what to do with all those emotions.

I had a friend who tried to tell me that for a lot of years, and I just didn't get it. I felt that if I really told Mike what I thought, he'd get mad. Women would get a better response from their men if they'd communicate more clearly on the front side. Don't nag, don't manipulate, and don't cry for effect. Just be courteous, respectful, and resolved in your desires.

Never underestimate the power of prayer. If the "rock" (your spouse) doesn't "get it," go to "The Rock." God has a way of bringing light to your issues— both you and your partner. You may even discover "at times" your hard-headed partner may even be right!

What did you learn about your spouse that caused you to love him even more?

I learned what I'm about to tell you in the very end days. Mike was actually more insecure than I ever realized. He had a lot of bravado that covered his insecurities, and I believe a lot of men do the same because their wives and family look to them for strength. So when their strength declines and they don't feel strong, they've got to put up a sense of confidence and bravado that they may not actually have. Looking back now, I think some of the problems we had were due to some of his insecurities that I never saw. That's why we need to ask God for more enlightenment in terms of who our spouse really is. What we see at first may not be who they really are.

I used to read a lot of psychology books because I was trying to deal with my own depression. Most of those books were clear to emphasize that when a person is telling you their problem, it's rarely the real problem. You have to dig through the various layers to get to the real problem. Problems are like an onion—many layers. You have to peel those onions to get to the core. We have to remind ourselves that everyone has problems going on.

Do you still think that marriage is a great idea?

Absolutely! God thought it was a great idea... so I guess I should. [laughing] And I really do believe it because it gives to you your other half... another person to bless, and to be blessed in return.

I'm very analytical, but early on after Mike died, I kept saying, "I'm here, but I'm not here." I couldn't understand why I was feeling that way. I ran into a friend one day at Wal-Mart and I told her that exact thing: "I'm here, but I'm not here." She said, "Jackie, it's totally understandable. You've lost a major piece from you life." And I thought how true it was what she said. I had lost my other half. When you lose your other half, you feel lost. I felt like I had never known him. Even looking at pictures of us as a couple, it feels like he never existed. And if you do get it into your head that he did exist, you're convinced he's been gone forever. That is how I feel right now. Like I never knew him, we were never together—he never existed. It's strange... very strange. I know he did. I have the memories, but it's what you feel. It's the weirdest thing. I feel lost in time. It puzzles me.

When you lose a spouse, you lose a major identity. Even though you may feel that you're very independent, and that's how we operated, I still feel that a major part of me is missing and I'm trapped somewhere in eternity. It totally changes your life perspectives. Not completely... but it does change you.

Any final words of advice for married couples of all ages?

Two words: Courtesy and Respect. So much of those two things are not happening in marriages. Give people a chance to grow. So you've been married 30 or 40 years—people are still growing through the various transitions of their lives. Whether you're with them every day or not, allow them to grow up. Allow them to change. Pray for change in them, and for yourself. And until they change, ask God to help you accept them for who they are—an evolving work in God's hands. I think it's a good way to look at life in general.

In Memory of
D. Michael Toby
February 18, 1947 - December 29, 2012

John

Introduction

It's hard to hear the name without your imagination jumping off course a bit. John Rambo spawns images of the 1980's Sylvester Stallone movie character grunting and slashing through the jungle. He's sweaty, conflicted, torn apart by war, and bent on revenge. Maybe your imagination could be lead astray, but don't go there. When you meet our John Rambeau, about the only similarity is that he too is intimately acquainted with the delicate veneer that separates life from death. Our guy is actually Pastor John Corwin Rambeau III. Although Pastor John is a different kind of warrior, make no mistake; he is a true warrior and a real man of God.

Being called a pastor these days can mean many different things. Rarely does the title reflect the true heart of a shepherd who really loves and cares for his people. Marketing slicksters, cultural appeal, and trendy whims leave many churches staffed with personnel, but without the true call and gifting of what a pastor is truly supposed to be. John Rambeau is graced with such a gift. Talk to anyone who knows him and they'll confirm what I'm saying in a heartbeat.

The courage on display in this interview is remarkable. John's story of growing in love with Anna Rambeau is quite amazing. Raising four kids together, being madly in love, and serving God in the ministry should be enough to grant the protection from the evils of this world. Wouldn't you think? The remarkable thing about life is that there are no guarantees about much of anything. Sometimes weeds just grow in the garden. Breast cancer is such a weed.

John agreed to share his intimate story. We got that and more. We also got his heart. He talked honestly about the woman who helped alter his life. Twenty years with one woman is a significant accomplishment, but for John and his kids, it wasn't near enough. The clock of time has continued to tick, life has moved on, and change has come, but Anna's impact will always be felt by the people who loved her the most.

As he and I sat in my man cave, there may have been cigars, and there might have been a bottle of wine, yet Pastor John led me into the wondrous memory of his days in the shadow with his girl. I am so grateful for that honor and privilege.

What a beautiful woman. What an amazing man. What an incredible family. Patti and I could not be more proud of them all. Thank you for taking the time to meet a dear soul with a true and brave heart: John Rambeau. –MDP-

Tell us about how you two met and fell in love?

After graduating from Baylor in 1987, I moved to Austin to start a job in banking. I was looking for a home church and was invited to visit Redeemed Christian Fellowship. I loved the church and started attending. It was there that Anna and I met. I had been attending Redeemed for a while, and I saw her in the church one day. She was standing at a distance away from me, but I could tell she had a small child on her hip.

She was on her way out of church one Sunday morning with her son Tyler on her hip, and I caught up with them and asked her out to lunch. I later discovered that Anna had gotten pregnant by her high school sweetheart while she was at the University of Texas. She was pressured to terminate the pregnancy, but after recently becoming a Christian was convicted to have the baby. As a result, their relationship ended, and with no support from her family at the time, she had to quit school. She started running a daycare out of an old home in Austin to make ends meet and save the money needed to pay doctor bills in preparation for Tyler's eventually arrival.

After that first lunch date, I found myself visiting she and Tyler every evening after I got off work. As crazy as it may sound, on our second or third date, I told her that she was the one I was going to marry. I realized we had just met, but I knew the Lord was prompting me that Anna was the one.

We were together every day for a couple of weeks, but I started to get cold feet. I had a previously scheduled trip overseas where I was going to be gone for two weeks, and during that time I started getting nervous about the idea of a marriage commitment. Anna had a distinct feeling I'd give her the "let's just be friends talk" when I returned.

Sure enough, when I got back, I went to her and told her that I just thought we should maintain a friendship. I was getting nervous about the idea. Everything I owned could fit in my car, but she had a home with furniture, a child, and I'm debating the whole idea of no longer being a bachelor. So we decided to just be friends and take the pressure off. Naturally we saw each other at church, but we basically avoided each other for an entire year.

So a whole year goes by, and one day I'm driving around and feel the Lord telling me that I needed to address this issue again with Anna. I just felt God was saying, "What's up with Anna?" Like he didn't know. **[laughing]** I knew he meant that I needed to resolve something there. So I drove over to my small group leader's home and asked he and his wife to pray with me about this issue with Anna. So we began to pray together. I prayed first, asking the Lord for some guidance and direction about what to do. Then my buddy and his wife prayed, and I definitely felt I heard the Lord say, "You will marry Anna." Clear as could be. I was so stunned that I had heard God. It really shocked me. I asked Dan, "Did you hear or sense anything while you were praying?" He said, "Yes, I did. I felt the Lord told me that he had given you the answer." So, now I'm freaking out. I've got God telling me that I'm going to marry someone that I really don't know, and another word confirming that what I had heard was my answer. So I left there and drove to the church to talk to my pastor. I told him what had happened and asked him, "What am I supposed to do with all that?" He said, "How about ask her out on a date, dummy?" **[chuckle]**

So I called her. She said she already had plans. So I said what all clue-less men say, "Cancel them," which she didn't appreciate. But as she told it, Anna had gone an entire year feeling that the Lord had said that I was the one for her too. Those two weeks we had together confirmed that. She never told me that. She had shared it with a few others in the church, but the counsel was always the same: If it's meant to be, God will talk to John about it, and he'll come back and begin to pursue. After a year of waiting, she was about done. Basically, she had resolved that she'd be fine as a single mother, she could raise Tyler alone, and it wasn't going to be a big deal either way.

One Sunday, a speaker came into the church and challenged the people about the things they felt God had promised to them. We were asked to sow a seed in faith for the remembrance of the things that God has promised. Anna took everything she had in the bank—I think it was $100—brought that as her offering, as a reminder to the Lord that he had made a promise to her concerning she and I getting married. About the same time, I'm getting in touch with this fresh word from the Lord about marrying Anna. So I start calling around trying to find her. I find her at a friend's house, go inside to where she is, and I begin to cry. I'm repenting, apologizing, and asking for her forgiveness. I said the words, "I know we're supposed to be married. I know you are the one." Anna starts crying. "God told me that you're the one." So I asked her how long she needed to plan a wedding. We were married 5 months later.

Honestly, we got married first, and then fell in love afterwards. I guess that's a little bit unusual, **[laughing]** but we got married and then fell in love. You can't make up a story like that. **[laughing]** She later joked with our children about how she got me for a hundred bucks!

So it wasn't love at first sight... kind of a crazy process?

Very crazy. I was attracted to Anna when I first saw her because she had so much life on her. She had a big love for God and people. She was beautiful inside and out. But I hardly felt I knew her until after we committed to get married. We both felt we had a word from God on it. We trusted that and had 20 wonderful years of marriage together.

When were you married? Where?

We had our wedding there in Austin at Redeemed Christian Fellowship, where we met. It was a huge wedding. In fact, it was one of the first weddings that involved a young couple from the church. What a blast, what a great memory. We had an awesome reception at the Austin Country Club. That was January 6, 1990.

How long were you and Anna married?

Just short of 20 years. She died right before our 20th anniversary.

What was the first year of your marriage like?

It was a bit crazy for me. Instant father and instant husband all at once was a bit nuts. We were having a blast doing ministry together, doing a lot of things at the church we were involved with, attending Bible School together—it was a lot of fun. We had a high level of excitement in our journey. We tried to get pregnant right away. After 5 months of pregnancy, we lost our first child, which was a little girl. We had named her Katy. That was a gut wrenching and painful thing for us. Eventually the pain from that subsided, and other than that, we were having the time of our lives during the first year! We were falling in love with each other. It was a definite honeymoon season for us—in every sense of the word.

How long did it take to figure out how to communicate?

Anna and I were both pretty good communicators. We did have some pre-marital counseling, but to some extent, we had a level of openness and honesty with each other that invited honest and frank conversations about the things that were bothering us. We didn't want to find out a month later that we were holding out on each other. We had made an agreement about that and felt that it was always important to share feelings and frustrations before they escalated or lead to unnecessary speculation about things.

How differently were you both raised?

I was a city boy, and Anna was a small town country girl. I came from a family that was very well off. I had the benefit of someone taking care of my college and graduate school expenses, where Anna had to take care of all those things herself. She was responsible for making her own way. In that sense, we came from different spectrums, but it was our spiritual commitment that linked us together. That was a singular path that we were both traveling on. We were both positive people and thrilled about life. We both always had a "glass half-full" outlook on life.

And even though our backgrounds were different, we loved the same things. Being outdoors, cooking, hanging with the kids, and doing stuff with our church were easy for us when we were together. We had very similar personalities. We fell in love easily because we had so many things that we similarly loved together. It wasn't the deal of opposites attract. We easily flowed together.

Early on, what were some of your toughest challenges as a couple?

Honestly, not many challenges. However, I will say that the transitional period of going from one child to four children was wild. We wanted to have a big family. Anna was one of four kids, and I was one of five kids. And let me tell you, life does get very interesting when you've got two boys and two girls, all at very close ages. Tyler was 5 years old when our first was born, but the rest came every couple of years. So there were definite challenges we had to face while raising kids. Overall I would say we had a normal marriage through all of that, but for the most part we experienced the same frustrations couples have trying to juggle family time and work, along with all the extracurricular activities of four kids.

I think one of the things that actually helped our marriage is that we were counseling a lot of couples at the church. We met with a lot of people who were facing hard issues. As a result, we learned a lot during that time, just by hearing other people's stories. We spent many hours doing counseling, and then we'd go home and thank God for our own healthy marriage. We were also growing and reading books together on how to help people. Guess we were helping ourselves in the process. In addition, we would frequently attend marriage retreats and seminars. It was a great investment for us—a good dose of preventive medicine.

I remember one of our first counseling sessions with a couple. I took the guy and went one way. Anna took the woman and went an opposite direction. After talking with the man, I was convinced that his wife needed to be shot and put out of her misery. After Anna heard the woman's side of the story, she was convinced that the husband needed to be locked up in prison. **[laughing]** That's when we realized we were each only hearing one side of the story. After that, we made the couples counsel in a room together with us both at the same time.

As a result, we drew some conclusions about marriage: It was always too soon to quit. You stay at the table. You talk it out. You don't run alone... team is better. And we stayed accountable to our pastors. We were frequently asked questions about how our marriage was going. It wasn't forced on us, but we chose to avail ourselves to the older and more experienced couples around us. That was very helpful to us.

Usually at the beginning of each year, we'd get together and share our dreams and goals for the next year. We'd write those out and pray for God's help fulfilling each other's desires. After a couple months, we'd pull those lists out to see if we were making any progress on those things. Sometimes we did, and sometimes we didn't, but we knew it was important to have a target out there. Both of us believed it was best to fire away at something.

What were your shared goals and ambitions?

Our daily declaration was, "God, cause us to fall more in love with you and more in love with each other." So first and foremost, we wanted a growing passion for God, and then for each other. In addition, we wanted to raise our children to hear God for themselves. We didn't want to control everything for them. As parents, our goal was to uncover their unique personalities and gifts, and then help facilitate their passions and desires. But most of all, we wanted them to be free to pursue the dreams in their hearts.

We also had similar desires to serve the Lord and the ministry. In 1992, we were both ordained through our church. I resigned from my position at the bank, and we accepted a ministry assignment in the Cayman Islands.

That sounds horrible John! [laughing]

There's nothing like suffering for the Lord! [smiling] It was the beginning of an incredible adventure in full-time ministry.

So as the marriage began to develop and mature, what did "normal" look like for John & Anna's relationship?

We had a real goal to raise the kids together. We agreed that Anna would be a stay at home mom. Whatever the kids were doing, Anna was there…a lot of sports and school activities. It seemed they did everything under the sun. Soccer, tennis, golf, and football, track—you name it. We shared responsibility in getting the kids to school. I'd head to the church office, and she would do whatever was needed around the house or town. We might meet for lunch 3 or 4 days a week while the kids were in school. And of course, we were always trying to figure out who was going to pick up a kid or take someone somewhere.

In general, the Rambeaus aren't morning people, so we tend to stay up late. We'd get the kids down for the night and we'd watch a movie, or just chill. We might read a book together and have discussions about that. If we had devotional time together, it was usually an evening activity.

How were you growing as a couple with all that stuff going on?

We were investing in the marriage. We'd read several different marriage enrichment books over the course of each year to help give us fresh things to focus on so we could grow our marriage. Life seemed like it was flying by with church, kids, crazy schedules, and life in general. We were still doing a lot of ministry together as a couple, and that helped sharpen the two of us.

What have you learned the most in your life that Anna taught you?

Compassion. We were both gracious people. In fact, her name meant, "God is gracious." Anna was a fighter. She'd never quit. She would do anything for anybody. Like most women, she would defend her kids, or me, to whatever measure was necessary. She was so passionate about life. Anna was the most tenacious fighter I have ever known. Her faith in God never wavered, and she never had a negative outlook in the midst of her battle. Like I said, she never quit, and would never give up when she had set her mind to something.

What do you think you taught her the most?

Hmmmm... I have no idea. Possibly it was to love every single moment of life. I am an encourager, and Anna was a mercy person. So if people had a problem, Anna could just jump right down in their mud puddle with them. She had this amazing ability to feel other's pain and love them right where they were. My strength was helping people get out of that pit. So we teamed up nicely. I think she'd say I taught her in that regard.

When did Anna's medical complications begin to surface?

In November 2006, she found a lump in her breast. So we had it checked out, and they did the biopsy on it. The surgeon was adamant that she needed a mastectomy a.s.a.p. She wanted to check the lymph nodes, and she was fairly certain it was cancer even before we got the test results back. The doctor went on to talk about the expense involved, right up front. That floored us—really rattled us big time. We knew we were called to live life together. There were so many things we had yet to accomplish together. There were kids to raise, weddings to do, and people at the church who needed attention and our love. In an instant we were rocked to the core. It felt very weird to think that we had to deal with this. This is the stuff that happens to other people... not us. It started in November of 2006, and Anna passed away in August of 2009.

Was there a progression to the illness?

Right after we got the diagnosis, I called my dad, who is a doctor in Houston, to see if he had any suggestions on where we needed to get the care. Did we need to go to M.D. Anderson? Within a couple days, Anna announced that she didn't want anyone changing their routines—her included. She would get up and make breakfast every morning until the last couple days. If she could drive the car, she would be driving to get the kids. She was determined to keep things on schedule. So for now, that meant that Houston was out of the question. Anna reasoned, my kids are here, you are here, so I'm getting what I need from here. And that was the underlying agreement we made. Obviously, we had no idea how things were going to turn out. We were feeling confident and thought: we can beat this thing.

Like the doctor suspected, the biopsy came back positive. That meant a radical mastectomy right away, chemo, and radiation (which we decided not to do). In addition, she was doing nutritional therapy. Our goal was to put as much good stuff into her as possible to combat the chemo. Now, keep in mind that Anna's mom died of breast cancer at nearly the same age. Anna was the youngest of her siblings, probably 10 or 11 years old when she lost her mom. With that thought in the back of her mind, Anna didn't want our youngest daughter Rachel, who looks most like Anna, to go through the same loss. [emotion pause] Her mom's cancer was extremely aggressive like Anna's. So we were fighting some horrible emotions in that process.

At each juncture where we had to make a decision about her treatment, we would come together and pray and then wait a day or so. Once we both had a peace about what direction to go, we would move on that. We'd then relay our decision to the doctor about treatment. I am really glad we did that. We didn't just robotically respond to the doctor's every thought for care. I'm thankful that we processed things that way.

In November 2006, she had the biopsy, in December, she had the mastectomy, and in January 2007, she started chemo. She did several rounds of 21 days of chemo. They did a biopsy of the lymph nodes to see if the cancer had spread. A large number of lymph nodes tested positive, but all other numbers looked good, so they declared that she was in remission the following year.

We felt we had won the battle. We were all excited that life would basically return to normal. That changed in November of 2008. Just prior to our annual family trip to Boerne, TX for Thanksgiving, Anna mentioned to me that she noticed a small lump in the area where the breast had been removed. I told her we would have it checked the next Monday when we got back. The doctor quickly confirmed it wasn't good news. He insisted we needed more chemo. When Anna had gotten her first round of chemo back in 2007, she got pneumonia and it nearly killed her. It wiped out her immune system. It was crazy to think we almost lost her in the first month of treatment.

While in the hospital for the pneumonia, Anna was reading a little book on healing by Dodie Osteen. Dodie had gotten healed of cancer. Somehow, a friend who had a friend, contacted Dodie, and Dodie called Anna to pray for her. Anna could barely talk she was so sick, but that really encouraged her. After Anna got past all of that, she wasn't sure she'd ever want to go through chemo again. So when the cancer showed up again, Anna was reluctant to do anything about it, and honestly I was too. We trusted the Lord, and we were praying, but I also wanted us to take advantage of everything we had with medicine in order to fight the cancer. She told me that she wanted to talk to

Dodie's daughter, April. She too was a pastor's wife. So I packed her up, and we went to Dallas in order to see April.

April told Anna about her mom's journey with cancer. Many good things came out of that conversation, but we found out that Dodie didn't do any treatment, no chemo—nothing. April looked at Anna and said, "My mom would have done anything possible in order to stay alive for her children. But the doctors didn't have anything they could do for her. If they would have suggested anything, my mom would have done it." That really helped us face the next big decision.

So Anna signed up for another round of chemo. Well, it wiped her out again. She got chemo-toxicity. Her liver couldn't flush out the chemo quick enough. She was in the hospital for over a month. Meanwhile, Tyler was about to graduate from the University of Hawaii. Anna told the doctor, "I'm going to that graduation." He said, "I can't let you out of this hospital." We had been there for a month, and she was starting to feel better, but she couldn't walk, and she was still on oxygen. Guess who won? [laughing] After getting special approval from the airline, we carried oxygen tanks, along with Anna onto the airplane. Went to Hawaii. We pushed her around in a wheelchair, but she was there to see Tyler graduate. She considered it a great victory.

Once we got back, we discovered that she was unable to flush the oral chemo out of her system that she was taking as we traveled. So she spent another 40 days in the hospital. By that time, Hilary was graduating from High School. To no surprise of anyone, Anna informed us that she was going to that graduation as well. The doctor thought it was a horrible idea. In fact, he said there was no way he could discharge her. I convinced him to give her a day. "I promised to bring her back in." So he relented, and I wheeled her out of that hospital. At that point, Anna looked nothing like herself because of all the fluid that had built up in her body, but she didn't complain a single time—always a smile on her face. So she made another graduation. She considered it another victory.

Once we got her back home, her condition worsened. The doctors in Waco were recommending another round of chemo, so at that point I felt we needed another opinion. We met with a specialist from Baylor in Houston who tried some experimental remedies. No success. So it was at that point that we decided to go for a week to M.D. Anderson for a battery of tests. It was then, about 4 months before she died, that the doctors at M.D. Anderson plainly said, "Any more chemo will kill you." Anna was like, "Praise God! No more doctors, and no more chemo." So we went home. She was thrilled. Privately, one of the doctors told me that she was amazed Anna was even alive and made it to Houston for all those tests.

During the last four months, we spent every day together. She maintained her routines. I started doing all of my church work from home, and she was happy. She was so glad to be done with all the needles and chemo, and Anna was starting to feel pretty good too. So at that point, the quality of life was actually much better.

We found out later that the cancer had spread to her brain and lungs, so the inevitable was progressing. I eventually called in hospice for what she needed. Anna would say, "You can talk to those people. I don't want to talk to them." After my first meeting with them, she said, "I don't like those people." She was being humorous, but serious at the same time. [laughing] Anna refused to have a conversation about the "ifs" and "when" of death. She gave me no indication of what her desires were in the event we didn't beat this. Even with the kids, she was insistent with, "I'm no good to God if I'm 6 feet-under." Our oldest, Tyler, went on to write a book entitled, "God from the Grave," in response to that comment. But she always felt she needed to be here on earth with her family, so we never talked about those possibilities. Even the times when I'd lose my composure and cry my eyes out, she would say, "John, it's going to be ok." And it was the same thing with the kids. Because she said "I'll be fine," they were convinced that God would heal her.

About a month before she passed, all the kids were home at one time. I pulled them into a room and said, "Short of a miracle, your mom isn't going to make it." They were absolutely shocked. I knew the score if God didn't do something quick. They cried, I cried, we all cried. I'm glad I did that, because it helped them prepare for the possibility. I knew they had a journey they were going to have to make themselves.

On the last day before she died, it was the first time that Anna said, "You know... I think I'm going to stay in bed today." [crying] I knew we had a shift. I brought food to her throughout the day, but she wasn't hungry and didn't want to eat. That evening, as the sun was setting and I was outside for a chore, I felt I heard the Lord say, "The sun is setting on her life." I got on the phone and called all the family and told them that they needed to come. They all made it in that evening.

Christian (our third child) was making his way home from an overseas trip, so he had been out of town for a little over a week. His plane was landing in Houston around 8:00 p.m. I told my sister, who lives there, to pick him up from the airport and get him home right away. He didn't get in until midnight. He hugged me and went straight to our bedroom, knelt by the bed, said some things to her, and when I entered the room, he had just laid his head down on her chest. [crying] I asked him if he was ok. He looked up and said to Anna, "Mom, did you hear what I said?" Anna reached over and put her hand on his head to confirm she did. He left the room, and I made sure that everyone had gone to bed.

I was pretty weary of the whole journey. [crying] There is a grace that comes to care for a loved one, but once its over, you begin to realize what it took out of you to stand in that role. Keeping the kids on their task, helping Anna, and praying to the Lord for a miracle—it was exhausting. I could not have done it without the support of my kids, family, and church friends.

Between 1:00 to 2:00 a.m., I'm laying next to her. I was listening to her breath and was thinking that her breathing seemed fairly normal. I had counted 18-20 breaths per minute. That's pretty good. So I started praying as I lay next to her: "Lord, thank you for every moment. Thank you for family and friends who have gathered with us. Lord, we need a miracle. If we're not going to get that from you, then take Anna home." I don't remember exactly how I said it, but it was to that effect. "If we're not getting a miracle from you, then take her on home." I was holding her hand and praying just loud enough for Anna to hear. The lights were out, and when I stopped praying, I realized that I couldn't hear her breathing anymore. So I got out of the bed, went to the other side to flip the lights on, and I said, "Baby," and she took a breath. I said again, "Baby, I love you, and I release you to go home to be with Him." She took one more breath and that was it.

So naturally I'm crying. It was 2:00 a.m. in the morning. The kids are all home, and we've got friends outside of the house praying for Anna. So I step outside and find about 30 people on our lawn praying. I said to them, "It's all good. Anna's home with the Lord." Some mingled for a while, we had other family members staying at neighbor's homes, which we got up, and they came to the house. The kids were up by now, so no one got any sleep that night.

It seemed so surreal—sort of foggy and an emotional blur. My oldest daughter Hilary was celebrating—thanking God that her mom was finally free from the disease that had wrecked her body with cancer and pain. But that wasn't what everyone else was feeling. As much as her response was right on, we all had our own unique response to the loss of someone we deeply loved.

Instantly, you are thrust into a world of making funeral arrangements and all that stuff. We hadn't made a single plan. We didn't have a plot. Didn't have any kind of arrangement whatsoever. So now we're making decisions about things we were not prepared for. Walking through a fog of the unfamiliar. How do people do this stuff when they lose someone they love?

In the days that followed, I'd have these dreams where Anna would show up. She'd be well and healthy. I'd be so excited that I'd want to tell everyone that she was healed and doing so good! Then I'd wake up, only to find out that reality was the nightmare. I continued to have the dreams, but somehow started realizing during the dream that it was just a dream. It's crazy, but you so desperately want to make a connection with the one you lost.

I had been a pastor for 20 years, and I was still questioning, "Where is she really?" and "Why?" I was thinking, "If anyone deserved to live, it was Anna." She was an amazing woman of prayer—a fighter for everyone who needed a defender. Anna was tenacious. She cared for others more than herself. I remember telling God one day, "Anna deserved to live," and I felt He said, "No John, she deserved to be with me."

I was studying in the book of Hebrews from the New Testament one day, and a parenthetical phrase about martyrs leapt off the page, which said, "Men of whom this world is not worthy." I felt strongly that was a truth about Anna. It was like God was telling me, "This world wasn't worthy of Anna." When you're trying to resolve the loss of someone, you're looking for anything to help you make sense of it. We think we're owed answers. Job tried that with God, and God said, "Where were you when I put the stars in the heavens? Where were you when I commanded the sun to rise?" [laughing]

Anna and I had been through some loss early on in our life together, so we had pretty much decided that all was gift anyway. Honestly, scripture didn't really make me feel any better. Things people said to me didn't really help. There aren't many words that really help people suffering with grief and loss. I was shocked. I was a pastor, but it's the truth. People do mean well, and I'd hear, "Be thankful for the years you had," but that message sucks. They do mean well, but you want to say, "Screw you," but you don't. There are no words that seem to help. Mow the grass, leave some food, let someone know you are there for them, but it's probably better not to say a whole lot.

How did she handle her complications emotionally?

Anna's posture the entire time was positive. I suppose that towards the end, as she looked at her own physical complications, there might have been questions, but she didn't voice them. It was always, "God is good. We've got another new day. I love the Lord. I love the kids. I love my husband. I love life." She handled her complications emotionally with a positive outlook. She never complained. I probably would have complained constantly. Not Anna.

How did you handle her complications emotionally?

At times I found myself mad at God, mad at cancer—just mad. You just want to be mad at something because you think, "This isn't right." That wasn't Anna's reaction, but it was hard for the rest of us to watch her go through something like that.

You've touched on this some, but was there a moment of communication when you both acknowledged the seriousness of her condition to each other?

I don't think there was a moment. Each hurdle we had to cross required us to face it, confront it, and pray through it for direction. Medical decisions and financial challenges had to be discussed. Our insurance didn't cover everything, so as a result we pretty much went through our life savings on this journey. But I'd do it again, no question.

We didn't know where this thing was taking us, but we were smart enough to know that cancer is a serious foe. We were learning as we went along. But Anna was insistent that we stay positive. She thought it best for us to trust God, and with that said, she placed her life in God's hands. That was how she achieved such peace, and it was her daily mantra. I absolutely respected her thoughts on that, but it didn't really make room for me to have hard discussions with her about the possible negative outcomes of the cancer. That wasn't her mindset. So we both believed for God to move, and that was the bottom-line.

So when the doctors suggested a third round of chemo was not a great idea, she was thrilled. But what was going on in your internal processing?

We knew the score at that point. We could see that our days together were numbered unless God moved miraculously. I could see what the three years with cancer had done to her body. Her energy levels were way down. It certainly doesn't build your faith to watch someone go through that. Try as you might, the tangible evidence wasn't good. She was honestly thrilled to be done with the doctors and all the medical stuff, but I knew where this thing was going without some divine intervention.

I didn't like crying in front of her. I knew it wasn't good for her mental state. But what I was looking at with her was brutally hard. I silently started doing some calculations on what life might look like without her. Your mind and your heart battle it out in those moments.

What kind of daily care did Anna need from you?

She pretty much didn't need much of my care early on. But later, there were some challenges for her. She'd get so weak, I'd have to help bathe her, get her clothes on, and get her from room to room. Her level of exhaustion was high. But once her clothes were on, I'd get her to where she'd want to be and serve her whatever meal she wanted. I had to give her shots and meds. She was taking blood thinners for blood clots. It was difficult for her because the chemo dries everything out. Since it targets the fastest growing cells in your body—your tongue, mouth, esophagus, and the stomach get torn up by the chemo (at least that was Anna's experience). Taking pills was hard for her because of how dry she was. One night, I had to do the Heimlich maneuver on this frail little body, because her meds got stuck in her throat. We're watching a movie, and all the sudden she motions that she's in trouble. Of course, I'm freaking out.

I was thankful that I was able to be with her through all of that. Thanks to the grace of our church, I had flexibility that allowed us that kind of quality time. In spite of it all, we did have a good time together those few months. The good thing was that I was in it with her every day. Looking back, I realized there is a definite identity in being the caretaker. I had a role to play. So when Anna died, in addition to losing the love of your life, a sense of purpose was lost.

Generally, what was Anna's response to your caretaking?

She was awesome. Our favorite all-time marriage book is called, *The Five Love Languages,* by Gary Chapman. Anna's love language was "acts of service." So because I was waiting hand-n-foot on her, that communicated love to her all day long. On the other hand, my love language is words of encouragement. So she'd thank me, and we were bouncing back and forth in love most of the time. Me serving her wasn't pestering for her. Anna also knew I needed a break from time to time, so friends would come over to serve her, and I'd go play nine holes of golf. When she was in the hospital for 40 days, I'd be with her during the day and evening, and others would come in for the night shift. We never left her alone. Everything was kept on a chart so there wasn't overlapping of meds, etc.

Anna was very responsive to all of it. Not everyone can handle that when they're sick. She could, and she was always thankful. I'd probably need a little more solitude, but she was great with it.

How much of that overall burden did you shoulder by yourself? For how long?

There's no way I could have done it without the help of our church family, my family, and our friends. I had a lot of help. Family would come in and stay weeks at a time. But I'm taking care of the kids as well. During the course of three years, I would say about seventy five percent of that time, it was just Anna and I doing the deal. That's probably a fair estimate.

How well do you think you did under that stress?

I think I did pretty well, but I'd have to give credit to God's grace. You do what you have to do. Looking back, I'm not sure how I managed all of that. I credit some to my job flexibility. If I hadn't been working at home, it would have changed everything. Obviously, it would have been much more stressful. We had a rhythm that worked for us.

Where did you find your strength and courage?

Of course the Lord, but I had my moments when I wondered where he was. I had my own questions. I knew God was real. I had my own relationship with him for a long time, but he felt distant to me at times during Anna's sickness. During that two-year process and even for a couple years after Anna died, I was doing my part to seek him, but I was really wondering where he was.

Thankfully, I had an awesome support system. Friends, family, and the kids were critical for me. And I always knew the church had my back. It was amazing the hours and resources that people sacrificed to help with Anna's care. During the last 5 months, we always had food in the house, and people were praying constantly for us.

What were your big "priorities" before you found out your spouse was sick? How were those things affected by the illness?

We had three major priorities: our marriage, our kids, and the ministry. When all this happened, the ministry took a huge backseat for me. Thankfully, our church gave us a huge dose of grace. They encouraged me to go spend time with my wife. I realize that most people can't do that. And as she became sicker, even the kids became less of a priority. I started finding ways to farm them out. She didn't want their schedules altered, so if they got invites to go skiing at Spring Break or things like that, we told them to go for it. We were handling things at the house as best as we possibly could, but honestly there was more going on with the kids than one person could manage. (Rachel 13, Christian 15, Hilary 18, and Tyler 23.)

Rachel, because she was the youngest, felt that she was really short-changed in her time with her mother. I totally understand why she would feel that way. For many months after Anna's death, Rachel would say, "Tell me something about mom. Give me a memory." Because she didn't have as much information as her siblings, and I could certainly understand her longing to have memories of her mom.

You asked about how priorities change. Well, priorities that you cared about before become things that you really could care less about—and that's putting it mildly. It's a strong lesson, but much more difficult to maintain when life is going great. It may sound trite, but during those times, you realize that every day is a gift. We squander too much energy on things that do not really matter. I'm thankful for what we learned in all of that.

Was there a point when you knew that your caretaking days were numbered?

Yeah. There were a couple times in the last weeks, where we were alone together, and I'd just break down. It had nothing to do with the caretaking, but the fact that she'd been through so much. I knew we had limited time. I'd never say anything out loud, but I'd cry. Not Anna. She wouldn't cry. She was an amazing support for me as I struggled with her condition. Anna knew I was crying about a situation that I couldn't control. It was out of my hands, and I so desperately wanted to keep her alive. I was staring at the inevitability of loneliness in the near future.

As I've already mentioned, I knew what was going down, and that is why I called the kids together.

Did you two ever talk about "your" future without Anna in the picture?

No. As I said, she didn't want to have that discussion, and so I honored her wishes.

Do you regret that?

Yeah, a little bit. There are new challenges to face after your spouse's death. I still cared about carrying out her hopes and dreams for the kids, and if I would have been in her position, I would have wanted her to continue to live, remarry, and find love again. She was such a blessing to me. I would have wanted her to be that for someone else. But Anna was strong-willed. Once she made up her mind on what she was going to do, it was a done deal. She might not have remarried. Who knows?

I was having my own battles with wondering if she would have been good with me meeting someone else. Initially, I didn't want to. For two years, I could have cared less about meeting someone. People wanted to set me up, and I heard, "You don't need to be alone." I wasn't ready to be with someone, and I really wondered if I'd ever be ready for all of that. I had four kids who needed me. I had more than enough to do. Anna knew everything about me—including my screw-ups. She knew the good, the bad, and the ugly. I didn't want to have to explain all of that again. I didn't want to pour my heart and life out again in order to get to know someone. It took 20 years to get where we were. I questioned whether or not my heart would be able to take all of that again.

Somewhere in our journey, we have to make choices concerning risk. Are we going to risk again? Are we going to open ourselves to love again? For me, it took three years to settle that question. Hilary, my oldest daughter (18) called me, 'an old fart,' but I was only 45 years old. [laughing] She promptly informed me that she didn't want details, but that I had certainly more than enough "fun" with mom in those 20 years—I didn't need any more touchy-feely stuff! [laughing]

To my amazement, within two years of Anna's death, all three of the oldest kids sent me letters, texts, or emails (all independent of each other) relaying basically the same information: "We know how much you loved mom, but you've got too much to offer to stay alone. If God brings someone to you—I want you to know beforehand—I've got your back, so go for it." That really helped me, because you don't want to hurt your kids. It released me from pressure when it was time to take the next step.

What was going on in your head and heart during the few final days with Anna?

I didn't want to lose her, but I was ready for her suffering to end. Although she did maintain some level of strength until that last day, it had been a brutal journey for her. That final day, I knew we were down to hours. My heart was already grieving the loss of Anna. It was a horrible thought to consider her not being there any longer. Maybe that was selfish on my part, but that's the truth of where I was towards the end. We were all fatigued, and that was a part of it, but grieving the thought of her not being around anymore was almost unbearable. How in the world was I to function in life without her around? I didn't want to live without my best friend and soul mate.

Looking back, how prepared were you to let Anna go?

I'm not sure there is a simple answer for that. We weren't prepared to be married, but we got married anyway. We weren't prepared to have kids, but we had kids anyway. Anna was dying, and I didn't really know what to do. I was just hanging on, one day at a time. Taking the steps that needed to be taken. Life's current moves you downstream.

That first year after she died, I was in deep depression. I ate too much, and instead of a glass of wine I would have several. A doctor friend suggested anti-depressants, but I decided against that. I'd muster up enough strength to get out of bed so I could get the kids off to school. Then I'd come home, get back in bed, and lay there for hours. I'd get up in time to put some clothes on, so it would look like I had been doing something all day before the kids got home. Some days I'd wake up and immediately begin to wish the day would end quicker. I didn't like today, and maybe tomorrow will be better. I was battling a monster I couldn't see. Loneliness and depression are ruthless.

Also, as I struggled with my own emotional issues, I wondered about how helpful I could be to my kids? I will say this though: having the kids around was helpful to me because they gave me a purpose. Without them, I would have looked for someplace to run to. That's how I felt. I really wanted to run.

A month after Anna died, I went to my boss at the church and said, "I'm leaving." A couple days later, another pastor friend in town said to me, "Now John, one thing you need to avoid is making big decisions for at least a year." **[laughing]** Too late! I had left the church and was actually thrilled about it. I needed a change. It was a weird season of change, which ended up being really good for me and the people that I was pastoring. We basically birthed a new church, and it really flourished. Some days I'd get in the pulpit and tell the people, "I feel like shit today. I'll give you grace, if you'll give me grace." Or I'd start preaching and couldn't finish because I was crying. But I started processing my grief journey with the church, and I found out that many were really identifying with my process. It was helping people with their own loss. Being honest about it was helpful.

Then I decided I wanted to sell our house. I was thinking strongly about it, and one day I was given the business card of a guy who had lost his wife seven months earlier. He had been through grief counseling, so eventually I decided to call him, and we talked on the phone for over an hour. I told him that I was thinking about selling the house. His response startled me, because it was so different from mine. He mentioned that he cleaned out his house as soon as possible, because he didn't want all the reminders around. That was not where I was. I would go to Anna's closet, grab as many clothes as I could, and just smell them. **[crying]** I couldn't imagine not having her pictures and things around me. So that pretty much did away with the whole 'selling the house' idea. The kids didn't need another huge adjustment that quick, and as it turned out that house ended up being the most peaceful place for me to be. I loved being in that house, and the kids loved being there also. It was life giving. It wasn't a place of sadness or sorrow. In fact, it was a real refuge for all of us. I'm really glad I changed my mind on that one.

One of the many things I learned is that grief is like a thumbprint. The way each person navigates through is absolutely different. Yes, there are similar touch-points, such as anger and loneliness, but ultimately everyone has to do grief in their unique way. I also realized that there is not a perfect way to do it. There is no formula that works for everyone. You're desperate for answers. Your fragmented heart is a mess. It's a scary and confusing time. But it's ok to realize that there aren't always clear answers.

So it's been almost 5 years since Anna passed. How are you doing?

I can honestly say that life is wonderful today. Of course I can still tear-up when I talk about Anna, because I still love her, and I loved my life with her. And we have these amazing kids because of that love. But after her loss, I discovered that there was more life to be lived. I found out that it is possible to be just as 'in love' with someone as you were the first time. That was a big surprise! I got hammered with crazy love. When I met Sherri and fell in love, I couldn't think, I couldn't drive straight—I felt like a kid again. But it wasn't until the beginning of that third year that I was ready. Something finally clicked between God, life, and me. I finally felt I had my A-game back. Before then, I was just getting by—existing only to help the kids. I genuinely did not think I'd live through that first year without Anna. I felt pretty crappy about everything.

Close friends and relationships are good medicine, but I didn't want to be close to anyone. I preferred to isolate. It wasn't the right response. I was a pastor, and I knew better; yet I was doing the very thing I would tell others not to do. Fortunately, I had people checking on me.

And now I've remarried a beautiful, awesome, and quite incredible woman who loves me and is an amazing partner in the ministry. She has two young men; my kids love them, so there are six kids now! Sherri loves having daughters. She went to my kids right after we were married and assured them that their mom's memory would never be replaced in our home. She offered herself as either motherly advice, or as a friend, but they got to determine that role. My kids absolutely love her. I used to get all the phone calls about stuff, but she gets them now. [laughing] I used to make the best egg sandwich. Not anymore. They want Sherri cooking their food. Honestly, it's all fantastic.

Do you ever sense that Anna is with you?

I have sensed that, especially before I met Sherri. A couple months after Anna died, I remember that I got a text from Rachel, asking me for advice on something. I instinctively called Anna on my phone hoping to get some advice. Only moments later realizing she's no longer here to help. I began talking to her anyway: "Honey, what do I do? I have a young girl here whose body is starting to change, and I have to go to the pharmacy to buy her lady products. I'm not equipped for this." I later told her older sister Hilary, "When you get home from college on your next visit, you need to talk to your sister a little bit. She needs some training." I was totally lost with all that.

Anna loved birds but her favorite was a red-tail hawk. A few weeks after she had passed away, I was out on a walk. As I was going, I was listening to a David Crowder song: *Oh How He Loves.* Then I noticed that there was a red-tail hawk hovering about 20 feet over my head. I burst into tears. I sensed that the Lord and Anna were just covering me with their love—like they were watching over me. It was an incredible comfort.

I found out later that Tyler had told his mom that he wanted her to communicate with him in order to let him know that she was ok. She said that she would. He had a vivid dream about a week after her death which involved him and Anna having a very long conversation.

I've decided that the veil between this life and the next is paper-thin. By God's grace, there are little things that happen that bring comfort and security, and we do have hope in what the Bible calls the great cloud of witnesses. Possibly our loved ones are watching over us—cheering us on. I've felt that. Now that Sherri and I are together, I'm in another place. The need isn't as great. I definitely think Anna helped get me to the next stage.

Most marriage vows contain the words: "For better or for worse... in sickness and in health... until death do us part." Describe what those words might have meant to John & Anna.

We all want someone to love us, value us, and care for us. But we soon discovered that having someone to love is the greater blessing. Giving is a powerful force. So we worked diligently to give love and serve one another. It worked for us in the good times and the bad times.

Those words mean you never give up on being together until your last breath. That's what we had. We literally walked that out.

From the Newlyweds:

Were there times during the illness that you didn't think you could do it anymore?

Yes, absolutely. I knew I was going to do what was absolutely necessary, but you do have those questioning thoughts.

How did your mate's condition affect your normal intimacy patterns as a couple?

It affected it. We were a very intimate couple. Between the medication and the fact that she felt like crap, it robs the desire. Anna was a passionate woman. She talked to the doctor about the complications the meds and chemo were causing to her anatomy. She was looking for help and solutions that were directly related to our being intimate together. Sexuality was still very relevant during her illness. So yes, it was hindered. It was still important to us. We both had sexual needs. But her issues with cancer took priority over my sexual needs and hers. That was the major concern.

How did you handle those changes?

It didn't feel like we had a lot of down time. Something needed to be done constantly. So I was fine with the changes. Anna was my passion, not just the sexual activity. Your desire is for the one who is sick. All you want for them is to sleep well tonight, get some food down, and feel better tomorrow. Small victories are still victories. You take what you can get. We were definitely still intimate, but less frequent. That's all.

Were you two still able to play together during your mate's decline?

Our play was to chill on the back patio or watch a good movie or comedy. We'd cook together at the house, but her physical strength was minimized due to the chemo. Her normal weight was around 125 pounds. She was well below 100 pounds. when she died. So she just wasn't strong enough to do a lot of things. Going to Hobby Lobby was a perfectly good outing for her. She loved to decorate and help other women do the same. She was very gifted with that.

How did you find joy together when so much time and emotion was filled with the illness, disability, and disease? How did you avoid not focusing on the bad all the time?

When you have four kids, it keeps you focused on other things. **[laughing]** We also realized that, in spite of the cancer, every day we had together was an undeserved gift from above. Having said that, it still wasn't easy to disassociate yourself from what's right in front of you. Anna wanted everyone to maintain their schedules, but because she had a regimen of shots, meds, and treatments that were fairly constant throughout the day, it kept us sadly fixed on the battle against this disease.

What was the dominant emotion during your season of caretaking with your mate—as compared to your emotional state now?

It would be fair to say that her condition did generate some fear—the fear of loss, and the fear of facing the future without her. She was really sick for those three years. We almost lost her a couple of times, and that really put me on edge. Thank God those are not issues I'm currently facing. When you go through a difficult loss, one of the positive things is that you realize you can handle just about anything. Right now, I'm excited and hopeful about the future.

What's the one piece of advice you'd give someone just starting out in marriage?

Find your commonality. Discover what you both love and can share together. Explore and find new things to do as a couple. Pay attention to your mate's love language. Make that book (*The 5 Love Languages*) the first book you read together as a couple. Being able to decipher what those differences are with a couple is huge! A little homework can transform a marriage, and tapping into what translates as love for your mate is extremely beneficial. Guys particularly need help with this. I learned that great sex starts in the kitchen. Since Anna was an "acts of service" person, doing the dishes and serving her had massive rewards for me. **[laughing]**

Another thing we realized is that from time to time you have a situation that needs to be mediated. We all need accountability. I suggest you have a pre-arranged mediator that either one can go to for counsel and support. If I wasn't listening to Anna, she had the right to call Dr. Bob Nichols and solicit help. That wasn't an intrusion by Bob—that was an investment into our marriage. Bob was my mentor. He had permission to kick my butt if needed. That's particularly helpful for women. Men can get into 'jerk' mode and need help in seeing another perspective. Usually, having that arrangement solves a lot of problems before it ever escalates to crisis.

What's the best thing a husband can do for his wife every day?

There is a principle called sowing and reaping. The 'seed principle' is one of the most powerful dynamics in life. Love is the most powerful force, but the seed principle is very legit. Once you know your mate's love language, sow into what feels like love for them! Without that knowledge, you only communicate in ways that feels like love to you. As a result, you're missing the mark, and you end up wasting a lot of time and energy. If men will sow into their wife's love language, it will enrich her life AND pay massive dividends for you.

Sherri's love language is physical touch. That doesn't automatically translate into sexual intimacy, but holding hands and hugs are extremely important to her. That's a huge target for me to invest in.

This also applies for parenting. Find out what love language communicates to your children. I quickly found out that when my kids were being unresponsive to me, it usually meant that their tanks were empty. I'd sow into what communicated love for them, and they'd respond immediately. It's amazing how that works.

What's the best thing a wife can do for her husband every day?

The same thing. Figure out what communicates love to him, and then sow there.

What is one piece of advice you would give to a newly engaged couple?

If you know you've found the one you want to marry, if possible, don't plan a long engagement. Get on with it. You're going to want to jump in the sack, and you'll probably regret that later. Just get on with it.

Knowing all that you know now, what would you have done differently in your marriage?

I would have appreciated every moment more fully. There are no guarantees in this life, and you never know when a moment with someone is your last one. I'm sure there were times where I took for granted the blessing that Anna was to me. I worked hard to appreciate every moment, but I'm sure I could have done better. I was very in touch with the fact that this life is brief and that life brings what it will. So seize the moment, live life fully, and love richly. Life's too short not to enjoy great friends, great food, and great wine.

Once I met Sherri, I was so thankful to be in love again. I felt reborn and was genuinely shocked that love came back and knocked on my door. Sherri had come from loss because of a divorce. We had both been through a long season of hurt and loneliness. So when we found each other, we couldn't keep our hands off each other. So excited and thankful we found each other. So much so, it was kind of uncomfortable for our kids. They were old enough to make their own comparisons. The love wasn't better between Sherri and I. It was just fresh and renewed. We felt very alive again.

Do you still think that marriage is a great idea?

Absolutely. I'm convinced it is a God thing. I think we're best when our soul is bound to another person in the right way. Anna was my soul mate. When she died, a part of me was fractured, broken—lost. I know what it's like to have that. I also know what it's like not to have it. Having it is better. God gave me Sherri as a soul mate to continue this wonderful journey. Yes, it's way better. Marriage is a fabulous thing. It's a gift, it's a mystery—one of the best things God did for us.

In memory of

Anna Laurie Plummer Rambeau

October 27, 1964 – August 6, 2009

Deane

Introduction

When Patti and I first started the discussions about doing a writing project together, we were motivated and encouraged to seek out the stories you've been reading in this book all because of one story — the one you're about to dive into. One of the grandsons of Loduska Deane Johnson recommended that Patti and I check out the new book that his grandmother had just written. Neither one of us were quite prepared for what we were about to ingest. We'll give you more details on her book as you move through Deane's story, but it wasn't necessarily the book (which is awesome) that caught our attention as much as the woman's courage to tell the whole truth about her journey alongside her beloved. Judge Joe Johnson's plight with Alzheimer's is a story definitely worth retelling, but it's only a part of what that disease has touched. Alzheimer's has stolen from a passionate couple, it has pained a loving family, it has taken what it wanted and never said, "I'm sorry." It's been a nasty bully and a vicious thief. But the grace that rests on this amazing woman would only lead you to believe that she's actually forgiven all, including Alzheimer's wrath on her man.

Not all loss happens at the grave. Not all grief begins once a battle is over. Alzheimer's is one of those cruel afflictions that slowly nibbles and chews at the memory health of its victim every damn day. In Joe Johnson's case, it's eaten much more than his memory, so much more. The man is alive, but there isn't much existing evidence of who he has been, or what he has accomplished except in the hearts of his family and friends. There are beautiful pictures and wonderful CD's of his music, but all of that now points to a time that seems so long ago.

On a good day, Joe might recognize the love of his life. Deane was the one who had his back as he offered himself to his nighttime fans and to his daytime clients. She was the magnet, home base and the one who held his due north in her heart. Those crystal eyes planted on her beautiful face are still very much on fire with passion and love. Joe has been in a care facility now for four years. The disease still eats, the pain is still real, but his final gig has yet to be played.

In 1950 when this love story began, Elvis was a freshman in high school, Chuck Berry was still working in an automobile plant in St. Louis, and John Lennon was 10 years old. We were still a good five years from Doo Wop and all that other devil music. In 1950, Big Band was still big business! Names like Tommy Dorsey, Count Basie, Louis Armstrong, Duke Ellington, Glenn Miller and Woody Herman dominated the radio and the record shops. The shock waves from the Great Depression, WWII and the post-war recession begged for crooners like Frank Sinatra, Bing Crosby and Nat King Cole to help "smooth" the way through some of the toughest times that America had ever known. We were on the verge of a major shift, but not quite yet. Smooth still worked.

Every now and then, once in a blue moon, a small country town can harbor solid local talent. In 1950, deep in the Heart of Texas, in the not-yet-infamous town of Waco, that meant only one thing: Joe Johnson and the band. Small places are usually always a little behind, but not always. Wherever Joe and the band were playing, that was the place to be. Deane surely thought so and she's never seemed to change her mind. This love story is like something you would read in a romance novel. Honestly, it probably should be a movie.

I must prepare you. This woman is full of life! Joe Johnson is and was a lucky man. She said things in this interview that brought tears to our eyes. Deane is as fearless as she is forthright. Open yourself to be touched by grace and seasoned wisdom. We could not be more honored to introduce you to Deane. What a gal! -MDP-

Tell us about how you two met and fell in love.

One evening I went into the Casa Blanca club in Waco, Texas, and I heard a trumpet player. When I walked into the ballroom, this man had his trumpet under his arm and he was singing. At that moment—I knew! It was that quick. I didn't know how it was going to happen, but it was going to happen. It took months for a relationship to actually materialize. I wouldn't accept a date unless we were going to Casa.

I never walked to the bandstand. I never went up there to meet him or introduce myself. In those days, girls didn't do that. We waited for the men to come to us. Finally, someone introduced us. I was absolutely speechless with awe. On December 31, 1950, he came over to my table and asked me if he could kiss me for Happy New Year! I said, "Of course!" Now, I had a date that night with a guy who was attending Rice University. He and his buddies were talking about splitting the atom. All of that was over my head. But I made my way to the bandstand at the appropriate time, and Joe kissed me Happy New Year.

Shortly after that night, I called local photographer Jimmy Willis and asked him to go take a picture of Joe. I thought, "If he never asks me out, at least I'll have a great picture of him." It was the end of April before Joe actually asked me out. We dated maybe six times. Joe was drafted, went to Ft. Sam Houston, and we would meet on the weekend. He asked me to marry him in July 1951, but because of his military obligations, we didn't get a lot of time together. His mother didn't think that marriage at that point was a good idea. The overall pressure was to wait until Joe was out of the service.

Around the end of August, Joe's brother came to me one day and said, "Joe is not going to set the date for marriage unless you are unavailable." So, I got on the bus and went to Dallas. I wanted to apply for an airline hostess job. A taxi driver took me out to Lemmon Avenue, and I walked the entire length of that road in high heels. I went into every business, every hanger, and Braniff Airlines accepted me for their January school, but I needed a job immediately. So I kept walking and Pioneer Airlines hired me that day! I was to report to work the next Monday.

I went back to Waco to gather my things. On that bus ride, I mentioned to a woman that I had gotten a job, but didn't have a place to stay in Dallas. She handed me a key and said, "I have a room, and I'm not home a lot, why don't you just stay at my house?" I said, "I'll take it!"

So I gathered my stuff and saw Joe over the weekend. He was really upset that I was moving to Dallas to work for an airline. He threatened to take the ring back. But I held my ground and got back on the bus and went to work in Dallas. I took the ring, put it on a chain, and wore it around my neck.

After my training, I was gone quite a bit. We didn't see each other for a couple months. I was just too busy, and it really got to him. Around October 21st, Joe called and said, "Let's get married next Saturday night." I said, "I will be there." The plan worked.

My kids tell me all the time, "We'll never know the kind of love that you and Dad have." It was a love that I never knew existed!

So, it really was love at first sight?

Love at first sight; and I think it was for him too. Joe was working as an x-ray technician at the time; he was on call a lot and his dad had just died, so he was spending as much time as possible with his mother. The weekends with his band was the extent of his social life.

We didn't get alone time. We might sit in the yard to talk, but there was no real privacy. I tell young couples all the time, "Keep sex out of your courtship. You need something to look forward to!" I couldn't wait to get Joe in the sack.

Someone asked me a couple days ago, "To what do you attribute your long marriage?" I said, "Two things: faith and sex.

When and where were you married?

Joe and I were married at my mother's house in Mt. Calm, Texas, on October 27, 1951. We immediately moved to San Antonio, and Joe was then deployed to France the following May. I joined him there four months later. We lived in France for almost a year. It was just the best for us! There were none of the normal distractions from here. No one was calling him for a job. We were in a foreign country with no T.V., no radio, and we became creative in our time together. Joe would play his trumpet, and I would guess the name of the tunes. That was our entertainment. We didn't need anymore than that!

How long have you and Joe been married?

Sixty-two years.

What was the first year of your marriage like?

We were alone and together. We were living the dream. There was no plumbing in that house. We had a two-burner propane stove. Bathing in a #2 bathtub, required us to heat our water on the stove. There was an outhouse on the back of the property. The heater didn't work too well, but being newlyweds, we didn't need a lot of heat **[laughing]**.

If a young couple could get married and be away from their family and friends for six months, it would be very helpful to them. We didn't want for stuff or things. Just being together was all we wanted.

How differently were you both raised?

Joe had two brothers and a sister. When Joe was born, his mother told Joe's dad, "You raised the other three. This one is mine (referring to Joe). I'm raising him." And that is exactly what happened. His siblings finished high school, and they all got married early. Joe lived at home until he left for the military in May of 1951.

One of his brothers had asthma. On a doctor's advice, his parents bought him a trumpet to help strengthen his lungs, but he never got interested in it. Joe picked it up and taught himself how to play. He was singing in schools around 8 or 9 years old with the Mary Holiday Talent Review. His father's failing health really put a financial hardship on the family. All the kids had to pitch in to help meet the needs. Joe's jobs, and his role with the band, were financially important to his family.

On the other hand, my dad died when I was 8 years old. The mustard gas in WWI was the origin of his tuberculosis. My mother was not inclined to nurture. When I got on that bus to go to Dallas to begin my work with Pioneer Airlines, my mother didn't ask me a single question about lodging, did I need money, or anything of the sort!

My mother married my stepdad in 1941, and he didn't have children of his own. I felt sorry for him that a preteen female moved into his house, along with his new wife [laughing]. I'm not saying that my mother didn't take care of me, but she was different. I remember as a little child that my dad would be in the hospital, and my mother would go out on dates with other men. Even as a little girl, I knew that was wrong, and I'd get very mad about all that. She said, "I love you," a lot. Times were different, and it may be that she wasn't raised in a nurturing environment either. So I was an only child. Joe used to tell our children, "Don't marry an only child. If you do, you marry a mental case." I'd respond with, "And don't marry the baby of the family, because you married the baby." [laughing]

Early on, what were some of your toughest challenges as a couple?

Once we had children, I had to get accustomed to his playing every weekend, and I couldn't go. While we were in France, I imagined a partnership where I'd be in the audience and I could watch him, and people would know I belonged to him. I had big visions of all of that. Joe said, "No, you're not going to work with me. Men don't take their wives to work with them. You're going to stay at home." And I accepted that.

When Joe was in Law School that was also a very tough time. He was also working as a Justice of the Peace during that season. Joe went to school in the mornings, worked as a JP in the afternoons, he studied at night, and he played with the dance band on the weekends. But he always kept Saturday open. That was the day he might take the kids and go to the airport, or the fire station, the zoo, or James Connelly air force base. Saturday was their day.

I was never jealous of Joe. I trusted him completely. There he was out there playing on the weekends, with good-looking women all around him! Maybe I should have been, but I wasn't. I decided one day that I needed to give him some reason to want to come home that night. So, I gathered every chiffon scarf that I had, stripped down to my bra and panties, and stuffed them full of those scarfs. I danced into the room where Joe was, and my 2 year old saw me. When the baby saw those scarfs, he grabbed me and wouldn't let Joe get near [laughing]. I was always trying to shock Joe so he wouldn't forget about coming home.

One time, the band was playing out at the Ranch House, and the owner of the place had a good-looking woman sitting with him. The woman stated to everyone at the table, that she wanted to take the trumpet player home with her. The owner said, "He won't go." She said, "I've never been turned down. He will go. Watch and see." He shot back, "I'll tell you what, I'll bet you a $100 that he won't go." She said, "I'll bet you $100 he does." So after the dance, the band members came to the table to collect their checks. That's when the woman propositioned Joe. He said, "That's very thoughtful of you, but my wife is at home." And Joe came home. Neither one of us ever did anything to make us question that part of our relationship.

Some women fall for their OB/GYN. I did have a thing for my doctor one time. I told Joe one day, "I'm not that bad looking am I? My OB/GYN totally ignores me." Joe said, "You've never given him the signal. That's why."

What were your shared goals and ambitions?

I'm not sure we had any. We got through the day. Being together was about my only goal. We were raising four kids. There was more than enough work to go around.

Joe didn't really want to go to Law School. He was working for a Television-radio station and applied at the local paper because it would pay $5.00 more a week than what he made. So he took that job, but applied again at the Connally-Compton Funeral Home, and he told Mr. Connally, "I need a job!" Mr. Connally said, "Joe, you've got too much on the ball to be working here. I'm not going to hire you. Go do something with your life." While working with the newspaper, he was covering the courthouse, and he became friends with Judge McDaniel. It was Judge McDaniel that suggested that Joe apply for Law School. With that counsel, we borrowed $500, and Joe signed up to run for Justice of the Peace. Joe won the election 2 to 1. Lots of people knew Joe from dancing to his music for years. People loved Joe, loved his music, and voted for him. He served as JP for 24 years while he was practicing law, and he loved it! He then ran for District Judge, and won that. He served 16 years on the bench as District Judge. In 2002, I think Joe knew he had some memory issues, because he resigned a year before his term was up. He was gracious and inferred that it was time for others to assume his position, but I think he knew something was going on with his health.

In 1955, we were attending a local Baptist church, and the minister came to our home and said, "Joe, you'll have to give up that band if you intend on bringing your family to our church." Needless to say, we changed churches **[laughing]**.

So as the marriage began to develop and mature, what did "normal" look like for Joe & Deane's relationship?

Saturday night! **[laughing]** The intimacy that we've had through the years has been the concrete of our marriage. We'd argue and carry on like normal couples, but the flame never flickered. The man was working three jobs, I'm at home with three kids—pregnant with the fourth, and we were desperate for a little tender loving care with each other!

Because of Joe's profession, he was invited to do a lot of outstanding things. He knew a lot of important people, and those relationships got him into quite a few amazing opportunities. It was easy in those days for me to play the "not fair" card. Pregnant, three little kids, and he'd be out running with the big dogs! He'd play golf, and I'd stay home. Do you know what Alzheimer's has taught me? There really isn't anything worth having an argument about. None of that is worth getting upset over. Stuff doesn't matter. Joe was a great provider, and we saved some money, but we needed to. His care is expensive. We had our differences, but we never allowed the differences to slice into the marriage. We worked it out.

Was Joe making room for the band also?

Yes. He had a standing weekend gig with the band for about 18 years, so I was at home with the kids a lot. A doting mother raised Joe, and it felt good to him for me to be home with the kids. I had other ideas about what felt good to me [laughing]. I didn't really ever go out with the girls. If Joe was at home, that was where I wanted to be. After he graduated from Law School, Joe dissolved the band. That was 1964. He didn't think it would look good to the community for him to practice law and play in a band at the same time.

What part of your life with Joe was the most rewarding for you?

Alzheimer's isn't rewarding [crying]. But, I've grown. I'm a changed person because of that [crying]. I'm not thankful for Alzheimer's, but I am thankful for the person that I've become because of Alzheimer's [crying].

Deane, not many people would be willing to say something like that.

In His own way, He has given me that opportunity to change [**crying**]. I've asked my kids to not judge me based on how I was, but how I am now. It's a horrible thing to say but, [**crying**] out of the 63 years with Joe, the past ten years have changed me the most.

I am so thankful that I've been allowed to grow—to have this comfortable feeling about who I am. I have found my mission. My mission is to be there for every spouse, for every daughter or son, who is also traveling this road with Alzheimer's. You can't go visit with your afflicted loved ones while carrying expectations. If you do, you're going to be disappointed. Kick all of your negative feelings to the curb. I have some of Joe's CD's in my car. When I leave his care facility, after I've seen this man [**crying**], and I get into the car and hear his music, I can then see him as he was on the day he recorded it. [**crying**] It allows me to leave *that* man in the facility and think about the man as he was. I think this process has helped me prepare for the final grieving season when it's over.

My son was here not too long ago, and he was dressed up for an event. He was standing in the den, all dressed up, and he had put on one of Joe's ties [**crying**]. I had to push him back. It was tough. He looked so much like Joe, and in an instant, I was back in 1960 [**crying**].

What have you learned the most in your life that Joe taught you?

Joe always said, "The man who knows he has enough is the happiest and content." I know right now that I have enough—I've had enough [**crying**]. I've had him, I've had children, I have grandchildren, and the means to take care of Joe now. The man who knows he has enough is content.

What do you think you taught him the most?

I'm not sure I taught him anything. Before Alzheimer's, Joe would say to me, "Honey, you can do anything. Everything you do is good, and you'll never get old." I'd say, "I'm old already." He'd shoot back, "You'll never get old."

As I've already mentioned, I did a lot to shock Joe. Joe was more of an old maid than I have ever been. One Halloween, I snuck out the back door and went to the front door. Of course, I was nude under that raincoat I had on. I met him at the door one night dressed only in Saran Wrap. I think I loosened him up a little bit. Once, I anonymously sent him love notes at the courthouse for about three months. No way was he going to forget about me at home!

When did Joe's challenge with memory begin to surface?

Joe retired January 1, 2003. That is when I began to notice little things. Men fail to realize that when they come home, they've now entered a woman's office.

Women assume that a man knows where everything is kept in the house. So he was asking a lot of questions, but it didn't seem to stick when I'd give him directions. That's when I began to realize that something wasn't right.

I'll never forget our first visit to the neurologist. The doctor asked Joe to draw a clock, and he drew all the numbers on one side. I wasn't really worried. I didn't react then like I would now when someone mentions "Alzheimer's." I wasn't blowing it off, but I had no idea of what I was facing. Ok, so he forgot phone numbers, or he'd forget to call me. Big deal. But I just didn't know where this thing was headed. Dr. Hurd told us his personality would change, he would lose his nouns, have anxiety, and begin sun downing. One thing I want to emphasize to all family members is that inside the plaque brain resides the man you know. Love him and be with him, as you said in your vows, "In sickness and in health" I will be by your side, today and always.

Joe was 75 years old. He quit a job he loved, he thought he wanted to play golf every day, but soon discovered he really didn't, and his strong embouchure was disappearing with his trumpet playing. Plus, he had to accept the fact that things were changing physically for him that affected our sexual intimacy. He was facing all of that at one time. That's when I realized that I needed to provide as much comfort as possible. Only two years ago, he handed me his trumpet and said, "Put this up. I can do better than this." So what he was hearing, he didn't like.

Early on, the doctor told me to keep him busy. Get him out of the house. Expose him to all kinds of environments. So I immediately booked us a trip to Europe. He loved poker, so next we went to Las Vegas. It got to when he played dice he wanted me to stand next to him because he couldn't remember which numbers he had covered. Then we went back to Europe twice. All of those were good trips. On the last big trip we took, Joe sundowned from the time we left Waco until we landed in Zurich.

I never realized how much God actually speaks to me. The past ten years has confirmed that to me over and over. One night, I was actually frightened at what happened. We were in the bed, and Joe was asking me questions. It was one question after another. He was hammering me repeatedly. It was like torture. So I said, "Joe, when I have a problem, I tell God that I'm going to give him that problem—I can't handle it." He said, "That would be good if it worked." I assured him it would, and suggested that we pray for God to answer his questions so that we could rest. For thirty minutes, there was not one sound in that room! It was quiet... almost eerie. I was looking around for a shadow or something. He'd been asking questions for over an hour. Finally, he excused himself to the bathroom. When he returned, he crawled back in bed, patted me, and said, "Thank you honey." I said, "That wasn't me. That was God. He did that for us."

He was subject to all kinds of forgetfulness, and I tried all kinds of things to help him remember. I'd make little signs, but he couldn't attach the message to the reality. I remember one time that he was mad at me when I got home from an errand. He said, "I've been calling you to see if you wanted a hamburger." And, as my habit at the time, I said, "Don't you remember that I told you my answer?" One night I was reminded by the Lord, "When you answer that way, it's demeaning to Joe. He will forget how you respond. You will never forget how you respond. Don't do that anymore."

One of the hardest things to deal with was the fact that he was sundowning so much. One day we took him out to eat, and he told our son that he had hurt his back. So he inquired. Joe responded, "I was skating with the Ice Capades, and the guy behind me told me if I wanted to win, I needed to turn a flip. I turned a flip and hurt my back." Now to him that was real. I caution caretakers that you can never go into their world. They can come into ours maybe, but we can't go into what they're seeing, thinking, or hearing.

When we moved Joe over to the care facility in 2010, he told our daughters, "Y'all have tricked me." He was still enough about himself that he knew we were making decisions without him knowing. We'd go pick him up from the facility and take him to eat, get a haircut, or a pedicure. But when he became incontinent we stopped taking him out.

(Deane has written a magnificent book, which is more or less comprised of her journal entries during the seven years she was taking care of Joe at home. *I'll Be Seeing You: A Wife's Journey With Her Husband's Alzheimer's* is a courageous and honest look inside of Deane's heart as she cared for her best friend while he declined of memory health. It is a mesmerizing reflection of a difficult season and a beautiful love story. The book is available in paperback and electronic format. www.deaneandjoe.com)

You've used the word "sundowning" twice now. What do you mean by that?

I think it is a lot like us having a dream that we can't get out of, and later we don't even remember having the dream. When the Alzheimer's patient is sundowning, they are in that dream—absolutely inside of that dream. Once they finally come out of it, they have no idea that it even happened. If you tell them they were sundowning—just like your dreams—they don't know what you are speaking about.

Was there a moment of communication when you both acknowledged the seriousness of the disease to each other?

No. Joe never acknowledged it, nor would he talk about it. He didn't allow the word "Alzheimer's." He was well read, and I'm sure he knew more than he probably wanted to. When it was time, he signed over Power of Attorney and never asked a question. I would email the doctor my notes from my journal prior to any visit. So there were no discussions about his condition in Joe's presence.

When we started going to see the doctors about the condition, Joe's stance was simple: "I'm not going to worry about anything that is happening to me." So I had much more data about his condition than he did.

One day, Joe told one of our doctors at church, "I can't seem to remember people's names!" The doctor said, "Oh, that happens to all of us as we get older." But there was a lot more going on than that. The thing about Alzheimer's is that you get settled in with them and the disease, and then they'll have lucid moments. And you let your guard down and begin to think that maybe it's not as bad as it seems. That is a faulty assumption.

The Alzheimer's patient does suffer with anxiety and frustration. About the only comfort you can gather about it is that they will forget about those times of fear and anxiety. Joe was really anxious one day and kept saying, "I've got to get out of this." I tried to comfort. He said, "The only thing I know to do is jump off of a building, and you're going with me." I said, "Okay." He snapped, "No. You're not going with me. I'm going by myself." Obviously, he knew he wasn't himself.

There are seven progressive stages with Alzheimer's. When you got new data on where he was, how did that affect you?

I never faced reality. I just wouldn't face it. I dealt with what had to be dealt with, and then dismissed it. I was probably just in crisis management. My kids were on the verge of taking over guardianship of their dad. They saw the toll it was taking on my health. You don't really ever sleep with an Alzheimer's patient in the house. Joe never wanted me out of his sight. If I was in the other room while company or our children were in the house, he'd whistle and say, "Deane, we have company in the house!" He wanted me right there at all times.

On the day I decided to move him to the care facility, I had prayed for some kind of signal, because I couldn't do it. I had visited the facility, it was a beautiful place, but I just couldn't pull the trigger on it. We were watching Glenn Beck on T.V. that day. Joe could not separate that Glenn was on T.V. and not in the room sitting with us. He accused me of having an affair with Glenn Beck. So I called one of the daughters over, and she took Joe outside to see if she could calm him down. He could hear my voice and would make the slashing motion on his throat. He was livid! My daughter came back in and said, "If he gets that gate open out there, what do you want me to do?" I said, "Nothing. He's too big, and we can't handle him." It was at that moment that I asked her, "Have you started filling out the paperwork for Soldalis Memory Care facility?" That was my signal [crying]. That was the hardest thing I've ever done in my life. I even think Joe knew what was happening [crying]. That night he wanted a hug and a kiss, and he patted me all night. I think he felt the change. My boys offered to put him in, but they were neck deep in work. My girls told me not to worry about it, and they came and got Joe to admit him in the facility [crying].

Generally, what was Joe's response to your caretaking?

I think he just expected it. As I mentioned earlier, Joe had full confidence in my ability to get things done. He didn't expect more from me, because he always had known what I was going to give him. In the beginning, he verbalized his gratitude. But he'd get so frustrated and agitated with me because he couldn't keep up with all the things that I was doing. Leaving him a note was useless. Joe couldn't remember that he couldn't remember. I had a hard time letting that soak into me. So he couldn't remember that he couldn't remember, and I didn't seem to remember he couldn't remember. [laughing].

It got to where I needed to be aware on an hourly basis of what he might need or want. It was an impossible task, but I tried my best to meet the needs most necessary. To a certain level, it was a guessing game, and most of the time Joe showed his gratitude. But he couldn't remember if he had thanked me or not. I took joy in serving my husband. I wasn't doing it for the thanks. I love this man.

One of the things I've picked up through all of this is a gratitude list. Every day, I write on a list all the simple things I'm thankful for during the day. Like your visit, or the grandkids drop by, or the crape myrtles that are blooming outside my kitchen window, or a red bird sings in a nearby tree, or the dogs hop in my lap—things like that. It has helped me zero in on all the joy in my life. It's stuff that would be easy to overlook if I didn't write it down. It really works! I'm thankful that one of my children called me to discuss a problem, and I just listened without offering advice. I'm thankful that I've grown enough to not have to give advice. I can just listen.

Joe and I always had different ways in dealing with our issues with each other. His tendency was to not allow his words to get away from him. He was an internal processor. He could keep his words to himself, or use very few words when needed. With me, it was completely different. I would let it all fly! I thought out loud. Once it got it out there, I quickly loved everybody. Once I vented, I wasn't mad anymore. Joe would pout because I had insulted him. How we worked all of that out—I have no idea, but we did.

How much of that overall burden did you shoulder by yourself?

All of it. I had people to come in and help with the house, but attending to him was my job. I might try to take him with me to the grocery store, but it would take a lot of effort to pull that off. One thing is for certain, after a visit to the grocery store, the females he met went home feeling good because Joe told them all how pretty they were [laughing].

How well do you think you did under that stress?

Looking back, I am content and happy with what I did, because I didn't know any different. During that season, I had Deep Brain Stimulation surgery and a double knee replacement. I think I stayed pretty dang strong through it all.

Where did you find your strength and courage?

I prayed. I'd wake up in the middle of the night, needing to go to the restroom, only to realize I was praying about something. I told my grandson just the other day that I had been thinking about Psalms 121. I didn't know the passage, so he read it to me. You don't get through something like this without knowing where your real help comes from! There isn't a human being on earth that can survive the pain of it alone [**crying**]. My kids are with me, but you can't make it alone. My Facebook friends have also been an incredible blessing to me.

What were your big "priorities" before you found out Joe's Alzheimer's, and how were those things affected by the illness?

For me, it was traveling. We both wanted to be able to do some volunteer work. Visiting with our kids was also very important.

I wrote a woman once and told her that young women spend a lot of their time and energy making preparations. We plan our wedding, we keep up with fashion, we want to stay current, we plan (or maybe not) our kids, and how we're going to raise them, and we plan about all that we're going to do when we get older—particularly retirement. But we don't plan for widowhood. We never make preparations for that. We're all going to be there at some point. It might be better if we faced that reality and made some plans. You never really know until you're there, but it might help to have a plan. I never saw Alzheimer's coming to us. Dreaming for the fun stuff is easy. Maturity pretty much declares that we need to face some harsher possibilities. We do not need to be in fear, but it's okay to do some due diligence with conversations.

Alzheimer's disassembled our priorities. Without Joe, why would I want to view the Alps or tour the world? I recently spoke in a class at Baylor on death and dying. I challenged them to watch their personal pronouns. Married people should beware of two particular pronouns: "I" and "me." The focus needs to move on "us." How does everything we're discussing affect us? A young mother in that class came up to me after the session. She was sobbing, and confessed that she and her husband were having problems. She said, "After hearing you today, I think I know how to fix this."

There really is no need for an argument, or even a deep discussion, if your motivation is to change your spouse's mind. Drop it, let it go, and go make love [laughing].

Did you two ever talk about "your" future without Joe in the picture?

No, and I know he never thought about living without me.

What was going on in your head and heart during the few final days with Joe at home?

We filled out the paperwork on a Tuesday, and by Friday the girls had dropped him at the care facility. Those few days in the interim were not days to remember, because you knew that everything that was happening was soon to end. I was pretty torn up by then, but I didn't want him to see me crying. If I did cry, I just told him it was allergies.

I wanted to make him a roast, because it was his favorite. One of the ladies who was working for me at the time made the worst roast I have ever experienced [laughing]. She chopped up the meat, along with the fat and gristle. Joe was not a fan of fat. Joe asked, "What is this?" I'm thinking, "Oh my God! It's his last meal at home, and I've served him this disaster!" [laughing] There is always humor, and you have to grab ahold of it when it floats through.

Looking back, how prepared were you to transition Joe to the care facility?

Oh, not at all. I did bring him home one night. One of the men at the facility was upsetting everyone else, so I decided to take Joe home for the evening. Although it was wonderful to have him at home, I realized that I couldn't do that. It wasn't fair to him or to me. You can't buy into their lucid moments. You just can't do that.

What is Joe's condition now?

He looks like he can't figure out where he is. If he eats, he eats with his hands. Sometimes he won't sleep, and he'll be up half the night. He walks a lot. There have been a couple times that he's gone 5 days without eating or drinking. I've shifted my gears for his final sleep. I must say, that has been much easier for me than when I was faced with putting him into the care facility.

How is his communication?

He doesn't say much. The other day he told me, "I need a buddy." And I said, "Well, I'm your buddy." He said, "Buddy." So I replied, "Ed Burleson is your buddy." He said, "Yeah." I said, "Nick Klaras is your buddy." And Joe said, "One of a kind." Then he drifted off to sleep. He sleeps most of the time. He dozes off often. Few words or sentences are intelligible. He babbles quite a bit. He no longer writes. He did know his birthdate not too long ago.

When I go into his room, I have to look for the Joe I knew. He may have Alzheimer's, but that is not who he is. Joe is still all the things that he once was. Somewhere inside is my Joe. When I sit by him, he'll grab and kiss my hand. I suspect that my presence sends him a signal that he's supposed to be doing something. He'll say, "Now you go ahead and do what you have to do." I truly think that my presence could be a bigger burden than help to him.

How often do you see Joe?

I'll go to his facility about four to five times a week.

Describe what a visit with Joe is like now?

I might be with him 15 minutes or three hours. It just depends. I'll just sit there and watch him—just look at him [crying]. I wish we could have a conversation. Then I could assure him he was safe and loved, and comfort him. All I can do these days is bring him candy. I like to think Joe knows me. I do know he knows me as the candy lady. I sit down and Joe holds out his hand and says, "Give it to me." He eats a couple of candy bars, drinks a bottle of water, and tells me often, "Thank you darling." That is my joy.

They keep a close eye on the residents. There are only ten residents at his facility, so Joe gets a lot of attention. There are always two attendants and a cook in the home. You never know where Joe is going to sleep. They'll swap beds with each other, so you just know they wake up not knowing where they are.

How much grief work have you done?

I've done some, but as I've already stated, I wasn't facing the reality of what we were dealing with. My kids would say, "Mom, you have to face reality!" I would say, "But you don't understand. Why would I face a reality when you have 24 hours in a day? He's going to sundown for three hours, and he's going to sleep for eight or nine hours. Why would I move him away and miss the few hours around here as a couple?" I wasn't going to do without him just because he was sundowning for two or three hours.

Most marriage vows contain the words: "For better or for worse... in sickness and in health... until death do us part." Describe what those words might have meant to Joe & Deane.

When I was saying them, I doubt I knew what they meant—not like I understand it now. Listen to what they mean. There is no way to get around those words. You have to be willing to ride it out and weather the storms. No matter what the problem is, it gets better if you give it a chance. I couldn't afford to tank the deal because I wasn't getting my way or not getting my point across. I was contending with a legal mind. You didn't get your point across with Joe Johnson [laughing]. Don't give up. Never give up!

From the Newlyweds:

Were there times during the illness that you didn't think you could do it anymore?

No.

If my spouse were just diagnosed with a terrible illness, what advice would you give me?

To be the caregiver, love isn't enough. You must be in love! There is a difference. Look at your relationship, and determine what it really means to you. Assess how you feel about yourself and this person that you're married to. Do you want to be there for comfort, support, and security? You wouldn't want to do anything that might mar your conscience. You stick with the person that you chose—you wouldn't think of doing anything different.

How did your mate's condition affect your normal intimacy patterns as a couple?

I think I miss that the most—the intimacy—just being able to feel his body. I miss feeling his hand on my back, to check if I was still breathing, or looking for that foot in the middle of the night. Waking up in the morning to thank God that we're both still alive today.

How did you handle those changes?

We never quit trying. We never gave up the feeling of skin on skin. Nudity was still good. I'd love to crawl into bed with him even now, but I dare not. He may not know who I am, and that would frighten him.

Were you two still able to play together during your mate's decline?

Yes. We made a couple trips overseas, but Joe wasn't really playful. I was much more playful than he was, but the changes were occurring too often. With Alzheimer's, you go steadily along, and then you dip. And then you go steady at that new level, and then you dip. Joe was making more dips than remaining steady. So I'd have to say that we were more in a maintenance mode than relax mode. We tried the movies, but he couldn't keep up with the plot. He'd ask, "Do you like this?" And then we'd have to leave. We'd go out to eat, and we'd go to church, but that was about it.

He came to me one day after church and said, "I don't know what is wrong with me. I can't even hang up my clothes." I said, "That's ok. It's my turn to hang them up."

How did you find joy together when so much time and emotion was filled with the disease?

It's a choice. The same way that I can enjoy going over to where he is now. I get to look at him. I'm thankful.

A wife at the facility told me that her husband hadn't talked to her in months, but he had winked at her the day before. I told her, "You take that wink, put it in your pocket, and never forget it! That wink said all the things he wanted to say, so you hang on to that wink."

What was the dominant emotion during your season of caretaking with your mate—as compared to your emotional state now?

You know, I never got angry with God, but I did get angry with Joe one time because he got Alzheimer's. I was like, "Why did you do this to us?" I was so engaged, trying to get through the day, to be too emotionally charged. Now, when he was sun downing, it could get wild. One night, he was talking to the pillows in this room and questioning, "Who started that fire?" He'd say, "Tell me which one of you guys started that fire! I am Judge Johnson, and I'm not going to hurt you!" That went on for an hour. I stood in the hall and listened and finally went into another bedroom and crawled into bed. He finally got in his own bed, and he was whistling for me to come and turn out the light [laughing]. Once he went to sleep, I went and crawled back in bed with him.

Another time, my daughter and her husband were at the house with us. Joe thought that he and I were going to have sex in the back bedroom. We were just trying to get him to go to bed [laughing]. He stood in the doorway and told my daughter and son-in-law, "I don't know what she's trying to do! I am paying for this room by the hour, and she won't come back here with me, and I am wasting my money!" [laughing]

You've seen my current dominant emotional state [crying]. I try not to think about his condition. I won't let myself go there [crying]. I won't allow myself to see him as he is. I look beyond Alzheimer's. I get in our car, play his music, and I'm right back in the recording studio with him [crying].

What's the one piece of advice you'd give someone just starting out in marriage?

Don't get so caught up planning the perfect wedding that you spend zero time thinking about the marriage.

When planning the wedding-reception, most young couples use the pronouns "I" and "me" way too much! Eliminate those pronouns now and forever more.

Most women began thinking about their wedding day as young girls. It wouldn't hurt for a young man to take that into consideration.

When we got married, Joe called and said, "Let's get married next Saturday!" I flew in on a Tuesday, borrowed a dress, ordered a cake and flowers, and hired a photographer. Joe came in from San Antonio on Friday, we got the license, and Saturday we had an amazing wedding.

Fancy Honeymoon? Joe borrowed a car, and we had one night at the Falls Hotel in Marlin, Texas. Our room cost $7.50. The 50 cents was to rent a radio. On Sunday, Joe went back to Ft. Sam Houston, and I went home with my mother. The next Friday, my mother took me to San Antonio to begin our marital bliss.

We still flourish in a love that has lasted 63 years (October 2014). Keep in mind how the vows give you a feeling of safety in your union. The wedding and reception are only fluff. Real marriage starts when you get home from your honeymoon.

Money seems to cause many problems for a couple. Remember "his" or "her" money is now OUR money! Joe and I each had our own checking account, but Joe's account was a business account for both the band and his law practice. Joe gave me ample money to run the house and etc. The only time I asked for extra money was Christmas and back to school necessities. If I wanted to buy curtains etc. or knock out walls like I did later on in our marriage, I got an estimate for it and saved the money. Every time Joe had to leave home for SLE hours, he got to where he would call me and ask, "What wall are you tearing out?" Our kids laughed—imagining his day— not knowing what to expect when he got home.

What's the best thing a husband can do for his wife every day?

She needs to feel safe. If she's secure in her marriage, it solves a lot of problems.

What's the best thing a wife can do for her husband every day?

Take care of him in the best way that you can. Know what he wants, and try to fulfill some of those desires. When it comes to the bedroom, you may not be turned on, but go ahead and move towards intimacy anyway. I promise you that you'll enjoy it in the end. Don't think for one second that it doesn't matter. It matters greatly! That's when you are literally one person and close. It's the bond of cement. It matters. I know I sound like a sex maniac, but I firmly believe it's so important for a solid marriage.

I walked up behind a young couple at the doctor's office a few days ago. I introduced myself and asked them, "Why are you two wasting precious time on your cell phones when you could be talking and carrying on without your kids present?" They both put their phones up.

What's one piece of advice you would give to a newly engaged couple?

Get on with it. What are you waiting on? You're wasting time, and time is precious! Get the preacher, find the church, and do it.

What are your most important memories of your marriage?

When we were in France, it was an incredible experience! I learned all of the tunes that he knew, and I got good at guessing what he was playing on his trumpet. It was just magic.

I remember when we had our first baby. Back then, the dad's couldn't be in the delivery room, but Joe managed to find his way in. I was holding the baby and Joe said, "Now don't mash on that soft spot on his head." [laughing]

When Mindy was born, she had Hyaline membrane disease. We were told that if she lived 48 hours, the statistics indicated that she'd make it, but we were warned not to get our hopes up. We were together through that crisis. I wouldn't go to Hillcrest Hospital at the time, because my doctor thought I needed to have my tubes tied, and I wouldn't agree to that. So I went to Providence Hospital. I remember looking at the crucifix and saying, "Thy will be done." I never asked for her to be saved.

I was praying to Joe's family the other night, and I said, "Nobia, would you please go talk to Jesus, and remind him that Joe's ready to come up there with you. It's time."

Knowing all that you know now, what would you have done differently in your marriage?

Absolutely nothing.

What did you learn about your spouse that caused you to love him even more?

My dad had died, and my mother wasn't an affectionate person. She was very critical and jealous of me. She was also possessive, but not in a loving way. Joe has filled all of those empty shoes! He brought me the security and strong love that I missed from my dad. Joe also provided the nurture and unconditional love that I missed from my mother. He was my husband, but he absolutely filled up my life.

Do you still think that marriage is a great idea?

I think it's the best thing in the world! I can't imagine living in this world without a mate. Children are also a must, but a mate is the best!

Any final words of advice for married couples of all ages?

Older couples need to marry because they're in love—not because they need someone to take care of them. When it comes to companionship, nothing can fill an empty spot like a mate. To know that you two are one, and that you're connected, is just the best.

When I go see Joe and he holds out his hand for that piece of candy, he knows it's me. Nothing is sweeter than love. You don't need stuff, but you do need love. I had to face Alzheimer's to learn it, and now I'm trying to pass on the message to whoever will listen.

I live by these sayings: Joe may have Alzheimer's, but that is not who he is. It is no big deal unless you make it a big deal.

In memory of

Joe Norman Johnson, Sr.
November 27, 1928 to January 31, 2015

Joe Johnson died peacefully in his care facility six months after this interview. Deane happily reports that he was comfortable and gracefully passed with a smile on his face. Joe and Deane's long battle with Alzheimer's is finally over. —MDP

Afterthoughts

Although the initial idea around this book was directed towards the development of married and engaged couples, we certainly see now see the advantage for everyone to peek into these amazing stories. Indeed they are beautiful and they are hard, but not really uncommon. These kinds stories are happening every day right before our very eyes, but are we willing to take note of them? Are we really allowing the linear string of moments in our existence to teach us our most valuable lessons for love and life? Sober questions for all of us!

It is quite possible that after reading these interviews that some hurt or pain has resurfaced in your heart. Unprocessed pain will usually find a way to show itself and those results are usually less than desirable. We'd like to offer a few brief suggestions for processing the grief or pain that you might be feeling:

First, writing in a journal might be one of the best ways to legitimize the pain that you are feeling. The fact that you recognize your hurt is one of the first steps to dealing with the pain. Hurt is common among all humanity. Your journal is a safe place to say what is real inside of your heart. Take your time and say it all. Getting real and truthful about your pain is a great first step towards healing.

Second, share your story of hurt with a good friend, a spiritual mentor or a counselor. Don't stuff, minimalize, or ignore your pain! Tell it to another person who can listen, ask questions, and then offer sound advice with a loving perspective.

Third, be willing to receive comfort and release from your pain. There can be great healing for us in not always having to be strong or stoic. It's okay to cry and we don't always have to be put together. Let someone minister to you. There really are trained people who'd love the opportunity to help you through your grief.

Fourth, for those of you who have also lost your mate, seek further help to process your loss. There are plenty of counseling professionals who can facilitate or steer you towards a local group that can help you on your journey. Grief isn't the same for everyone. Everyone processes his or her grief differently. It can be very helpful to find a safe environment of people who know some of what you're feeling. They want to know your story and they'll offer their story in support.

We also want to offer you a vehicle for sharing how Til Death Do Us Part has impacted you, your mate, or your marriage. If you are willing to share please go to: www.everytribeinternational.org and find the SHARE YOUR SCOOP page. Please do tell us what is on your mind. We eagerly await your scoop!

Thanks for joining in this beautiful journey with us!

Mike & Patti

A Few Additional Thoughts...

Honestly, there wouldn't be a book without the cooperation of the people you've met in these interviews. We have known some of these people a very long time. The rest are newer friends. All of them are now a part of our own story. Their transparent courage has shown us all something really special about a lifetime of love and marriage. We have felt the direct effects in our own marriage because of our time with these people. The esteem that we feel for each of them is surpassed only by our gratitude for their trust. They have shown us the brutal truth of what unflinching commitment looks like in the best and worst of days.

It's not that our marriage has been saved by this project, for we have always had a strong connection of commitment to each other. We've always been deeply in love. But with the passing of time, which becomes shrouded within the various battles of life, a couple can become numbed by life's droning hum. It takes a lot of work to continue a marriage with transparency, honesty, and fearless intimacy. Hearing the words of these widows and widowers through their cracked voices and falling tears caught us totally by surprise. We did feel the pain of the loss of their best friend, but the ultimate challenge they hurled at us—to be more intentional with our love and tangible affection—really hit our hearts. To the outside observer, things probably don't look much different. But our inner resolve to do better with our presence and intentionality for each other has definitely gone to another level. Frankly, that is the whole point of this book: pay close attention, talk about it, and then take decisive action. We did, so you can too.

The traditional temptation is to summarize and compile a list of bullet-points from what we gleaned while on our journey with these people. Naturally, that is what experts do: reduce it down to manageable bites for your consumption. We are tempted to do what has always been done, but we shall pass. There is a staining messiness in traipsing through people's pain. It's supposed to leave a residue. Therein lies the overarching hope that these interviews will move you enough to change that status quo in your most significant relationship or relationships. Inspiration and conviction demand that we change, and change is usually uncomfortable. Obviously that explains why change is so difficult and deep ruts form. If your marriage is in trouble or in a rut, maybe it's time to reboot the system. It could be that your marriage is good, but you have a longing for it to be even better. Whatever the case may be, someone must at least pose the questions: Can we do better? Should we have a discussion? Is this the best we can do? Two hearts in agreement at that point is a favorable chemistry for positive change.

The dynamics of what makes a marriage is different for every couple. The effects of these multiple conversations inside the interviews will land on each couple uniquely. Here is to brave listening and moving resolutions. More love, more caring, more passion—more oneness. Til Death Do Us Part.

—Mike and Patti

Authors

After 30 years of full-time ministry, Mike and Patti Paschall have a tremendous desire to be an encouragement and help to married couples of all ages. They married in 1977 and remain best friends. They have two daughters (Nicole, married to Steven Brewer, and Paige, married to Jon Egan) and five grandchildren (Isabel, Jones, Lewis, Grace, and Esther), all of whom live in Colorado Springs, Colorado. Mike and Patti currently reside in Waco, Texas.

Patti was born and raised in Waco, Texas. Patti greets everyone with a warm smile, a big hug, and lots of love. Mike is quick to point out that Patti has the heart of a true pastor servant. She now spends most of her days taking care of her mother who suffers with memory loss.

Mike was born in Pine Bluff, Arkansas, but raised in Texas. He is a graduate of the University of Arkansas with a BSEd. He also has a Mdiv from SWBTS in Ft. Worth, Texas. Mike loves any opportunity to mentor young pastors, missionaries, men and women who are passionate about ministry and Kingdom. He also loves preaching, teaching, and writing. He is also particularly fond of a good hang with family, a cigar with a great friend, his Indian motorcycle, and an occasional trip to the golf course.

He previously published the daily devotional RAW TALKS WITH WISDOM: Not Your Grandma's Devo (www.rawtalksdevo.com).

Mike Paschall - mike@everytribeinternational.org
Patti Paschall – patti@everytribeinternational.org
http://mikepaschall.com, http://everytribeinternational.org, @m.d.paschall

Resources

BRUCE
Field of Dreams. Dir. Phil Alden Robinson. Perf. Kevin Costner, James Earl Jones, Ray Liotta. Universal Pictures, 1989.

MIKE
Siddhartha Mukherjee, M.D., The Emperor of Maladies (New York: Simon and Schuster, Inc. 2011) pg. 6.

TOMMY
Peterson, E. H. (2005), The Message: the Bible in contemporary language. Colorado Springs, CO: NavPress.